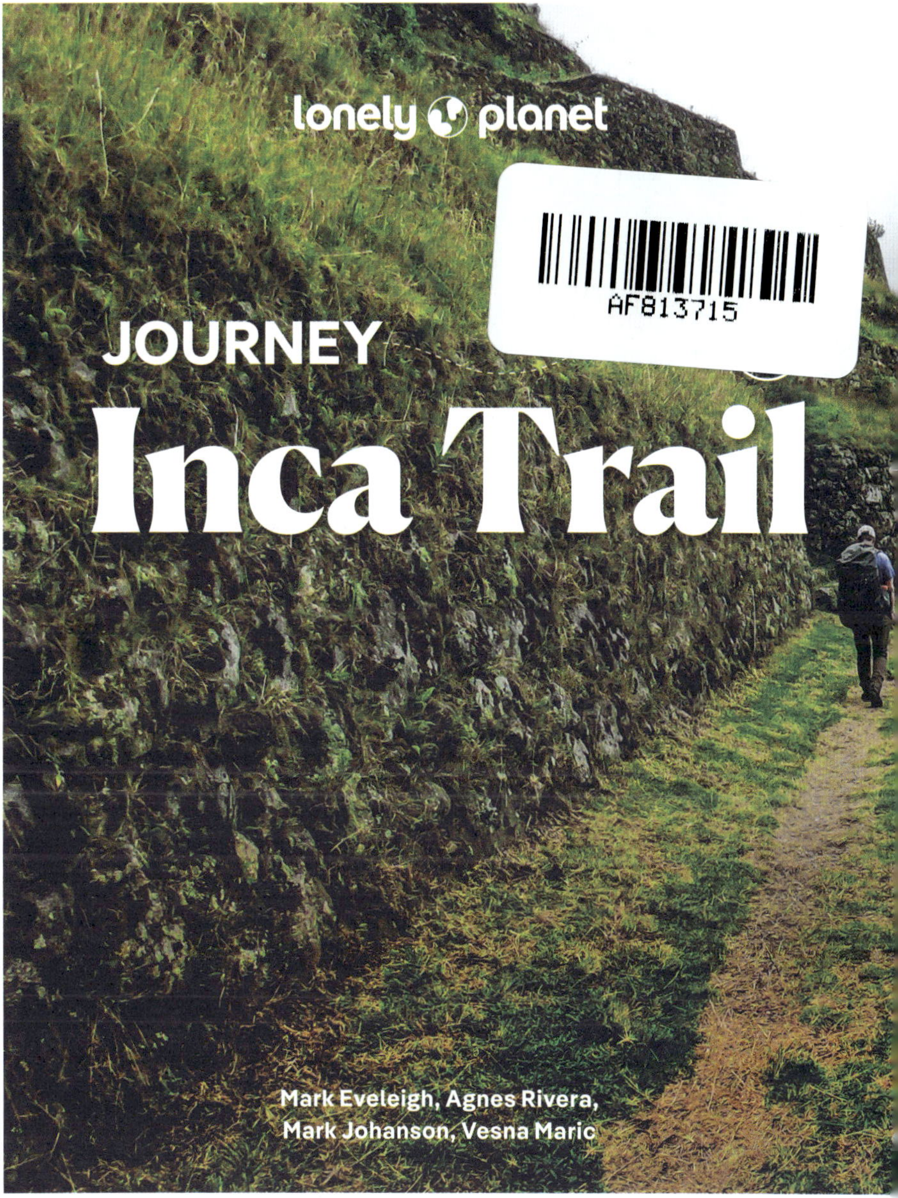

lonely planet

JOURNEY
Inca Trail

Mark Eveleigh, Agnes Rivera,
Mark Johanson, Vesna Maric

CA TRAIL
Km 82
Camino Inka - Inca Trai
START
PATALLAQTA
WAYLLABAMBA

Contents

Plan Your Trip

Go to p30 for the full route map

The Walk

BCHYLA/SHUTTERSTOCK

Llamas, Lares Tek (p220)

INSIGHT ESSAYS

Toolkit

Previous page: Hiker, Inca Trail
ANTHONY GC/SHUTTERSTOCK

My Inca Trail

Mark Eveleigh @markeveleigh

It makes me feel particularly ancient to admit that the first time I walked the Inca Trail was 'at the turn of the century.' I was on a six-week assignment, traveling with an overland truck, and we had enough energy to burn to kick a hacky sack around on the summit of Dead Woman's Pass. Much has changed on the Inca Trail, although walking the route again at the ripe old age of 57, I had no urge to burn off surplus energy. Having visited Machu Picchu six times over the decades, I'm still astounded by how many questions that uniquely spiritual site raises.

Mark Eveleigh is the author of 14 Lonely Planet guides, including the Journey Camino de Santiago *guide.* Vagabond, *the story of his 1225km coast-to-coast hike across Spain, was ranked among National Geographic's top six travel books of 2024. Mark covered the last three legs of the Inca Trail, Machu Picchu site and Pueblo, four insight essays, Toolkit and planning chapters for this book.*

Mark Eveleigh on an earlier Inca Trail hike in 2001

MARK EVELEIGH

MY BEST INCA TRAIL MOMENTS

Machu Picchu Mountain

While hundreds of people flock up Wayna Picchu, few are even aware of the trail up this majestic mountain. p172

Machu Picchu Pueblo

This is a unique and fascinating town for anyone who takes the time to get to know it. p180

Llactapata Ruins

The hike to Llactapata ruins is an ideal follow-up to the Inca Trail. p186

AGNES RIVERA

Agnes Rivera, Casa del Colibri (p62)

Agnes Rivera @wagnesthedog

In 2023 I got my first taste of the Inca Trail with the two-day option and was mesmerized by the remote archaeological site Wiñay Wayna, but, minutes later, was overwhelmed by the nearby campsite full of hikers and exhausted porters. When it came time to book my Classic Inca Trail experience, it was important for me to choose a company with sustainable operations that capped the group size at 12. In the end, I was accompanied by just four other hikers and we truly bonded while deeply connecting to the surrounding sites and nature.

Agnes Rivera is a freelance writer and proud Oregonian based in Peru. She has been a contributor to Lonely Planet for over a decade (including the 2025 Peru *guidebook). She covered the first four legs of the Inca Trail and four insight essays.*

MY BEST TRAIL MEALS

Crema de Zapallo

Warm squash soup while facing the Patallaqta terraces.

Pancakes

Fluffy flapjacks at 6am as clouds hover around the Phuyupatamarka.

Lomo Saltado

Steaming steak stir fry with a view of Machu Picchu mountain.

Vesna Maric @vesnamarx

Hiking in the Andes was a monumental experience – the high altitude notwithstanding, walking in clouds was incredibly life affirming (though possibly more so in retrospect!). I imagined it to be every bit as hard and incredibly beautiful as it turned out to be. Being amid those gigantic mountains, feeling so tiny and so out of breath, was such a reminder of the miracle of existence and the beauty of our planet. Seeing the locals trotting about the mountain sides, passing by and shouting out an encouraging 'Vamonos!' while I huffed my way up the hill was pretty hilarious (for them).

Vesna writes literary fiction and non fiction, and essays. She has written travel guides for Lonely Planet since 2004, including work on the neighbouring country, Bolivia. For this guide, she wrote the Salkantay and Lares Trek routes.

MY BEST BEANS

Cusco

Tasting outstanding Peruvian coffee in the many, trendy specialty coffee cafes. p37

Coffee Farm, Lucmabamba

Have a cup at a coffee farm in the Amazon, on day three of the Salkantay Trek. p203

Chocolate

Taste a bar or a cup of Peruvian 100% cocoa bean – it's top stuff.

Scott Montgomery

It wasn't until I arrived in Cusco for the first time more than 15 years ago that I began to grasp the famous Qhapaq Ñan's reach and complexity. The road isn't an archaeological relic from the past: it's still in use, maintained and traveled by villagers and locals. While walking the Inca Trail to Machu Picchu is the experience of a lifetime, there are many trails in the region, such as the route between Cusco and an archaeological site known as Huchuy Qosqo, where I've felt myself most in awe.

Scott Montgomery, a North America-born writer, coach and guide, has been a resident of Peru's Sacred Valley for over 10 years. He has a Master's degree in creative writing, and is passionate about helping travelers connect with the landscapes and people of the Andes mountains. He wrote 'A History of the Inca Trail' for this book.

MY BEST HOT SPRINGS

Lares

A great place to relax after completing the Lares Trek, which starts in the Sacred Valley. p224

Cocalmayo

Several large pools with crystal-clear water, located in the jungle, a short distance from Machu Picchu.

Chimur

A rarely visited gem in the Mapacho Valley.

Mark Johanson
@MarkOnTheMap

I first hiked to Choquequirao for Lonely Planet when we placed it atop our Best in Travel list for 2017. Nearly a decade later, I could see the difference that publicity had made. There are now cabins, restaurants, hot-water showers, even satellite wi-fi – all things that didn't exist on my earlier visit. Back then, I did the roundtrip hike in three days. A decade older, but with more trekking experience under my belt, I opted for the same. Reader, beware: it was a terrible mistake! I seem to have completely forgotten just how grueling that experience could be.

Mark Johanson is the author of Mars on Earth: Wanderings in the World's Driest Desert. *He's co-authored nearly two-dozen guidebooks for Lonely Planet, and regularly contributes to publications such as* National Geographic, AFAR, Outside *and the BBC. He hiked and wrote about the Choquequirao Trek for this book.*

MY BEST VIEWPOINTS

Cocamasana
Searching for condors and hoping the clouds will break so you can spot the Padreyoc Glacier. p212

Ushnu
Surveying the ruins of Choquequirao from a lofty vantage point prized by the Inca. p216

Playa Rosalinas
Standing by the Río Apurímac and gazing at the canyon walls above. p213

Mark Johanson, Choquequirao Trek (p206)

MARK JOHANSON

James Gulliver Hancock @gulliverhancock

James is a well-traveled illustrator known for his playful illustration style. His obsession with drawing everything in the world has seen him work around the globe, with his work appearing on everything from train carriages to books, clothing, ceramics, boardgames, billboards and animations. His 'How Things Work' series spans a wide range of subjects, from space stations to trains.

James drew the illustrated map at the start of this book.

Majesty of the Andes

Before hiking the Inca Trail, it is useful to get a sense of its geography within the greater context of the Peruvian Andes mountain chain.

WHEN THE CONQUISTADOR Francisco Pizarro returned to Spain from Peru, the king asked him what the landscape looked like. Legend has it that Pizarro scrunched up a piece of parchment and dropped it on the table: 'It looks like that,' he said.

To someone raised on the flat plateau of Spain's Extremadura province, the Andes must certainly have looked like that. While the entire range stretches almost 9000km from the southern tip of South America almost to the coast of the Caribbean, the entirety of what geographers refer to as the Central Andes lies within Peru. The country's highest mountain is Huascarán (6768m), which lies about 700km north of the branch of the Andes known as Cordillera de Vilcabamba, along which the most famous section of the Inca Trail runs.

The Spanish soon learned of Tahuantinsuyo – the Inca's name for their empire with its 'Four Nations.' Pizarro's 'informers' – acting under who knows what 'incentive' – warned the Spanish falsely that Antisuyo (the easternmost of those nations) was home to a bloodthirsty cannibal tribe who ate their victims while still alive. The tribe, so they said, were called the Antis. Some linguists believe that this is the origin of the name Andes.

Land of the Mountain Spirits

To the Incas, their mountain home was a deeply spiritual place. Among the many all-powerful *apus* (mountain spirits) two were paramount: Mt Ausangate, the great glacial mountain that feeds its waters into the Río Urubamba, and Mt Salkantay, which gives birth to the Río Ahobamba.

For anyone walking to Machu Picchu, even in the Inca era there would have been little reason to walk along the twisting, turning highland path that we know now as the Inca Trail. Far easier and less daunting was the relatively direct 'trade route' that hugged the Urubamba riverbank – the route by which Hiram Bingham III, the US explorer who introduced Machu Picchu

SCOTT BIALES DITCHTHEMAP/SHUTTERSTOCK

ICONIC PEAKS

Salkantay

This great rearing glacier rising to 6271m (p199) is one of the Inca Trail's most unforgettable natural sights.

Nevado Veronica

Mt Veronica was named by the Peruvian-Dutch-Swiss team that summited the risky 5860m peak in 1956.

Machu Picchu Mountain

This is one of Peru's iconic mountains (3082m; p172), yet it's entirely free of the crowds who queue to climb neighboring Wayna Picchu (2693m; p175).

MATYAS REHAK/SHUTTERSTOCK

Left: Hikers, Mt Salkantay (p199)
Right: Hikers, Machu Picchu Mountain (p172)

to the rest of the world, reached the ruins in 1911. Yet the great Sapa Inca (Inca emperor) Pachacutec constructed this ornate and beautiful trail as a pilgrimage route ending at the mountain city he had built in around 1450. Just a short distance from the confluence of the Ríos Ahobamba and Urubamba, the city lay in an isolated spot that was almost entirely surrounded by a great switchback of the sacred Urubamba (sometimes called Río Vilcanota). While it seems unlikely that any of this was coincidental, archaeologists still debate why exactly the trail and city were built.

Machu Picchu's 'Lost City' Status

The Incas, under their great conquering leader Pachacutec, built a network of roads known as the Qhapaq Ñan, that stretched for 30,000km or more and allowed them to dominate the mountains until the Spanish conquest of 1532. Machu Picchu often seems to float on a sea of clouds, a near-mythical place that must have seemed to be a bridge between the three domains – *ukhu pacha* (the underworld), *kay pacha* (the world of men) and *hanak pacha* (the world of the *apus* – mountain spirits). The way that the sacred Urubamba encircled the plateau must have convinced the Incas that the powerful highland spirits intended to protect the area for them.

KATH WATSON/SHUTTERSTOCK

GLEAMING TROPICAL GLACIERS

A clear morning in Wayllabamba (the first camp for most Inca Trail itineraries; pictured above) reveals jaw-dropping views of Salkantay, one of the most revered peaks for the Incas, and the foreboding Mt Veronica. These glaciers feed the sacred rivers and, as the Incas were aware, give rise to much of the region's natural wealth. Peru is home to over 2000 glaciers – two-thirds of the world's tropical glaciers.

INCA TRAIL 'HIGHPOINTS'

Abra Warmiwañusqa, p80

Known as Dead Woman's Pass, this is the Inca Trail's highest point at 4215m above sea level and the most challenging stage of the route.

Runquraqay Pass, p93

At 3950m above sea level, this pass is particularly dramatic because of its alpine lakes.

Intipunku, p147

Much lower at 2720m, the Sun Gate is nevertheless the bucket-list viewpoint that lures hikers to the Inca Trail.

NATURAL WONDERS OF THE INCA WORLD

1 Cordillera de Vilcabamba (p9)

This most easterly branch of the Peruvian Andes was the last domain of the Inca civilization.

2 Mt Ausangate (p232)

The sacred mountain drains its glacial waters into the tumbling Río Urubamba. To visitors today, Ausangate's lower slopes are best known for the photogenic 'Rainbow Mountain'.

3 Cusco (p34)

The capital of the Incas was the central point of Tahuantinsuyo (the Inca empire). These days, it's a favorite base for visitors exploring this section of the Andes.

4 Mt Veronica (p111)

The jagged snowcapped peak – actually a range of saw-toothed peaks – of Mt Veronica frequently forms a spectacular backdrop to Inca Trail views. The first recorded summit of its treacherous glacier was in 1956.

5 Mt Salkantay (p199)

Another of the Incas' most powerful *apus* lies directly south of Machu Picchu. Its lower slopes are a major drawcard as an alternative to the Inca Trail.

6 Río Ahobamba (p174)

The icy waters of the Río Ahobamba meet the Río Urubamba near Machu Picchu. The confluence of these two sacred rivers would have been a place of great spiritual power to the Incas.

FROM LEFT: GABRIEL RIBEIRO VALLIM/SHUTTERSTOCK, DANIEL PRUDEK/SHUTTERSTOCK, BETO SANTILLAN/SHUTTERSTOCK

FROM LEFT: ERIK LLONTOP MARTINEZ/SHUTTERSTOCK, XANDERDEL/SHUTTERSTOCK, MARK EVELEIGH

Wildlife of the Inca Trail

With Peru ranking fifth in the world for mammal species and second for birds, the Inca Trail is home to some unexpectedly dramatic species.

Iconic Mammals

The Inca were so in awe of their mystical mountain lion that they built Cusco, their capital city, in the shape of one. Also present in the Andes, the jaguar might be the holy grail of Peruvian wildlife watchers but the enigmatic puma is equally hard to forget if you've ever spotted one bounding lithely along a remote highland trail. One of the most widely distributed terrestrial big cats, the puma's status is officially listed by Convention on International Trade in Endangered Species (CITES) as 'least concern' yet it is so elusive that the chances of encountering one in the wild are close to zero.

You do have a very good chance, however, of spotting the elegant white-tailed deer, one of the puma's main prey species, and the extremely cute viscacha (similar to a rabbit, but with a squirrel's tail). Spectacled bears are also sometimes seen by lucky hikers. To the Incas the bear was believed to be an alter-ego of the high priests who prayed to the *apus*. Popular folklore stories feature a sort of 'were-bear' known as *ukuko,* in an Andean love story involving a highland maiden and a bear that protected her.

You're more likely to see guinea pig as domesticated livestock in Quechua homes, though populations of smaller brown montane guinea pig *(Cavia tschudii)* continue to exist in some areas. The domesticated species *(Cavia porcellus),* used as a food-source since around 5000 BCE, is distinct and doesn't exist in the wild.

There are several members of the camelids family too (see p134), some of which still run wild. Woolly alpacas graze on the alpine meadows of the Inca Trail while llamas inhabit the warmer cloud forest sections, specifically on the invasive kikuyu-grassed terraces of Intipata and Machu Picchu.

Entering the cloud forest areas you might also be lucky enough to see the nimble little agouti (like a long-legged guinea pig), a family of coatis (sometimes described as a South American raccoon) or the arboreal chinchilla rat *(Cuscomys oblativus),* which was first recorded in 2020. You might even become one of the few people

GALYNA ANDRUSHKO/SHUTTERSTOCK

NOTABLE LOCATIONS FOR SIGHTINGS

Abra Warmiwañusqa (p80)

Camera-trap images of, and spoor from, puma have been found on the peak immediately to the west of Dead Woman's Pass.

Runquraqay Pass (p93)

The *mirador* (lookout), accessible via a steep scramble up the southern side of Runquraqay Pass, is one of the most likely places from which to spot spectacled bears.

Wiñay Wayna (p132)

An excellent place to see families of coatí, the raccoon-like creature known locally as *capiso.*

MAPHKE/SHUTTERSTOCK

Left: Alpacas
Right: Viscacha

ever to see *Incanomys mayopuma* – a member of the rodent family which could be described as an 'Andean platypus.' Discovered in June 2025 near Wiñay Wayna, its rather formidable name derives from the Quechua *'mayopuma,'* meaning 'river puma.'

Sacred Reptiles

Hiram Bingham III, the US explorer who in 1911 brought Machu Picchu to the notice of the rest of the world, suggested – apparently without a shred of evidence – that Inca priests probably predicted the future by watching which holes 'trained snakes' would emerge from. Despite also being represented in Inca mythology as the creatures that represent *ukhu pacha* (the underworld), snakes – 'trained' or otherwise – are rarely seen in the highlands.

Rather than being seen as a sinister and devious creature, the snake has very positive connotations in Andean belief. Even today some Quechua people name their kids Amaru (snake), since the reptile symbolizes wisdom, while at the same time being a connection between man and Pachamama (Mother Earth).

Feathered Gems

Among Peru's estimated 1892 bird species there can be little to match the effortless soaring of the mighty condors (which, it's believed, can reach altitudes up to 8000m). To an avid birdwatcher the flight of a giant hummingbird is just as mesmerizing. In 2024, scientists realized that the slightly bigger northern giant hummingbird (resident in Peru) is a separate species – it has

MILTON RODRIGUEZ/SHUTTERSTOCK

THE REAL PADDINGTON BEAR

Contrary to popular belief it's very unlikely that a spectacled bear was ever spotted at London's Paddington Station but they are sometimes seen prowling the ruins of Machu Picchu. In fact, there are around 45 spectacled bears (South America's only bear species) living in the vicinity of the historic sanctuary. With a total wild population of 18,000, Peru is home to the largest population on the planet.

BEST BIRD-SIGHTINGS

Andean Condor

Only rarely seen on the Inca Trail, the Incas believed condors were immortal and that they were the embodiment of *apus*.

Giant Hummingbird

About the size of a small thrush, *Patagona chaski* hovers at a fairly sedate (for a hummingbird) 15 wing-beats per second.

Sword-Billed Hummingbird

Perhaps the most spectacular of Peru's 400 or so hummingbird species, this one is unique for being 'more beak than body.'

GALLO IMAGES/GETTYIMAGES

Green jay

been named *Patagona chaski,* after the fleet-footed Inca messengers (usually spelled *chasqui*) who used to run the highland trails.

The Andean cock-of-the-rock *(Rupicola peruvianus)* are occasionally seen in the cloud forests and along the valleys. Listen out for the pig-like squeal that earned this spectacular scarlet bird its slightly disrespectful Quechua name *'cuchi pishku'* (pig bird), though it's more often known in Peru simply as *tunki*. The rarely-spotted quetzals are famed for their jewel-like iridescence, while gorgeous green jays, known sometimes as Inca jays or onomatopoeically to locals as *querrequerre,* are likely to brighten your hike from time to time with their vivid plumage. Yet even these avian beauties look drab next to the versicolored barbet *(Eubucco versicolor),* which looks like it must have been present at a riot in a kindergarten art class.

Motmot

A spectacularly colorful bird with a distinctive racket-shaped tail and an unmistakable hooting 'mot-mot' call.

Andean Gull

You might be surprised to see what appears to be 'seagulls' flying along Urubamba Valley but this is their natural breeding ground.

Mountain Caracara

A spectacularly large falcon often seen above Dead Woman's Pass with black and white plumage and a vibrant red face.

Taste of the Highlands

It will surprise noone that the World Travel Awards' 'World's Leading Culinary Destination' has a lot to offer the adventurous foodie.

CUSCO IS ONE of Peru's gastronomic powerhouses (p37), but even smaller towns like Urubamba (p51), Pisac (p45) and Ollantaytambo (p53) offer incredible culinary diversity. Little Machu Picchu Pueblo (often known as Aguas Calientes; p180) is an unexpectedly cosmopolitan town where menus feature regional cuisine alongside delicious international offerings.

More than Guinea Pig & Alpaca

Few tourists can resist the opportunity to sample *cuy* (guinea pig) at least once during their Peruvian highland adventure. A decade ago, the domesticated Andean rodent was an unappealing prospect, with its clenched claws and rat-like grimace. These days many tourist-level restaurants will prepare choice cuts that are served and presented like particularly tender and delicious crispy belly pork.

Alpaca, too, is served in countless ways that pleasantly surprise international visitors. For those who just want the merest sample, you'll even find alpaca and guinea pig served as a topping for pizzas.

Beef, lamb and the ubiquitous *chancho* (pork) are also widely available. Trout is a regular fixture on menus and is served as irresistible ceviche or found in its smoked form on hotel breakfast buffets.

Fruit, Veg & 4000+ Potatoes!

Traditionally a staunchly carnivorous society, the rich agricultural areas of the Andean valleys also produce some of the world's finest vegetables, so finding good vegetarian meals is no hardship here. Dinner at tourist-style restaurants is often accompanied with seven or eight varieties of what are described as 'native potatoes.' There are over 4000 varieties in Peru and some restaurants even have 'potato-tasting experiences.'

Be sure to look out for *causa limeña*, mashed yellow potatoes seasoned with chili and lemon and stuffed – often with meat or tuna but frequently also with other vegetables. *Causa*

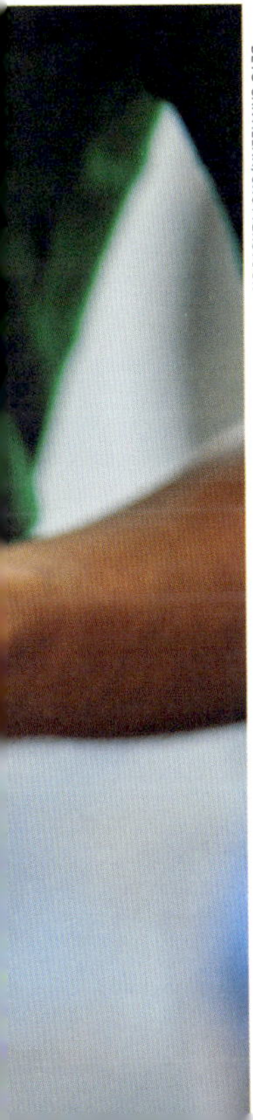

BETO SANTILLAN/SHUTTERSTOCK

BEST EATS

Mercado San Pedro, Cusco (p38)
Look out for smoked cheese and the great wheels of bread known as *chuta de Oropesa.*

Mercado San Blas, Cusco (p43)
Great vegetarian meals but best known for the most delicious, and most affordable, ceviche in the city.

Chuncho, Ollantaytambo (p52)
The tasting plate (with alpaca and guinea pig) is a regional favorite.

Kampu, Urubamba (p52)
A Sacred Valley hot spot, featuring the freshest ingredients – some plucked directly from the owner's garden.

KAROL MORAES/SHUTTERSTOCK

Left: *Causa limeña;* Right: Woman with traditional bread

cevichado combines this Andean staple, which some say derives its name from a Quechua word meaning 'giver of life,' with a topping of ceviche.

Even the most fleeting glance around local markets will reveal an amazing diversity of fruits and vegetables, along with a mind-boggling variety of cereals and seeds, some of which, like quinoa, have been a staple since the time of the Incas. Innovative Andean fusion dishes include vegetarian specialties such as quinoa risotto and cassava casserole.

Street Food

Even at the street-stall level Peruvian cuisine is typically freshly prepared, healthy and appetizing. Try a lunch of fresh ceviche in Cusco's San Blas market (p43), served with *leche de tigre* (tiger's milk), the deliciously tangy, spicy sauce made from evaporated milk. There's something to be said for supporting grass-roots local industries such as the women who sell *choclo* (boiled corn cobs) or empanadas (meat- or cheese-filled pastries) on street corners. The humble *classico,* a ham and cheese roll sold by vendors outside Machu Picchu archaeological site, makes for an irresistible and affordable picnic supplement in an area that's famously expensive.

You'll find that variety is fairly limited in the most remote rural communities, with potatoes, rice and chicken being staple fare. *Cuy* (guinea pig) might be served during festivals and celebrations. Thanks to the Sacred Valley's popularity with tourists, however, you'll find a varied and tempting culinary scene in all areas frequented by tourists.

BLKG/SHUTTERSTOCK

CHICHA

Traditionally, the active ingredient in the fermentation of the corn drink known as *chicha* was human saliva. Its fermentation was started by women who chewed the corn and spat it into *aribalo* (an urn with a conical bottom that was sunk in the soil, perhaps so that Pachamama – Mother Earth – played a part in the process). Non-alcoholic *chicha* (produced by more hygienic means) is still a popular staple for Inca Trail porters.

UNEXPECTED LOCAL SPECIALTIES

Pachamanca
Pachamanca feasts, with meat and vegetables roasted in a ground oven, are particularly popular around Ollantaytambo.

Lechón
The town of Huarocondo (close to Urubamba) is known as Tierra del Lechón for its slow-roasted pork.

Puca Picante
While *puca picante* (a stew of beets, peanuts and potatoes) is most famous in Ayacucho, you'll also find it in *cuzqueña* restaurants.

ARTURO LOPEZ LLONTOP/SHUTTERSTOCK

Pachamanca feast

Dining on the Inca Trail

Inca Trail tour operators pride themselves on serving abundant, healthy and delicious meals. If you're expecting basic camping-style fare, you're likely to be very pleasantly surprised. The camp chefs (who also double as porters) are among the hardest-working members of the Inca Trail teams. Normally they begin preparations for breakfast – which might include hot drinks, eggs or omelets, and bread – at around 4am.

They then have to race ahead to fix a hearty sit-down lunch, then overtake you again on the trail so that they can prepare a three-course dinner – perhaps corn soup, mushroom ceviche, excellent guacamole or *lomo saltado* (stir-fried sirloin strips with vegetables). In between these meals, juice and snacks will be served, in the form of popcorn, biscuits, fruit or the irresistible *tequeños* (pastry wraps filled with white Peruvian cheese).

Most hikers enjoy custom-mixing their own trail mix with dried fruit, nuts, chocolate, cookies and jelly sweets for sustenance on the trail, but hunger is unlikely to be part of the Inca Trail challenge. Many hikers feel that, despite the rigors of the trek, you're more likely to put weight on rather than lose it!

Pisco Sour

Peruvian mixologists pride themselves on serving delicious and potent pisco sours – a ubiquitous treat that rarely disappoints.

Fruit Juices

Be sure to head to any local market for a breakfast of super-vitamin juices, often served with milk, wild honey, pollen, maca and even beer.

Coati Poop Coffee

Some Peruvian baristas have jumped on the *kopi luwak* (civet coffee) bandwagon.

Floral Kingdom

Landscapes and vegetation change rapidly – often by the hour – as you hike through a series of biomes along the Inca Trail.

'IN INCA LAND one may pass from glaciers to tree ferns within a few hours,' Hiram Bingham III wrote of his first expedition along the Urubamba Valley in 1911.

One sweeping glance at the brutal ridges of the Sacred Valley is enough to convince anyone that the highland people have learned to survive here only because they're attuned to the natural environment.

The great feat of engineering that is the Inca Trail climbs, swoops and weaves through a whole spectrum of botanical biomes including high *páramo* grasslands, alpine tundra, highland jungles and cloud forests. The vegetation – often changing dramatically within the course of an hour's hiking – is a constant fascination on the Inca Trail. The trail is frequently brightened by flashes of red from flowering banks of Bolivian fuchsia and Chinese lanterns *(Abutilon)* or the multicolored glow of lantana *(Lantana montevidensis)*. There are ever-changing scents too with wild sage, thyme and the Andean mint known as *muña (Minthostachys mollis)* constantly reminding you to take deeper gasps of reinvigorating oxygen out of the rarefied air. Less appealing, the poisonous *Arum italicum* is for obvious reasons often known as the 'corpse flower.'

MIROSLAV SRB/SHUTTERSTOCK

NATURAL DIVERSITY

High Puna Grasslands
Characterized by stiff ichu grass that was used by the Incas for thatching.

Woodland
Riverside forests of deciduous Andean alders *(Alnus acuminata)* and hardy unca trees *(Myrcianthes oreophila)*.

Ceja de Selva
Descending from Phuyupatamarka you enter the cloud forest area known as the 'eyebrow of the jungle.'

Cloud Forest
Known in Quechua as '*yunka*,' the moist jungle trails are lined with *curcur (Chusquea delicatula)* cane and some 30 species of orchids.

Left: Rusty flowerpiercer on *kantu*
Right: Andean cloud forest

Orchids

Peru is said to be home to around 10% of the world's orchids and about 400 species have been recorded in Machu Picchu Historical Sanctuary alone. Nearby, Inkaterra Machu Picchu Pueblo Hotel runs afternoon tours through tropical gardens that boast a spectacular collection of 372 species.

Useful Plants

Among the dry montane forests take note of the tough hardwood trees known as *chachacomos (Escallonia resinosa)*, which were harvested by the Incas to make tools and to carve the ceremonial vessels known as *kero*. The Incas didn't take all their secrets with them: ichu grass is still

MARC MORAITIS/SHUTTERSTOCK

used for thatching in remote mountain hamlets and even for making rope bridges, and the little green globules of llullucha *(Nostoc sphaericum)* – a gelatinous algae that grows in high-altitude wetlands – is still collected to enrich soups.

Sacred Plants of the Incas

Along with the world famous – some might say notorious – coca (see p112) *muña* has been used since the time of the Incas to counteract the effects of altitude sickness. You're sure to have a chance to drink *muña* tea (often combined with coca leaves) while on the trail.

Look out too for the elegant trumpets of the fuchsia-like *kantu (Cantua buxi folia),* Peru's national flower and one which featured in many Inca ceremonies. Spanish chroniclers wrote that its petals were used to decorate the roads upon which the Sapa Inca would pass. According to Inca chronicler Inka Garcilaso de la Vega, *kantu* blooms were used as military insignia by Inca nobility and even today the flower has spiritual importance and is used to adorn traditional offerings. The pisonay tree *(Erythrina falcata),* of which there's a spectacular specimen in the heart of Machu Picchu, is also still considered sacred.

FRIDA MARTHA/SHUTTERSTOCK

THE 'FOREVER YOUNG' ORCHID

In 1942 Peruvian archaeologist Julio C Tello was studying ruins behind Machu Picchu Mountain when he noticed some beautiful orchids *(Epidendrum secundum).* His Quechua guide told him they were known locally as Wiñay Wayna – which means 'forever young' – because they bloom almost year-round and the flower lasts for up to three weeks. Inspired, Tello decided it was the perfect name for the newly excavated archaeological site.

ORCHIDS TO LOOK FOR

Platystele Peruviana
It's hard to spot one of the smallest in the world, with the entire plant measuring just a few centimeters tall

Phragmipedium Caudatum
You're more likely to notice the Mandarin orchid, a local giant which is famous for having petals that stretch up to a meter long.

Masdevallia Veitchiana
Known as the Waqanki orchid, the name (meaning 'You Will Cry') derives from a Quechua Romeo and Juliet-style myth.

Pisonay tree, Machu Picchu
MARK EVELEIGH

A History of the Inca Trail

To walk the Inca Trail is to traverse a 500-year-old engineering marvel that's full of mystery and awe-inspiring sights. From its 15th-century origins as a sacred 'Road to the Sun' to its long hibernation following the Spanish Conquest, and its 20th-century emergence as a global trekking icon, the trail continues to encourage a sense of adventure.

The Royal Road: Building the Trail

Many centuries before worldly adventurers began trekking the iconic Inca Trail, this 44km path was just a minuscule part of an ancient road network spanning more than 30,000km. The Quechua people called it the Qhapaq Ñan (p68) – the royal road – a network that spanned large parts of present-day Peru, Colombia, Ecuador, Bolivia, Chile and Argentina.

Messengers known as *chasquis* (p84) ran along these roads carrying messages. Armies made their way from one side of the empire to the other. Administrators and laborers traveled between state centers such as Quito and Cusco.

Ruling over the empire was Pachacutec, the ninth Sapa Inca (Inca emperor). This influential leader whose name loosely translates to 'transformer of the earth,' orchestrated his peoples' vast and rapid expansion beyond the Cusco region. In a matter of decades, the Inca rapidly expanded their territorial reach by

BROOKLYN MUSEUM, PUBLIC DOMAIN, VIA WIKIMEDIA COMMONS

400–700
The Wari build roads across present-day Peru

500–1000
Tiwanaku, near Lake Titicaca, reaches its height

C 1200
The Inca found Cusco

C 1438
Pachacutec leads an Inca expansion across the continent

thousands of square kilometers. If Pachacutec was unsuccessful in conquering territories and people through political means, he called on his growing army to seize them by force. He compelled conquered people to pay tribute through labor, with many playing a part in the construction of the citadel now known as Machu Picchu (p166), which Pachacutec used as his personal refuge.

The complex also housed administrators, astronomers, priests and workers, all of whom traveled along the Inca Trail on their way to and from the site. The route's enormous stone gateways and elaborate terraces indicate ancient travelers viewed the journey to Machu Picchu as a spiritual experience. Access routes into the citadel were carefully planned. Approaching from the highlands, travelers would have passed through a sequence of way stations and ceremonial sites. Complexes like Wiñay Wayna combine agricultural terraces with ritual spaces, suggesting both practical and spiritual functions were intertwined along the route.

In this early phase, the Inca Trail was not a destination but a single thread in a complex web. Instead, it was the city of Cusco, which the Inca believed to be the navel of the world, that was at the center of the Qhapaq Ñan.

Pachacutec

PACHACUTEC

The ninth Sapa Inca, Pachacutec transformed the Inca Empire from a regional kingdom centered around Cusco to Tahuantinsuyo (Land of Four Quarters), a vast empire that extended from modern-day Ecuador to Chile. Credited with founding the citadel we now know as Machu Picchu, establishing the Inti Raymi festival (p44), and constructing vast irrigation networks, agricultural terraces and roads throughout the lands he conquered, Pachacutec was a shrewd and strategic ruler. In addition to expanding his empire through diplomacy and force, Pachacutec enacted a system of forced migration by which colonists from Cusco were sent to populate unstable regions, embedding Inca culture into far-flung societies.

C 1450
Construction on Machu Picchu begins

1493
Inca Huayna Capac continues Qhapaq Ñan's expansion

1532
Spanish conquistadors arrive in the Andes

1544
Manco Inca is assassinated

Conquest & Decline: The Trail is Lost

The short-lived golden age of the Inca came to an end with the arrival of Spanish forces in the 1530s. Under Francisco Pizarro's leadership, conquistadors shattered the political world that had built the road system. First he captured and murdered Atahualpa, the Sapa Inca who had taken the throne just months before. Next, his forces captured Cusco.

The conquistadors then consolidated power by replacing Inca rulers with handpicked puppet leaders. Manco Inca, one of the rulers chosen by the Spanish, eventually turned against them. During the course of the Inca's staged rebellion, they intentionally destroyed key parts of the Qhapaq Ñan, including the Inca Trail, in an effort to protect their hidden strongholds and armies from being attacked.

The Inca rebellion rocked the conquistadors on their heels, but ultimately failed, marking the start of the colonial era. Reliant on horseback, the Spanish found the Qhapaq Ñan's precipitous, stepped footpaths challenging for the animals to navigate, so rather than travel on preexisting Inca paths, they built and used their own roads.

Now devoid of its administrative and ceremonial functions, the Inca abandoned Machu Picchu and the jungle quickly reclaimed the stone steps. For nearly four centuries, the royal route to Machu Picchu was swallowed by the dense canopy, remembered and known by only a few.

HIRAM BINGHAM III, PUBLIC DOMAIN, VIA WIKIMEDIA COMMONS

Local man, Machu Picchu, early 20th century

Back in the Spotlight: From Lost City to Global Icon

In 1911, American explorer and Yale academic Hiram Bingham III brought the ruins of Machu Picchu to the attention of the outside world (p164). While many people associate his name with the site's 'discovery,' it would be a mistake to do so: local Quechua families, who had been farming the citadel's terraces, guided the explorer to the ruins. The site and its surrounds had never been 'lost' to these farmers or their ancestors, who lived in the area for hundreds of years.

In the years following Bingham's famous expedition, the trail remained a local path used by farmers and occasional foreign visitors. In 1940 and 1941, Hungarian archaeologist Paul Fejos led the Viking Fund Scientific Expedition to unearth large sections of Machu Picchu. Like Bingham, his team depended on the knowledge of local guides. This expedition meticulously cleared away and documented parts of the Inca Trail and nearby archaeological sites such as the stunning agricultural terraces of Wiñay Wayna, later meticulously excavated by Peruvian archaeologist Julio C Tello.

1874
Mapmaker Herman Göhring notes location of Machu Picchu

1911
Quechua farmers lead Hiram Bingham to Machu Picchu

1941
Inca site Wiñay Wayna is uncovered

1948
Hiram Bingham publishes *Lost City of the Incas*

HISTORICAL HIGHLIGHTS

Wiñay Wayna (p132)
A terraced agricultural complex and ritual site whose existence illustrates how the route linked sacred landscapes with working settlements during the Inca Empire.

Intipunku (Sun Gate; p147)
The ceremonial entrance where trekkers first glimpse Machu Picchu is a testament to how the Incas designed the journey itself as a dramatic and symbolic arrival.

Runquraqay (p93)
This semicircular stone structure perched high above the valley likely served as a resting place and relay station for *chasqui* messengers carrying imperial news.

By the early 1970s, independent travelers from around the world were traveling to Machu Picchu, many inspired by the advocacy of local Peruvians who recognized the area's potential as an adventure travel destination (p98). Early travelers typically carried simple, hand-drawn maps they bought in Cusco's markets. As word about the complex spread, more travelers arrived and in the 1980s, having now recognized the trail's tourism potential, the Peruvian government began to restore large sections of the original stonework.

Becoming a Popular Trekking Route

By the late 1980s, the trail emerged as a globally recognized bucket-list destination. Thousands of visitors walked the route annually. The trail's popularity brought significant pressure. The heavy foot traffic caused problems with erosion, waste and challenges with the preservation of archaeological sites.

In response, the Peruvian government began to regulate activity in the area. Regulations introduced in 2002 established a permit system and in 2005, the number of people entering the trail was limited to 500 (including porters) each day, while daily visitor numbers to Machu Picchu were capped at 2500. The trail is closed during the month of February (the height of the rainy season) for maintenance each year, while conservation efforts, such as weight limits for backpacks and a prohibition against plastic water bottles, aim to protect both the historic path and the surrounding environment year-round.

This modern phase has also reshaped the trail's human history. Today the Inca Trail exists simultaneously as archaeology, adventure and cultural landscape. Trekking tourism supports thousands of guides, porters and cooks, many from high-mountain communities. Their ancestors once traveled this same route in very different circumstances, and their labor and knowledge underpin the modern trekking experience.

1970S
International hikers begin following Qhapaq Ñan segments

1981
The Machu Picchu Historical Sanctuary is established

2002
Peruvian government introduces Inca Trail permit system

2014
The Qhapaq Ñan is designated a UNESCO World Heritage Site

6 Ways to Do the Inca Trail

It's often said that there are only two ways to reach Machu Picchu: take the train or walk. Actually, it's a little more complex than that, so we've delved into the options to help you find the way that suits you best.

1 Classic Inca Trail

Time *4 days*

Best for *The full experience*

The Classic Trail takes you over mountain passes, through cloud forests and past Inca ruins before greeting the sun at Intipunku on your final morning, then descending to the iconic citadel. The trail can only be walked with a certified operator and a maximum of 500 people (including guides and porters) may start the trail each day.

Possible overnights Wayllabamba, Paqaymayu Alto, Wiñay Wayna

See p30 for the full route map

MARK EVELEIGH

2 Two-Day Inca Trail

Time *2 days*

Best for *A taste of the trail*

The two-day Inca Trail (p148) offers a more affordable and accessible 'taster' of the Inca Trail experience, though hikers no longer spend a night on the trail due to overcrowding at Wiñay Wayna Camp. Instead, the two-day option involves an 11km (six- to eight-hour) one-day hike to Intipunku, followed by a bus to a hostel/hotel in Machu Picchu Pueblo. On day two, guests are transported back up to Machu Picchu archaeological site for a tour.

Possible overnight Machu Picchu Pueblo (aka Aguas Calientes)

3 Five-Day Inca Trail

Time *5 days*

Best for *In-depth exploration with fewer crowds*

This less rushed option with more time to explore is available through many operators and has the benefit of avoiding the most crowded camps. Your last night is typically spent at the idyllic Phuyupatamarka – one of the most spectacular (but chilliest) spots on the route.

Possible overnights Patallaqta, Wayllabamba, Paqaymayo, Llactapata, Llulluchapampa, Phuyupatamarka, Machu Picchu Pueblo

Hikers, Inca Trail near Llulluchapampa (p79)

BETO SANTILLAN/SHUTTERSTOCK

Train to Machu Picchu Pueblo (p176)

Go to p193 for other treks in the region

4 Rail & Bus

Time *1-2 days*
Best for *Machu Picchu visits without the strenuous hike*

Most people arrive in Machu Picchu Pueblo by rail (p176) from either Cusco (3½ hours) or Ollyantaytambo (two hours). From the train station, you need to book return bus tickets *(comprar.caminoalamaravilla.com)* for the 25-minute ride up the grandly named Hiram Bingham Hwy to the archaeological site. It's possible to do this in one day, but staying overnight ensures you have a full morning to visit the site you've traveled so far to see.

Possible overnight Machu Picchu Pueblo

5 Budget 'Backdoor' Route

Time *1-2 days*
Best for *Budget travelers*

Catch a bus from Ollantaytambo to the railhead north of Machu Picchu at Hidroeléctrica (S70, 8:45am). You can then either take a train from 'Hidro' to Machu Picchu Pueblo (S130) or enjoy a beautiful hike. The first 2½ hours of the trail runs alongside the cascading Río Urubamba and the last 1½ hours climbs the steep steps up to Machu Picchu ruins.

Possible overnights Mandor Pampa Lodge

6 Salkantay Trek to Machu Picchu

Time *5 days*
Best for *A road-less-traveled experience*

The Salkantay Trek (p194) is the only non-Inca Trail trek that ends at Machu Picchu ruins. Feasible as a self-guided walk, highlights of the 74km hike include the little-known Llactapata ruins (p186) and an overnight stay at Llactapata Lodge (p205) with views to Machu Picchu. After descending the Ahobamba Valley you arrive at Hidroeléctrica where you can follow the walking trail along the Río Urubamba.

Possible overnights Soraypampa, Collpapampa, Lucmababamba, Machu Picchu Pueblo

WHEN TO GO

Jan–Mar
Rains can be heavy but crowds are limited. In February the Inca Trail closes for maintenance, although Machu Picchu remains open.

Apr–May
Good dry-season hiking with lush vegetation and misty mountain views at their most spectacular.

Jun–Aug
Winter months are usually dry and are the most popular time to visit. Book six to nine months in advance.

Sep–Dec
Rains begin and the trail becomes quieter. Rise early in the morning for optimum walking conditions, coupled with warmer nights.

Intipunku to Machu Picchu, p154
Machu Picchu, p166
Machu Picchu Pueblo, p180
END
Machu Picchu
Intipunku (Sun Gate)
Wiñay Wayna to Intipunku, p138
Wiñay Wayna
Phuyupatamarka to Wiñay Wayna, p122
Phuyupatamarka Camp
Sayaqmarca to Phuyupatamarka, p102
Sayaqmarca
Abra Warmiwañusqa
Warmiwañusqa to Sayaqmarca, p86
N
0
5 km
0
2.5 miles

The Walk

A stage-by-stage, kilometer-by-kilometer account of the route. Your journey begins here.

CUSCO & THE SACRED VALLEY

Welcome to the altitudinous Cusco region, the cradle of the Inca Empire. The mountains will steal your heart – but only after they've taken your breath away. Here, living local traditions thrive next to caravans of sleekly dressed tourists. Agricultural communities continue to work in fields beneath blazing Inti (sun god) and words with Quechua origins like *choclo* (corn) and *chacra* (cropland) are woven through daily language, keeping native Andean ancestry unquestionably present. Home to the imperial capital Cusco and the Sacred Valley, this is where your journey into Inca heartland begins.

Conical terraces, Moray (p53)
SAIKO3P/SHUTTERSTOCK

CITY GUIDE:

Cusco

More than a capital, Cusco was the axis of the Inca universe, spiritually and politically. Wandering the city's narrow streets – where Inca foundations underlie colonial facades and temples crown the surrounding hillsides – elevates your Inca Trail trek to a passage through a living empire.

WORDS BY **AGNES RIVERA**
Agnes remembers sliding down the rock walls (rodaderos) *near Sacsaywamán on her first Cusco visit in 2007.*

Arriving

Plane The gateway to Peru for international travelers, Lima's **Aeropuerto Internacional Jorge Chávez** connects to Cusco's **Aeropuerto Internacional Alejandro Velasco Astete** with a short, one-hour flight. Authorized taxis waiting just outside baggage claim charge S35 to S45 to the historic center, while taxis found on the street charge S15 to S25.
Bus Direct bus rides from Lima to Cusco are possible with Cruz del Sur *(cruzdelsur.com.pe)*; however they take nearly 24 hours. Scenic hop-on, hop-off services are available with **PeruHop** *(bushop.com/peru)*, extending the commute to at least three days.

HOW MUCH FOR A

Coffee S10

***Cuy al horno* (roast guinea pig) S50-70**

Qoricancha entry S15

Getting Around

Take it slow as you acclimate to being nearly 3400m above sea level, allowing a day or two to settle in if you have the time. Hop in a taxi if you're feeling any effects of altitude sickness and consider staying in the lower altitudes (below 3000m) of the Sacred Valley (p50) if symptoms persist.
Walking Most of Cusco's main attractions are clustered in the historic center or in the blocks surrounding it. Many streets have sidewalks, but are sloped. It's not a bad idea to walk around in your hiking boots – in fact, you'll see a majority of other travelers doing just this.
Rideshares Rideshare apps like Uber and taxis circulating the historic center are handy if you'd rather save your legs for the trail or if you are feeling the effects of altitude sickness. For safety reasons, such as theft, and to avoid paying exorbitant rates, stick to the rideshare apps.
Buses Figuring out the operations of Cusco's inner-city buses isn't worth the hassle for short-term visitors, but *combis* (shared minivans) to the Sacred Valley are handy and cheap (between US$2 to US$4). The white vans depart from Puente Grau, a 20-minute walk from Plaza de Armas.

Calle Pumacurco, Cusco

FROM LEFT: EDUARDO VIDAL GUTIERREZ/SHUTTERSTOCK, CRISTI CROITORU/SHUTTERSTOCK

GOLD
GARDEN

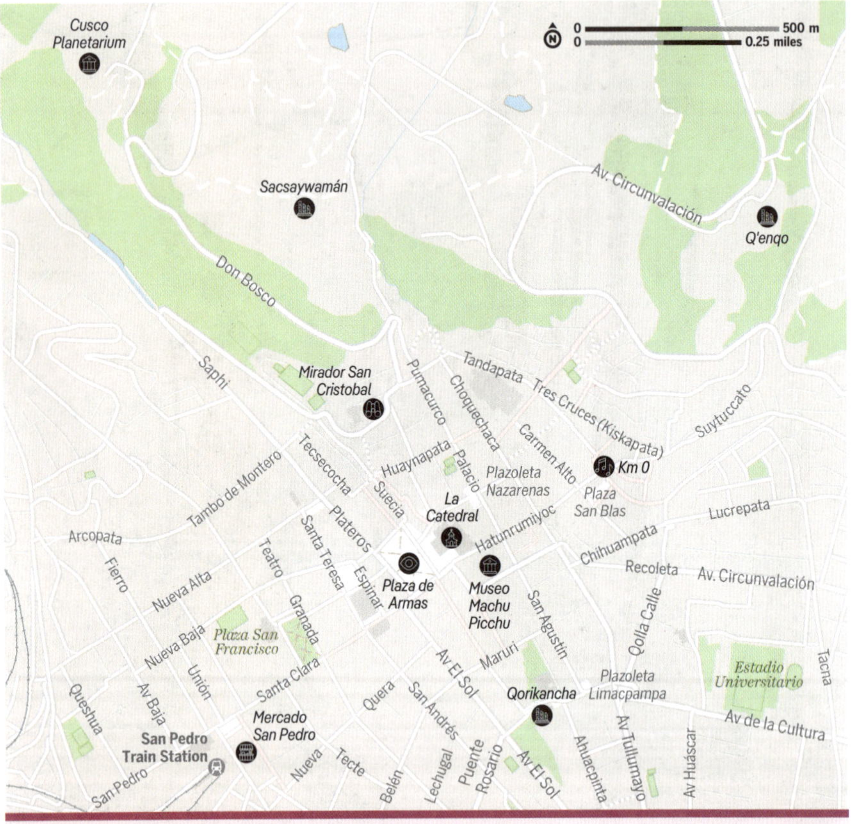

A DAY IN CUSCO

Follow the morning sun to **Qorikancha** (p40), the foremost Inca temple and ode to the sun deity, Inti. Head to **Plaza de Armas**, where a golden Inca Pachacutec rises from the central fountain, then stroll through **San Blas artisans' quarter** (p43), before heading to **Mercado San Pedro** (p38) to sip on an exotic juice and shop for souvenirs.

Climb stone stairways or opt for a taxi to reach the stunning **Sacsaywamán** (p39), where impeccable afternoon views of the city below are an added bonus. Laze in the site's open fields or continue exploring labyrinthine **Q'enqo** (p38) or get a taxi (15 to 20 minutes) to the advanced aqueducts of **Tambomachay** (p38).

At **Cusco Planetarium** (p42), gaze at 'dark constellations' in the Milky Way above, celestial beings that will accompany you on the trek. Afterwards, peruse concept stores and dinner spots in the trendy San Blas neighborhood. A nightcap at tapas bar **Km 0** could not be more fitting.

Where to Stay

Cusco has hotels for every budget, but don't base your pre-trek lodging solely on price: party hostels are not going to give you the restful sleep you need. Stick to the historic center and surrounding neighborhoods – San Cristobal and San Blas – so that you can easily stroll to major attractions or get a taxi for a reasonable price. The night before your pickup for the trek, request a box breakfast from your hotel. If you are struggling with altitude, consider staying in the Sacred Valley (p52).

BEST PLACES TO STAY

Niños Hotel Meloc $$ Charming hotel and restaurant supporting underprivileged youth. *ninoshotel.com*

La Bo'M Backpacker $ Calm hostel above San Blas crepe shop. Has trekking gear for rent. *labohemecusco.com*

Casa Tunki $ Upscale hostel with spacious pods and private rooms. Superb breakfast. *casatunki.com*

Tierra Viva Cusco Centro $$ Colonial building with double-glazed windows for light sleepers. *casa-andina.com*

Where to Eat

Cusco may not be Peru's culinary capital, but it has quietly built for itself a scene of go-to classics alongside tucked-away bars and cafes worth seeking out. The Plaza de Armas has plenty of tourist traps, but there are also some gems where traditional flavors are enjoyed in a casual fine-dining setting. San Blas is brimming with aesthetic cafes, while delicious budget bites can be found in the food stalls of Mercado San Pedro (p38) and neighboring Mercado Cascaparo.

JANA BURYSKOVA/SHUTTERSTOCK

CUY AL HORNO

For many visitors, the guinea pig conjures up childhood memories of a furry household pet; for *cuzqueños* (inhabitants of Cusco), it's a delicacy of long-running tradition. Originating in the Andes over 5000 years ago, the domesticated species *(Cavia porcellus)* was raised to be a food source and has been a high-protein, low-fat staple in the highlands ever since. The mainly plant-based diet of the Incas incorporated *cuy* (pictured right) during ceremonies and celebrations. Today, rural families commonly share portions of their abode with the timid creatures, feeding them a diet of foraged greens until plump enough to cook. The regional classic *cuy al horno* (roast guinea pig) begins by rubbing the rodent with a mix of herbs (heavy on the *huacatay* – Peruvian black mint) and spices, then bathing it in a citrus dressing. Slowly baked to crisp perfection then served whole – tiny claws and teeth included – this is a dish best approached with a sense of curiosity.

BEST PLACES TO EAT & DRINK

Cusqueñisima Picanteria $$ Taxi 15 minutes from Plaza de Armas to try *chicha de jora* (corn beer). Reservations required. *11am-5pm*

Limbus $ Cocktails and pub food with a view at golden hour. *Calle Pasñapakana 133; 9am-midnight*

Pachapapa $$ Cozy atmosphere. Contact to order roast guinea pig in advance. *@pachapapacusco; noon-10pm*

Florencia y Fortunata $ Specialty coffee harvested and brewed by women. *@florenciayfortunata.cafe; noon-11pm*

BETO SANTILLAN/SHUTTERSTOCK

Fruit stalls, Mercado San Pedro

Mercado San Pedro

Peruse over 1000 stalls in Cusco's oldest market, the centenarian **Mercado San Pedro** *(from 6:30am),* a 10-minute walk from Plaza de Armas. Piles of coca leaves, sea shells and huayruro seeds – bundled as *pagos a la tierra* (offerings to Mother Earth) – will pique your curiosity. Sip on Amazonian flavors from the juice bars, where vendors can prescribe healing concoctions. Bulk bins of Peruvian superfoods, dried fruit and nuts are ideal for making a personalized (Inca) trail mix. Browse potential souvenirs toward the back, but don't skip the curious vendors along the market's periphery.

BIG CAT CITY

According to chroniclers such as Garcilaso de la Vega and local tradition, the Incas designed Cusco in the shape of a puma, a creature symbolizing strength and protection in Andean cosmology. Alongside the condor (sky) and serpent (underworld), the puma represented the earthly world *(kay pacha)* for the Incas.

Two rivers – the Saphy and the Tullumayo – once flowed above ground, forming natural boundaries that helped define the cat-like outline. The head of the puma is the mighty fortress of Sacsaywamán, with its zigzagging stone walls evoking the animal's teeth. The body stretches across the city center, while the tail extends southeast along what is now Av del Sol. The Plaza de Armas, once called Huacaypata, formed the puma's 'belly' and the ceremonial center for the Inca capital.

Whether the city was deliberately planned this way or the resemblance is symbolic rather than literal, the story adds another layer of mysticism to your visit. With a bit of imagination, trace the puma's outline while soaking up panoramic views of the city from **Mirador San Cristobal**, a 15-minute walk uphill from the Plaza de Armas along Calle Resbalosa.

TRAVELVIEW/SHUTTERSTOCK

Q'enqo & Tambomachay: Ceremonial Places of Stone & Water

Meaning 'labyrinth' in Quechua, the **Q'enqo** ceremonial site is characterized by stepped rock carvings, zigzagging water channels, a limestone block turned sacrificial surface and subterranean tunnels that, from the Inca worldview, connect the earthly world with the world of the dead. Whereas Q'enqo is a 20-minute walk from Sacsaywamán, **Tambomachay** is a 20-minute taxi ride away. Built upon the Río Tambomachay and underground springs, theories of the site's purpose vary from military post to Inca spa, yet there is one certainty – the two fountains, a feat of pre-Columbian hydraulic engineering, flow year-round.

Left: Tambomachay

Marvel at Sacsaywamán

A feat of Inca engineering, stand next to colossal stones measuring over 8m tall and weighing tons as you overlook the city from the hilltop site.

HOW TO

Getting here: Sacsaywamán is a 15-minute taxi ride (S20) from Plaza de Armas. Starting from the San Blas *barrio* (neighborhood) and walking through Calle Siete Borreguitos, the archaeological site can be reached in 25 to 35 minutes via multiple stairways.

Cost: Included on the full (S130) or partial (S70) Boleto Turístico *(cosituc.gob.pe)*.

Opening hours: 7am-5:30pm

Tip: Hire a guide at the entrance, but linger on the lawn after the tour.

What had long been considered a fortress, Sacsaywamán is now seen by many archaeologists as the *hanan* (upper half) sacred temple to Qoricancha's *hurin* (lower half). Elevated terraces may have functioned as natural observatories for tracking the sun's path and aligning rituals with solstices that structured the agricultural calendar.

You'll feel like an ant as you walk beside its iconic three-tiered, zigzagging walls built using the Inca's masterful cyclopean masonry, where massive stones lock without mortar. These structures are said to outline the puma's head in Cusco's sacred animal layout.

During an Inca rebellion in 1536, Sacsaywamán was stage to a bloody battle between the Spanish and Inca. After weeks of siege and eventual Inca defeat, the site was rampaged by the Spanish for constructions like the plaza's cathedral. What remains today are the colossal stones – some weighing over 100 tons – that were simply too heavy to move.

Time your visit to finish on the expansive lawns just before sunset.

Right: Tourists, Sacsaywamán
Above: Doorway, Sacsaywamán

FROM LEFT: RAFAEL MARTIN-GAITERO/SHUTTERSTOCK, CHRISTIAN VINCES/SHUTTERSTOCK

Revolve Around Qorikancha

Once sheathed in gold and silver, the Incas most important temple continues to radiate power. Qorikancha – literally 'golden enclosure' – may not be as recognizable as Machu Picchu, yet it remains one of the best places to understand the empire's expert engineering that aligned spirituality and astronomy.

HOW TO

Getting here: Qorikancha is a 10-minute walk southeast from the Plaza de Armas, along Av El Sol.

Opening hours: 8:30am to 5:30pm Monday to Saturday, from 2pm Sunday

Cost: S15, cash only

Facilities: A small cafe, restrooms and a gallery are all found inside.

Guides: English-speaking guides congregate at the entrance, with fees hovering around S40.

Tip: For an extra S5 (cash only) you can climb the bell tower for panoramic views.

Dedicated to Viracocha, the creator god, and Inti, the sun deity, Qorikancha was the center of Inca cosmology. From here radiated 41 *ceques,* conceptual lines linking hundreds of *huacas* (sacred spaces) across the empire. These included mountains *(apus),* rivers and stones, along with other natural elements imbued with spirituality. While the Qhapaq Ñan bound the Inca realm with roads, Qorikancha connected it through conceptual sacred pathways.

The *ceque* system wasn't just spiritual. By organizing members of the empire tasked with maintaining and honoring the sacred spaces, the lines also became a social and political tool.

Golden Days

Step inside the sacred temple and you'll see fine ashlar masonry, where niches once held gleaming altars honoring members of the celestial pantheon, such as Killa (the moon deity). Chroniclers describe walls plated in precious metals and a roof of gold straw that shimmered in sunlight. The very rays of the sun were carefully harnessed by way of windows and walls aligned with solstices and equinoxes. In turn, the temple served as an astronomical observatory and solar calendar, essential for timing agricultural practices and festivals like Inti Raymi (p44).

Pause in the garden, where native flowers like cantu *(Cantua buxifolia)* bloom in hues of red and pink. During the empire,

LOVELYPEACE/SHUTTERSTOCK

THE KILLKE

Before Inca Wiracocha commissioned Inticancha – the House of the Sun – around 1200 CE, and long before Pachacutec transformed it into the lavishly decorated Golden Enclosure, the site was sacred to the Killke. Using ground-penetrating radar beneath the Church of Santo Domingo, archaeologists have uncovered crypts, ceramics and buried walls from the 10th to 12th centuries, evidence of the Killke culture that flourished in the Cusco Valley before the rise of the Inca.

Left: Iglesia de Santo Domingo, atop Qorikancha stonework
Below: Inca stonework, Iglesia de Santo Domingo

the lush area was filled with life-size golden figures of llamas, maize and pumas, symbolizing the gifts of the sun's abundance.

A Layered History

After the Spanish conquest in 1533, the Dominicans built the Iglesia de Santo Domingo directly over Qorikancha's foundations. The Renaissance-style structure acquired baroque features following the 1650 earthquake, while the original stone foundation remained intact. Inca stonework below, Spanish architecture above – visitors are witness to a striking showcase of Cusco's quite literal layered history.

SEEWHYBEE/SHUTTERSTOCK

MARCO TULIO FARFAN/SHUTTERSTOCK

Señor de los Temblores, Holy Monday procession

Illuminate Dark Constellations

Look to the night sky to read the invaluable celestial map of Inca astronomers (p150). Guided by experts at **Cusco Planetarium** *(planetariumcusco.com; adult/child S85/60; 6pm Mon-Sat)*, peer through a powerful telescope lens for an up-close look at the Chakana (Southern Cross). Mirroring the four directions of the *suyus* (regions), the constellation helped the Incas track seasonal changes. A projection inside the site's dome touches upon 'dark constellations,' which the Incas believed shaped earthly life. Transportation from the historic center to the planetarium's hilltop location is provided.

INCA FOUNDATIONS: SHAKEN, NOT DESTROYED

Cusco's dramatic history is written not only in stone but also in numerous earthquakes that, for centuries, have repeatedly shaken up (and torn down) its cityscape. The most catastrophic struck on March 31, 1650, when an estimated 7- to 7.5-magnitude tremor toppled colonial churches, convents and homes. Much to the chagrin of the colonists, their newer constructions turned to rubble, while Inca walls stood firm.

Inca's extraordinary engineering featured trapezoidal doorways, inward-leaning walls and massive, interlocking polygonal blocks that naturally absorbed seismic shock. Another powerful quake in 1950 destroyed or damaged one third of Cusco's colonial and republican-era buildings with the Inca foundations once again withstanding.

Step inside the city's **Cathedral** – built of 'repurposed' Inca stone – and you will come across an ex-voto commemorating the tragic 17th-century shakedown. In the bottommost plaza depicted in the oil painting appears Señor de los Temblores – Cusco's patron saint of earthquakes, whose figure is still carried in procession every Holy Monday.

LEONARDO DIAZ ROMERO/ALAMY

View Bingham's Photo Collection

Southeast of Plaza de Armas, in the colonial-era Casa Concha, **Museo Machu Picchu** *(museomachupicchu.com; 9am-5pm Mon-Sat)* houses artifacts from the 1911 Yale Peruvian Scientific Expedition led by Hiram Bingham III (p164). Photography was one of Bingham's principal methods of documenting his 'scientific discovery' of Machu Picchu, and some of the thousands of photos he took are on view here. You'll also see handwritten journals and sketches, as well as typed letters – including an amusing list of goods to be supplied by Abercrombie & Fitch – and field party etiquette. Note the origin of excavated artifacts, all found at Machu Picchu yet reflecting the wide span of the Inca Empire.

Left: Museo Machu Picchu

Stroll An Artisans' Quarter

Until the Spanish conquest, San Blas was known as Toqacachi, home to farmers and makers. Despite its name change, the neighborhood continues to be an artisan quarter filled with timeless artifacts.

HOW TO

Getting here: From Calle Choquechaca, climb a set of stairs up Siete Angelitos to officially enter the neighborhood of artisans, San Blas.

Fueling up: Sip an energizing cacao at Xapiri Ground, which supports Amazonian artisans, near Museo Hilario Mendivil, or head to the San Blas Market for delicious and affordable eats.

Tip: Spot seven snakes (and then some) carved into the stonewall of the narrow Siete Culebras passageway.

Exploring San Blas is as much about appreciating the colonial architecture and Inca stonework on the streets as it is about what's behind the walls.

Peruse the boutique shops of **Calle Carmen Alto** where fashionable **HILO** continues the *barrio*'s tradition of handmade items, with a contemporary twist.

In the Plazoleta San Blas you'll find **Museo Hilario Mendivil** *(9am-8pm Thu-Mon, 8am-7:30pm Tue & Wed),* dedicated to the late religious sculptor and neighborhood native. On Calle Hatunrumiyoc, look for the massive 12-angled stone in the wall of Inca Roca's former palace, now the Archbishop's Palace or **Museo de Arte Religioso** *(8am-6pm Mon-Sat),* where carved wood ceilings and colorful tiled floors frame Cuzco School art.

Upon the neighborhood's northern outskirts, browse the collection of artifacts at **Museo Inka** *(S20; 9:15am-4pm Mon-Fri, 8:45am-1:45pm Sat)* and admire the immaculate **Museo de Arte Precolombino** *(S20; 8am-10pm),* in the tranquil Plaza Nazarenas.

FROM LEFT: CAROLINE MORLEY/ALAMY, BETO SANTILLAN/SHUTTERSTOCK

Above: Llama pottery, Museo de Arte Precolombino
Right: Calle Hatunrumiyoc

Celebrate Inti Raymi

Meaning 'Festival of the Sun' in Quechua, Inti Raymi honored the sun and sought agricultural abundance. Each June 24, a reenactment of the winter solstice celebrations takes place in Cusco.

HOW TO

When to go: 9am to 4:30pm June 24. Arrive at least an hour early to secure a 'front row' standing spot.

Tickets: While tickets to the finale in Sacsaywamán are required, the first two stages of Inti Raymi – Qorikancha and Huacaypata – are free for bystanders, though a good view is not guaranteed. Prices for the finale range from US$160 to US$225, not including transport or guide. Purchase tickets at least one month in advance.

Don't forget: A hat and sunscreen for the strong Andean sun.

Tip: If you can't make it for Inti Raymi, the solar path – Qorikancha, Plaza de Armas and Sacsaywamán – makes for a great self-guided walking tour.

More info: www.entradaintiraymi.com

Dating back to the 15th century, Inti Raymi is believed to have been one of the most important events on the Inca calendar. The Sapa Inca presided over as many as 10 days of ceremonies to give thanks to their ancestor, the sun. What may have included llama sacrifices, toasts of *chicha* (fermented corn beer) and dances drew crowds from across the four regions of the Tahuantinsuyo.

Though banned after the Spanish conquest, Inti Raymi lived on in oral tradition. In 1944, writer Faustino Espinoza Navarro staged its revival, which today attracts thousands of Peruvians and visitors each June 24. More than 300 actors and dancers bring the pageantry to life.

The reenactment begins at 9am in Qorikancha's gardens, where the Sapa Inca appears to honor Inti. By 11am the procession reaches Huacaypata (now the Plaza de Armas), with symbolic coca ceremonies and dances. The finale unfolds at 2pm in Sacsaywamán: a 2½-hour spectacle of Andean rituals, offerings and traditional flavors (food not included with festival finale ticket).

STEFANOLAROSA/SHUTTERSTOCK

Inti Raymi procession

INCA TRAILS, UNDERGROUND

Underground Inca tunnels that connect sacred sites have long been the stuff of legends kept alive through local oral tradition and alluded to by early travelers – legend, that is, until recent findings dug up some truth about these secret passageways.

Since the early 2020s, archaeologists Jorge Calero Flores and Mildred Fernández Palomino have used ground-penetrating radar (GPR) to find and map deep cavities and linear voids extending from the Sacsaywamán area. In early 2025, they reported evidence of a nearly 2km subterranean passage beginning near the hilltop complex and pointing toward Qorikancha, suggesting the two major temples – one in the upper half of the city and the other in the lower half – may have been connected through the realm of *ukhu pacha* (the inner or underworld). This temple-to-temple tunnel is one of several Inca systems referred to as *chinkanas,* a Quechua term meaning 'a place to get lost.' But rather than host impractical wanderers or escapees, the lead archaeologists believe the *chinkana* was restricted to the elite and used for ceremonial purposes.

CRISTI CROITORU/SHUTTERSTOCK

Parque Arqueológico de Pisac

Day Trip to the Sacred Valley

Take a dip in altitude with a day trip to **Pisac** (2972m) in the Valle Sagrado de los Incas (p50). One hour northeast of Cusco by taxi (S80), the town is known for its vibrant artisan market, an international community of New Age earthlings and the mid-15th-century terraced archaeological site, **Parque Arqueológico de Pisac** *(8am-4:30pm),* whose partridge-shaped layout gives the town its name. A challenging two- to three-hour ascent from the plaza brings you to the Intihuatana, a sun stone surrounded by other exquisitely carved rocks. A taxi (S30 to S40) is wise for those short on time.

Weave a Memory at CTTC

Fiber work is one of Peru's oldest cultural expressions (p134) and evidence of its continued importance can be seen on just about every street corner in Cusco. Preserving the art form of using hand-spun naturally-dyed fibers while directly supporting women from over 10 weaving communities in the Cusco region is the **Centro de Textiles Tradicionales del Cusco**, located at the base of the Qorikancha lawns. Half-, full- or multiday workshops led by a local artisan are a restful and creative way to acclimate. There's also a **textile history museum and shop** *(www.textilescusco.org)* on site.

LUIS VINE/SHUTTERSTOCK

Right: Textile weaving

Río Urubamba
ALEXANDRA LANDE/SHUTTERSTOCK

INSIGHT

Yanantin: Sacred Principle of Duality

For the Inca, the universe was governed by *yanantin*, the sacred principle of complementary opposites – a living concept experienced on the trek to Machu Picchu.

WORDS BY **AGNES RIVERA**
Agnes studied yanantin *while working with the K'acllaraccay community in Maras, Cusco.*

WHILE WALKING THE Inca Trail you are suspended in a cradle of juxtaposition. Dry puna and humid subtropical rainforest, blazing sun and soft mist, introspective solitude and the shared company of fellow trekkers.

Natural Dualities

Worshiped as cosmic partners were the masculine sun god, Inti, and the feminine moon goddess, Mama Killa. Temples to both existed across the empire, for example the golden Qorikancha (p40) in Cusco is dedicated to the sun, while the Acllahuasi at Machu Picchu, where chosen women prepared sacred offerings, is dedicated to the moon. Their union represented a universe in which masculine and feminine were not opposites, but complementary energies sustaining all creation.

Finding unity in parity, the Andean year itself was divided into two great halves – the wet and dry seasons – governed by the celestial forces. Rising in the east, Inti brought forth new beginnings. During the dry months, the earth rested beneath his warming rays. Mama Killa, shining against a blackened sky, marked the end of another cycle. She presided over the rainy season, drawing fertility and growth. Together they kept the world in balance: rain ensuring sown crops would germinate and come to fruition, and sun preserving goods after harvest. While the Inti Raymi festival shines a spotlight on the divine sun, the abundance that is celebrated and hoped for wouldn't be possible without such complementary forces.

> The Incas believed that harmony came from duality and that wholeness required two sides: male and female, sun and moon, upper and lower.

Fed by seasonal rains and nourishing fields with its floods, the Río Urubamba, or Willkamayu (sacred river), was more than an irrigation source. In Andean cosmology, rivers and stars were often understood as mirrored forces, linking the earthly and celestial realms. Flowing through the Sacred Valley toward Machu Picchu, the Urubamba came to embody this connection – binding landscape, sky and ritual life into a single sacred system.

For the Inca, not all was divided by two. According to their worldview, the universe was divided, yet interwoven by a trilogy of realms, or *pachas: hanan pacha,* the upper world of gods and stars; *kay pacha,* the human world; and *ukhu pacha,* the inner world of ancestors and seeds. Along the trail, travelers symbolically move through these realms, ascending from fertile valleys to high passes, between earth and sky.

No Better Half

Balance was not just a metaphor, it was the organizing principle of Inca life. The Incas believed that harmony came from duality and that wholeness required two sides: male and female, sun and moon, upper and lower.

One half of Cusco, the capital, was *hanan* (upper), the other *hurin* (lower). Political and geographical, the dual structure was less about dominance or status and more about allowing balance to govern local life. Representing the higher, more elevated sector, *hanan* was often associated with power, the sun and the masculine principle. *Hurin,* set lower in the city, symbolized the moon, fertility and the feminine.

The Sapa Inca and his *panaca* (royal family) resided in *hanan,* but would carry out rulership and ritualistic obligations in the shared space of Huacaypata (now the Plaza de Armas). Though it may seem counterintuitive, Qorikancha sits in what was considered *hurin,* underscoring the Andean obsession with equilibrium whereby the upper world (in this case, represented by Inti) manifested physically in the lower section. Perched on a hill in the *hanan* area, Sacsaywamán, neighbored by the Temple of the Moon, is considered the complementary opposite of Qorikancha (Temple of the Sun).

In line with this societal equilibrium, was the practice of *ayni,* the ethic of reciprocity: today I help you, tomorrow you help me. Widely understood without the need of a written contract, *ayni* was present in every social act, from politics to agriculture. *M'ita,* a kind of taxation used by the Inca Empire, can be seen as a form of *ayni* as well: in return for services and working for the state – laying stone highways, constructing temples, weaving textiles, farming – people would receive goods, such as food and raw materials. Today, rural Andean communities continue to be strengthened by *ayni,* mutually helping one another from season to season. One day you lend your hands to a neighbor preparing fields for sowing; months later, those same hands return to help you harvest.

Engineered Balance

As you visit more Inca archaeological sites, it becomes clear that the Incas saw no separation between architecture and landscape. In fact, as you walk the Inca Trail the very ground beneath your hiking boots reveals the Inca attentiveness to harmony. Terraces such as those at Patallaqta (p66), Intipata (p147) and Wiñay Wayna (p132), and Sacred Valley sites such as Moray (p53), transform steep, unstable slopes into practical yet aesthetically pleasing designs. The Incas built these agricultural steps to manage water, prevent erosion and extend the growing area for crops. Honoring natural form through advanced engineering, each terrace wall adapted to the curves of the mountain, allowing the land to breathe rather than break.

Machu Picchu (p166) itself is a striking symbol of this balance. Sitting between a teeter-totter of two peaks, Machu Picchu (old peak; p172) and Wayna Picchu (young peak; p175), the location of the sacred citadel was no coincidence. One represents wisdom and age, the other renewal and vitality. Guarded by these two mountains, the citadel balances sacred and agricultural sectors, open plazas and enclosed temples, all designed with precision to mirror or honor celestial movements above. Every terrace, temple and stone in harmony and with purpose.

Incas saw no separation between architecture and landscape

The trail's final climb to Intipunku (Sun Gate) reveals this balance in motion. Maybe you don't make it through at dawn when – if you're lucky and there is no cloud cover – light spills over the mountains and strikes the ruins below, but you'll have transitioned up the angled slope, feeling the warm sun kiss your cheeks after the previous

Above: Intipata terraces (p147) Right: Wiñay Wayna (p132)

FROM LEFT: DIOGENES LAERTES/SHUTTERSTOCK, NIARKRAD/SHUTTERSTOCK.

steps beneath subtropical rainforest. And then, just when you think you've finished walking, it's time to head down to the citadel itself. From there to here, dark to light, path to entryway, the moment captures the Inca understanding of time itself: cyclical, not linear, where every end is a beginning.

Five centuries after the fall of the Inca Empire, the Quechua word *yanantin* may rarely be uttered, yet the concept of complimentary dualities continues to maintain balance in traditional Andean communities. Farmers still read the stars to predict rain, rotate crops with the seasons and practice *ayni* through collective labor. Even belief systems have, over time, become a duality: Catholicism and ancient devotion to living nature merging and coexisting in festivals like Qoyllur Rit'i (Star Snow Festival) or Corpus Christi.

Along the Inca Trail, the external transitions are harmoniously reciprocated in internal shifts for the mindful trekker.

AREA GUIDE:

Sacred Valley

Adjust to the altitude in the Sacred Valley, where a string of Inca towns rise and fall with Andean slopes and trace the bends of the Río Willkamayu from one terraced fortress to another, from abundant crop fields to colorful artisan markets, and, eventually, from Km 82 to Machu Picchu.

WORDS BY **AGNES RIVERA**
For the past five years Agnes has called the Sacred Valley her home.

Arriving

Elevations in the Sacred Valley range from 2800m to 3000m above sea level, making it a good place to acclimate to the Andes' breath-taking (literally) heights.

Bus Pisac is a scenic 45-minute bus ride from Cusco (S5). Buses depart from Calle Puputi, a 20-minute walk east of Cusco's Plaza de Armas.

Shuttles Departing from Puente Grau, a 20-minute walk south from Cusco's Plaza de Armas, shuttles to Urubamba (S7) and Ollantaytambo (S10) take 1½ hours. Shared car services also depart from this area (Urubamba S10).

Taxi Use a rideshare app or ask your hotel to book a secure ride from Cusco to Pisac (S80), Urubamba (S120) or Ollantaytambo (S150). Prices vary according to season and hour.

HOW MUCH FOR A

Coffee S8

Three-course set lunch S15

Boleto Turistico de Cusco Integral ticket S130

Getting Around

A 58km stretch between the major sightseeing towns of Pisac and Ollantaytambo, the Sacred Valley is one of the safest areas in Peru. Don't be shy to ask locals to help point you in the right direction.

Walking All valley towns are compact and walkable. That said, few streets have proper sidewalks and you'll want to wear proper footwear.

Taxis Hop in and out of taxis to tour the Sacred Valley in one day. From Pisac's main square, walk to the main 'highway' that connects all of the valley. Drivers can take you to Urubamba for around S60. In Urubamba, taxis wait directly in front of the gas station at the intersection with Av Mariscal Castilla and charge S40 to Ollantaytambo.

Combis *Combis* (shared minivans) pick up and drop off passengers at *paraderos* (bus stops) along the main road. There is no direct bus from Pisac to Ollantaytambo; instead, get off in Urubamba (S7, 40 minutes) and transfer to another bus (S5, 40 minutes) at the terminal.

ERIK GONZALEZI/SHUTTERSTOCK

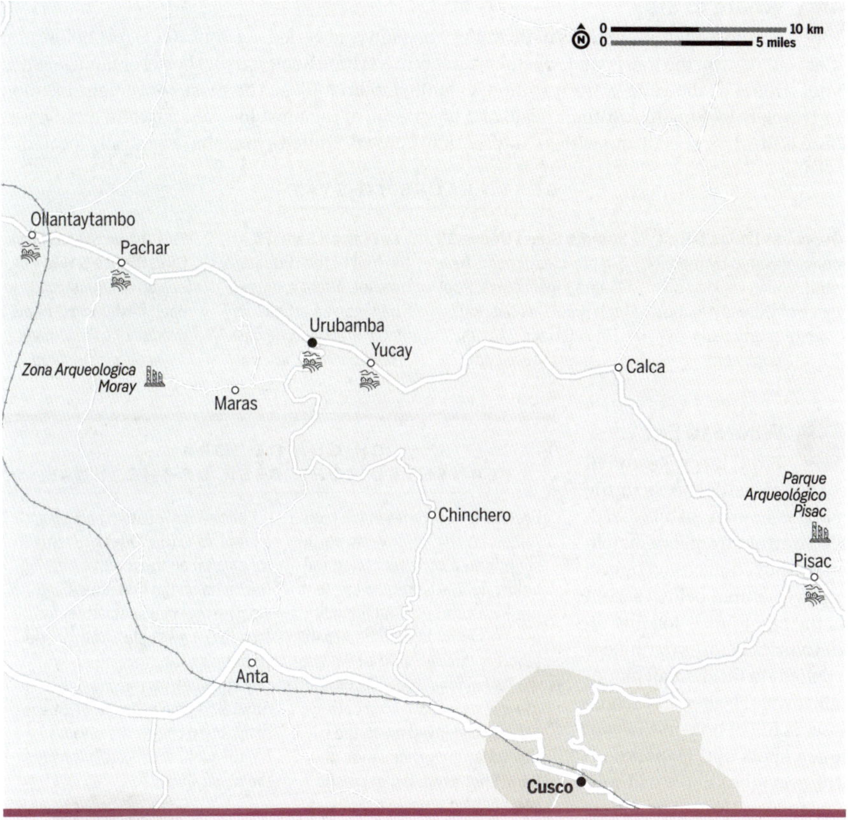

A DAY IN THE SACRED VALLEY

Begin in historic and now-bohemian **Pisac** (p43), exploring the town's Parque Arqueológico Pisac, a multifunctional fortress and strategic checkpoint hugged by steep, curved terraces. Fuel up with a superfood smoothie at Kula Cafe then peruse the vibrant artisan market.

Work your way west (and downward in altitude), passing through quaint **Yucay**, once an Inca resort. Zigzag through the lively produce market of **Urubamba** or the renowned handicraft workshop, Cerámicas Seminario. After lunch at AMA Restaurant, your journey continues west – but not before an award-winning pint at Cerveceria del Valle Sagrado brewery in **Pachar**.

Scramble up the imposing terraces that once defeated the Spanish in the living Inca town of **Ollantaytambo** (p53). Upon your descent, catch your breath meandering narrow streets that keep to original Inca urban planning. Admire the textile collection at ALQA Museo before a dinner of traditional flavors and lively ambiance at Chuncho.

Where to Stay

Accommodations options in the valley are many and varied. A comfortable rest before and after your days on the trail is vital, whether you stay in a private home, quality hostel or family-owned hotel. Home to the valley's train station, Ollantaytambo may be the most convenient location for travelers looking to rest their head, and boasts one of the most low-key, peaceful ambiences. Pisac is ideal for socializing with an international crowd, while Urubamba is centrally located.

BEST PLACES TO STAY

Quechuas Lodge $ Basic rooms elevated by friendly staff. Within walking distance of Ollantaytambo's center. *peruquechuas lodge.com*

Kamma Guest House $$ Simple, clean rooms near Ollanta's main plaza. Rooftop breakfast overlooks Inca terraces. *kamma guesthouse.com*

La Maison Samaï $ At the foot of the Urubamba market, bright rooms sit between an art gallery and a French-style cafe. *la-maison-samai.com*

Wolf Totem Steam Punk Guesthouse $ Hike 150 steps up a mountainside to reach flashpacker dorms overlooking Pisac ruins. *@wolftotemnomad*

Where to Eat

Find large-kerneled corn with salty cheese in the markets, a variety of tubers saddled by trout from local hatcheries, hearty quinoa and squash soups (pictured below) served as the night falls – loading up on calories before your hike is a delight in these small mountain towns. Flexiterian-friendly Pisac is full of hole-in-the-wall lunch spots and giant woodfire ovens baking bread and empanadas. Urubamba's sheer size means more culinary variety, while tiny Ollantaytambo, boasting riverside bistros and farm-to-table restaurants, is big on good vibes.

CHICHA DE JORA, FERMENTED CORN BEER OF THE INCAS

Brewed for centuries in the high Andes, *chicha de jora* – an earthy, slightly sour corn beer (pictured below right) – is a liquid link to pre-Inca cultures. Traditionally used in ceremonies and to sustain laborers through long workdays, the low-alcohol brew of sprouted, ground, then fermented corn kernels is enjoyed much the same way today in the highlands of Peru. Spot a red flag or plastic bag hanging outside a doorway, and you've found a home serving the cloudy-gold elixir in large glasses for S1.

Follow local custom and pour a bit of *aqha* (the Quechua term for *chicha*) on the ground, offering Pachamama the first nourishing sip. The regional specialty is *frutillada* (S2) – a sweeter, frothier and pretty-pink variation infused with tiny strawberries *(frutillas)* that grow along the valley floor. Seeds of *ayrampo* cactus are often blended into the mix to intensify the blushy hue.

FROM LEFT: BETO SANTILLAN/SHUTTERSTOCK, JHONATAN OLMEDO/SHUTTERSTOCK

BEST PLACES TO EAT & DRINK

Chuncho $$ Outstanding bar stocked by its sibling distillery. *@chuncho.pe, Ollantaytambo, closed 4-6pm*

Doña Clorinda $$ Order the trout – grilled or ceviche-style – in the garden. *+51 984 769 058, Pisac, open to 5pm*

Kampu $$ Lunch on Thai, African and Peruvian daily specials. *@kampu. restaurante, Urubamba, Tue-Sun*

Monkey Coffee $ Specialty coffee and all-day breakfast with co-working space. *@monkeycoffee cusco, Urubamba, Mon-Sat*

INCA BREADBASKET

The Sacred Valley's legacy as an agricultural hub is written across the landscape. Fed by the Río Urubamba and blessed with fertile soils, the valley once served as the Inca Empire's breadbasket, yielding maize, quinoa, potatoes and other highland staples that sustained Cusco and distant ceremonial centers. Ingenious terracing, irrigation canals, and experimental sites like Moray allowed the Incas to manipulate micro-climates and cultivate crops at varying altitudes. Many valley towns, including Pisac, Maras, Yucay and Ollantaytambo, remain rooted in farming traditions that trace back centuries.

Don't miss a Sunday visit to **Urubamba's Mercado de Productores** *(5am-4pm)*, a large open-air market found one block from the bus terminal. Farmers from across the valley haul in their goods, be they bundles of freshly picked medicinal herbs or sacks of freeze-dried potatoes. Arrive early to witness the incredible bounty of Valley-grown products and the haggling action between *caseros* (a term used between buyers and sellers) as you snack on a warm corn *humita* (pudding) with *ponche de habas* (sweet fava-bean breakfast drink).

RAFAEL SACCHETTI/SHUTTERSTOCK

Parque Arqueológico de Ollantaytambo

Ollantaytambo's Terraced Wonders

At the west end of the valley, **Parque Arqueológico de Ollantaytambo** *(7am-5pm)* rises above the town with a steep set of 17 terraces that roughly outline a llama. Though stage to a 1537 Inca victory, its finely cut, unfinished temples and royal fountains suggest it had a role other than military. Admission is included in the **Boleto Turistico de Cusco Integral** *(S130, cosituc.gob.pe)* and guides are available for hire at the entrance. Walk 10 minutes to the **Pinkuylluna** *(free)* storehouses to enjoy a panoramic view of the town backdropped by the historical terraces.

Maras & Moray

Just when you think you've seen enough terraces, the most unusual appear near **Maras**, a 30-minute bus ride from Urubamba (S4). **Moray** reveals a series of conical terraces once used as an Inca agricultural laboratory. Each level created a distinct microclimate for experimenting with crops and seed selection. Entry is included in the Boleto Turístico de Cusco Integral.

About 50 minutes away by taxi (S30 to S40), a sodium-rich harvest is practiced. Over 3000 pink-and-white saltpans cascade down the mountainside, forming the **salineras** *(S20, cash only)*. The strictly communal harvest maintains this landscape much as it was in pre-Inca times.

Right: Salineras de Maras

279PHOTO STUDIO/SHUTTERSTOCK

INCA TRAIL

The 42km Inca Trail takes you through a dizzying array of landscapes and vegetation as you pass impressive Inca ruins and spot enchanting Andean wildlife. Though the altitude and terrain can prove a challenge, your journey is made surprisingly comfortable by the team of guides and porters that accompanies you en route to your ultimate goal: Machu Picchu, justifiably one of the world's great bucket-list travel destinations. You might have seen a thousand photographs but nothing can prepare you for the spellbinding moment when you first stand on the terraced viewpoint with the whole city laid out before you.

Hiker, Phuyupatamarka ruins (p127)
PAUL SOUDERS/GETTY IMAGES

KM 82

Most travelers begin their journey in Cusco or Ollantaytambo, from where they are ferried by car to the furthest point of the Urubamba Valley for a gentle introduction to the Inca Trail. Walking your way west, the undulating first kilometers are what tour guides jokingly describe as 'Peruvian flat.' The curves of the footpaths are initially determined by the snaking Río Urubamba, the sound of its rushing waters urging you along until you make your way inland towards the Andes. Use your first day to ease into a pace that suits your acclimatization to the altitude.

Agnes Rivera

Río Urubamba, KM 82 (p60)
SHARPTOYOU/SHUTTERSTOCK

Patallaqta

6.4KM

3 HOURS' WALK

THIS LEG:

- KM 82
- Canabamba Viewpoint
- Casa del Colibri
- Patallaqta Viewpoint
- Huillcaraccay
- Patallaqta

Walking Notes

After the two-hour (86.9km) drive from Cusco, you will clear the initial checkpoint in Piscacucho with your passport in hand, snap a photo with the iconic Km 82 sign and step onto the trail. The first day's trek follows gravel and dirt pathways – the original Inca stones long ago buried beneath centuries of pounding steps. Until the small gorge of Miskay, it's not uncommon to be left in the dust by a local riding a motorcycle.

Breaking Your Journey

Shaded rest areas with toilets are abundant throughout the initial kilometers, as are homes selling packaged snacks, bottled water and soft drinks. Take note of the prickly dry-climate flora that will disappear by the end of the day's trek.

Agnes' Tips

BEST VIEW The lookout point above Patallaqta.

FAVORITE STOP Casa del Colibri, where a bouquet of bright flowers draws a performance of nectar-hungry hummingbirds.

TIP Breakfast is on you this morning, so ask your hotel for a boxed breakfast and stay hydrated in preparation for the extreme elevation gain tomorrow.

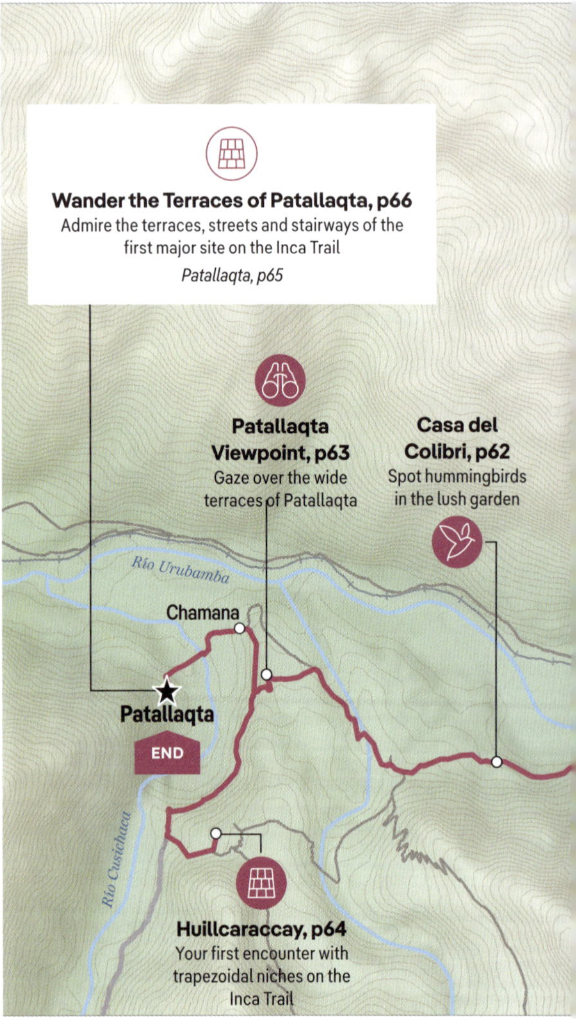

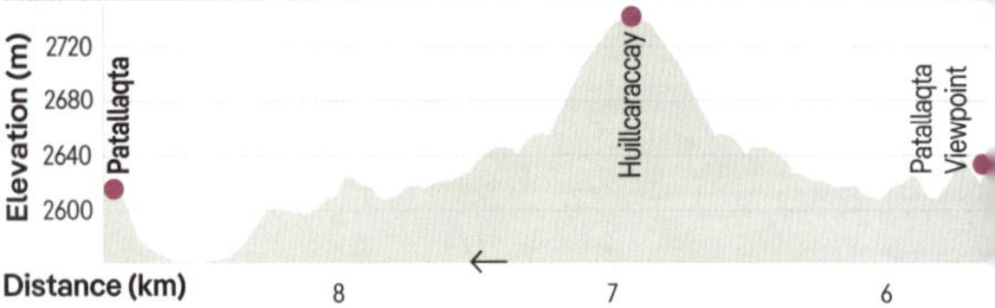

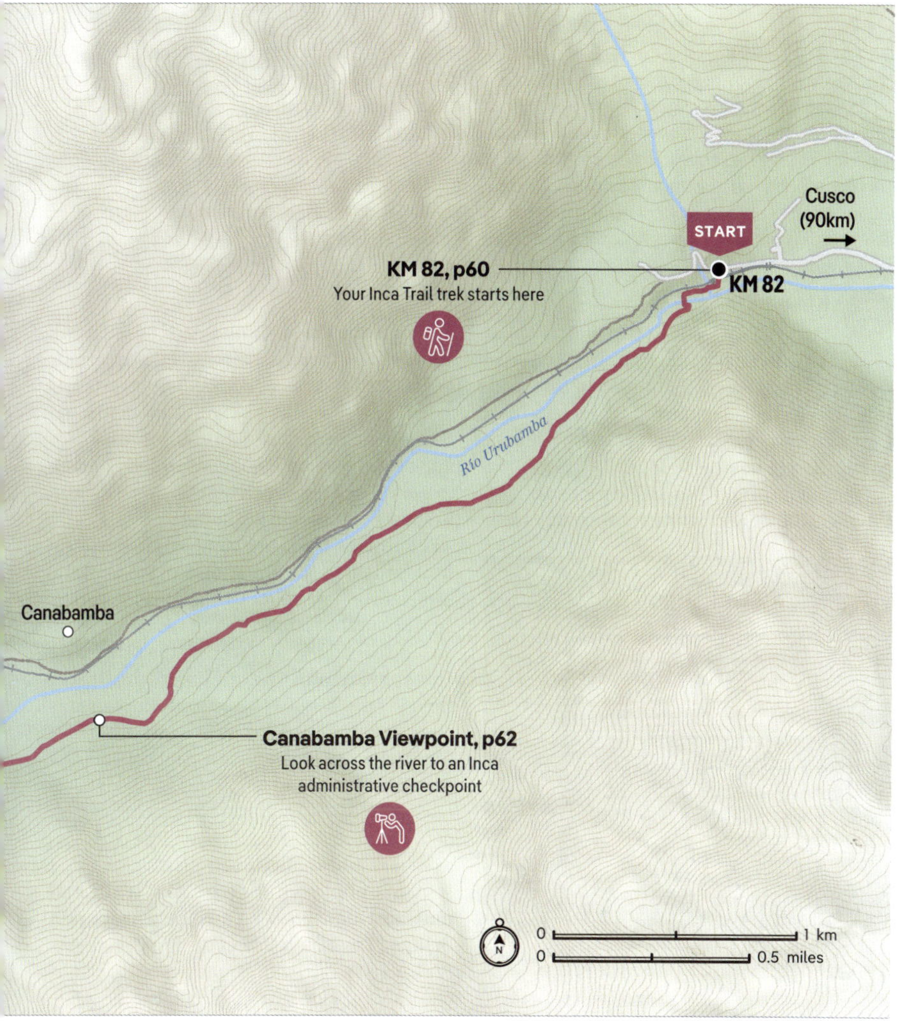
Cusco
(90km)
START
KM 82, p60
Your Inca Trail trek starts here
KM 82
Río Urubamba
Canabamba
Canabamba Viewpoint, p62
Look across the river to an Inca administrative checkpoint
N
0
1 km
0
0.5 miles

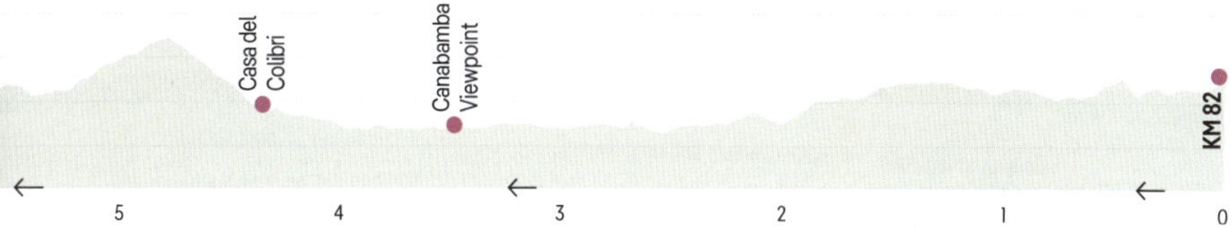
Casa del Colibri
Canabamba Viewpoint
KM 82
5
4
3
2
1
0

GETTING THERE Indulge in an early morning hot shower – your last for the next four days – before your agency picks you up from your Cusco hotel, transferring you to Km 82 by road. After exiting the city, curves hugged by two-story adobe homes give way to the patchwork fields of Chinchero. The snaking road temporarily uncoils when you reach Ramal. With the Urubamba mountain range radiating in front, you'll begin your descent into the valley upon switchbacks carved into the red clay mountainsides. Once in Urubamba, it's a (comparatively) straight shot to Ollantaytambo, where your chauffeur may stop for snacks and a bathroom break, but will more likely drive around the town, following the banks of the Río Urubamba.

SUSIE HEDBERG/SHUTTERSTOCK

KM 82

Piscacucho (*'pisca'* is five and *'cucho'* is corners in Quechua) is the last town you'll drive through before reaching the official trailhead. It is here, 82km along the railroad tracks from Cusco city, where you will meet your team of porters and hand over your bag.

A maximum of 500 Inca Trail permits are allocated each day, and when your agency's van pulls into the Visitor Center parking lot, it will become clear that the majority of those permits are allotted to porters. As the porters expertly assemble their rucksacks with bags, tents and cooking equipment, use the on-site restrooms or mingle with your trekking companions. Be sure to keep your passport on hand as you will need to show it in order to begin the trek.

MARK GREEN/SHUTTERSTOCK

Official trailhead marker

Before your boots are baptized by the dusty trail, walk beneath the wide wingspan of the Andean condor, a protagonist of the center's facade mural, and into the open arms of a Spectacled Bear statue as you enter the **Centro de Interpretacion** (Visitor Center). Just paces from the trailhead, all hikers pass through this bite-sized museum. Peer into a replica of an Inca water mirror or flip through a giant pop-up book of regional flora and fauna. A scaled down 3D model of the Inca Trail gives you a birds' eye view of the route and terrain that you'll be covering, as well as interconnecting trails.

Snap a photo with the **official trailhead marker** before crossing a bouncy pedestrian **bridge** to the south side of the Río Urubamba. Rock walls stacked with geranium and the clover-like leaves of a low-growing oxalis species guide

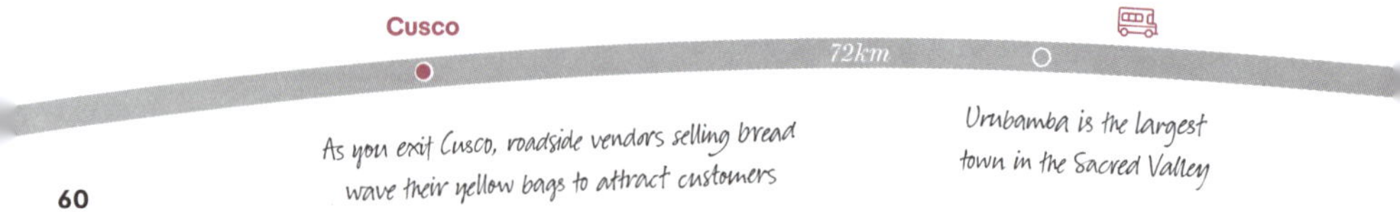

Bridge spanning Río Urubamba, KM 82

you along a dusty footpath as you head west, away from the morning sun. As you steady your excited feet, you may be wondering where the hand-laid stone paths have gone. Much of the original stone in the lowland sections, as you'll be able to compare days from now, have crumbled due to modern use. In the wake of post-pandemic government stimulus packages, the use of motorcycles by local villagers along the trails has substantially increased.

Keep your eyes out for cochineal, a tiny white insect covering the broad leaves of the tuna cactus. Avoiding the thorns of the prickly pear plant, scoop up a patch of cochineal and give the dusty bugs a squeeze, releasing their vibrant purple hue, which is used as a natural dye (p134)

LOOK FOR TARA TREES

Hugging you through the first days of the trail is a peaceful army of tara trees *(Caesalpinia spinosa)*, native to the Peruvian Andes. Small round leaves decorate the upright branches that rise from the knotted, bumpy trunk of this leguminous tree. Their pink-red pods have long held a place in Andean apothecaries' remedies, being crushed into powder to soothe skin ailments or steeped in hot water and then gargled to ease sore throats and canker sores, to name a few. If you've ever seen 'tara gum' listed on a cosmetic or food item, these seedpods are its source.

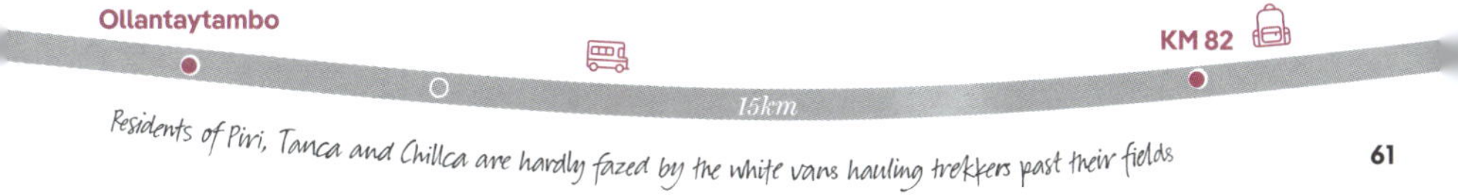

Northern giant hummingbird

throughout the Andes. With each step tara trees, bearded with *sunka sunka* (a hanging moss), become increasingly present.

Canabamba Viewpoint

A local **cemetery** on your left is noticeable not for its quantity of graves (few), but for their traditional positioning: all facing east, eternally connected to the sun. The graves are also pointed in the direction of the glacier and a major Inca *apu* (mountain spirits), Waqaywillka (Sacred Tears), now known as **Mt Veronica**.

Minutes later, a roofed seating area looks out towards **Canabamba**, an Inca administrative checkpoint on the opposite side of the river. Squint your eyes to make out a litter of rectangular chambers, the largest of the set determinedly holding onto its exposed 2nd-floor lintels. A portion of the stone buildings may have served as a *tambo* (resting post) for the foot messengers, known as *chasquis*. To the upper left of the site are circular remains of *qolqas* (storehouses) where staple crops such as potatoes, corn and pseudo-cereals, such as quinoa, would have ensured food security for surrounding inhabitants.

Casa del Colibri

Stands selling the same packaged snacks and offers of toilets (S1) dot the path, but hold out until **Casa del Colibri** for clean bathrooms and a lush **garden** that attracts hummingbirds. Here,

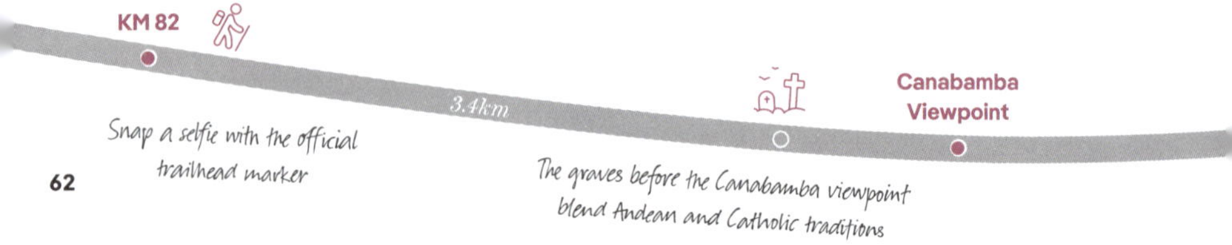

PEDER BJUREKE IHLE/SHUTTERSTOCK

the endemic green-and-white hummingbird *(Elliotomyia viridicauda)* and non-migratory northern giant hummingbird (the largest in the world) dip their beaks into trumpet-shaped flowers and feeders. A lookout spot has a clear shot of the **Río Urubamba**, which disappears the moment you pick up your walking sticks.

From an area known as **Miskay**, you'll head down and up a small gorge, crossing a tributary. Above the river once again, tree trunks are wrapped in a chartreuse blanket of lichen.

Patallaqta Viewpoint

Breathtaking Patallaqta (also referred to as Llaqtapata, but not to be confused with the site west of Machu Picchu of the same name) comes into view for the first time as traces of the original stone path of the Inca Trail arise in the dirt pathway. Fanning out like retreating tide waves, the wide terraces of the archaeological site bend across the landscape with a fish-eye lens effect – but you'll want to zoom in.

A winding descent from Patallaqta Viewpoint brings you down to the small town of **Chamana**, the gateway to Patallaqta. From here, groups will visit either Patallaqta or nearby Huillcaraccay, two Inca sites divided by the Río Cusichaca yet facing one another at staggered heights. Due to time constraints and the need to reach the first camp before dark, it's highly unlikely you will be able to visit both sites. But whether your group visits Patallaqta along the valley floor

Along the Way We Met...

FINN ANDRESEN The morning we drove to the trailhead at Km 82, I had an upset stomach, so my main focus was on surviving the first day's walk. The next day, after drinking a soda to settle my tummy, I felt much better – despite the longer hours and higher altitude. Uphill sections on the first days naturally spread the group apart, and in the fog of the mountains I walked some sections alone. It gave me time to reflect on life issues, which was very positive.

Finn Andresen is a retired entrepreneur from Stockholm, Sweden. After completing the Inca Trail he went whitewater rafting down the Río Urubamba.

FINN'S TIP: *I'd have to say the best part of the entire trek was Patallaqta, since we were completely alone with our guide. Honestly I think it was more impressive than Machu Picchu, which was overflowing with other tourists.*

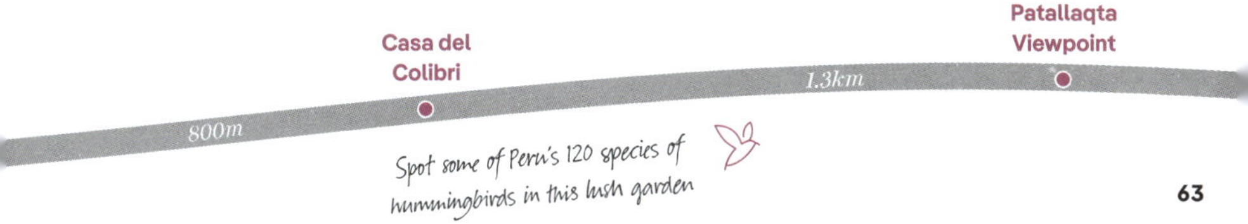

Along the Way We Met...

ED PREVATTE I'm sure everyone's excited when they take the first few steps of this life-changing journey, but my level of excitement was through the roof! Of course, there was also a fair amount of apprehension as I didn't know exactly what to expect. The first day in as we visited Patallaqta, an incredible Inca ruin, I knew that I was in for the adventure of a lifetime and an experience that would live with me forever.

Ed Prevatte is a semi-retired doctor based in Florida. He travels (and hikes) the world with his wife, María.

ED'S TIP: *Find your own pace. The altitude affects everyone differently but, as our guide would say, 'there's only one way: forward.'*

MARK EVELEIGH

Hikers approach Huillcaraccay

or Huillcaraccay sitting above, both are early proof that there is no such thing as a bad view on the Inca Trail.

Huillcaraccay

From the terraces of Patallaqta, gaze eastward and towards the skyline to spot the broad, seemingly continuous curved wall of Huillcaraccay. Also spelled Willkaraccay, the name is often translated to mean 'sacred enclosure.'

Taking advantage of its top tier seat on a promontory, Huillcaraccay was most likely an Inca checkpoint, where foot traffic below could easily be under surveillance. Dozens of buildings are aligned neatly and near one another so as to create a series of narrow alleyways. If you visit, this will be the first place on the Inca

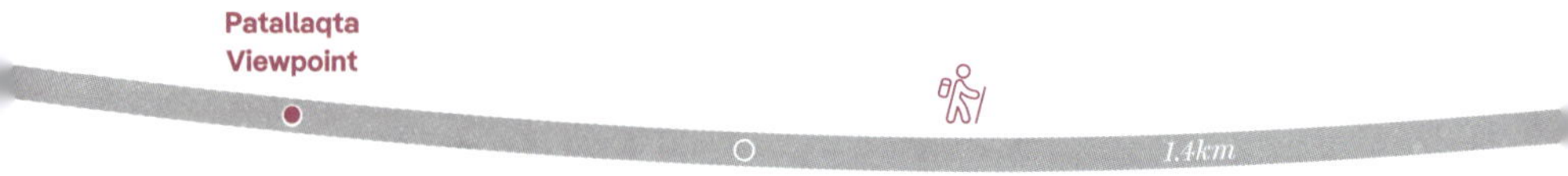

Enjoy the last few kilometers of relatively flat path

MARK GREEN/SHUTTERSTOCK

Patallaqta

Trail where your hands are able to trace the shape of **trapezoidal niches**. As you make your way down towards the Río Cusichaca, keep your eyes out for a rounded **burial site** nestled in an opposing cliffside: some guides say it was crafted especially for an engineer from Tiahuanaco.

Patallaqta

From Chamana, walk up a short, rubble-strewn path to rise to the base terraces of Patallaqta (p66). A massive bedrock crowned with a semi-circular wall will draw you in, but save it for the end of your unhurried visit and continue towards the terraced town.

The name itself – *pata* (terrace) and *llaqta* (town) in Quechua – could surely be used to describe many an Inca site; nonetheless, it perfectly captures this riverside site's design – an urban center perched above what once reaped extensive cultivation. Over 100 stone dwellings border open plazas, while a distinctive curved temple at the base stands as its ceremonial focal point.

Wander the Terraces of Patallaqta

Set at the confluence of the Ríos Cusichaca and Urubamba, Patallaqta is often the first major site visited along the Inca Trail. Here, at this vast terraced settlement, agriculture, ritual and trade converged at one of the empire's most important valley junctions.

HOW TO

Nearest stop: Patallaqta Viewpoint
Getting here: From Chamana, walk up a short path to the ruins
Fun fact: During the Inca empire, the population of Patallaqta is estimated to have neared 1000, while the food procured from its terraces would have fed those in Ollantaytambo all the way to Machu Picchu.

Signs of a Once-Thriving City

As you approach Patallaqta, agricultural terraces stretch wide to meet bulging mountainsides then unfold in an urban layout of ruler-straight pathways crisscrossing from the plaza, which then give way to rows of houses with hollowed 'shelves.' The mud plaster that once smoothed the walls of residences and storehouses has faded to faint patches, yet the stonework and stairways remain remarkably intact.

Red Andean flowers known as *ñucchu* (*Salvia opositiflora;* pictured left) peer down from the top terraces and white lilies bloom across the grassy expanse at the site's base. Large boulders are strewn at staggered heights across the site, with some incorporated into the terrace outline.

Analysis of food remains from nearby sites in the Cusichaca Valley suggests Patallaqta may have served as an occasional market for exchanging produce during the Inca period. Late 20th-century excavations revealed diverse crops from multiple ecological zones (such as high-altitude tubers), pointing to active exchange and redistribution along this section of the trail.

Sacred Spaces

Canals would have channeled water diverted from the river into the tiered agricultural sector.

FROM LEFT: FABGONZALO, CC BY-SA 4.0, VIA WIKIMEDIA COMMONS; AGNES RIVERIA

A TOWN OF MANY HATS

British archaeologist Ann Kendall, who directed the long-running Cusichaca Archaeological Project, saw Patallaqta as a strategically placed Inca settlement that combined agricultural and administrative functions – its incredible irrigation system pointing to it as a farming hub for the surrounding valley, and its position along the classic Inca Trail hinting to its role as ritual waystation marking the start of the pilgrimage to Machu Picchu.

Left: Patallaqta
Below: Hikers approach Patallaqta

At the base of the site, you can follow the centuries-old flow of an elegant stone-lined watercourse to the curvy eye-catcher, **Pulpituyuq** (an allusion to a 'pulpit,' also referred to as the Temple of the Sun). Facing the rising sun, the raised shrine or *huaca* is surrounded by rooms at staggered levels. Even before you step through the narrow trapezoidal entrance, the high-quality ashlar masonry clearly distinguishes this sacred place from the domestic sector. A series of elongated trapezoidal niches, each flanked by bar holes, may once have secured ritual offerings – or even ancestral bundles (aka mummies).

GEOFF MARSHALL/ALAMY

Qhapaq Ñan near Cusco
JERENY/SHUTTERSTOCK

INSIGHT

Qhapaq Ñan

The picturesque 43km of the Inca Trail are but a minuscule fraction of the vast Andean road system, Qhapaq Ñan. If Cusco was the heart of the Inca Empire, then the roads of Qhapaq Ñan – stretching over 30,000km – were its veins.

WORDS BY **AGNES RIVERA**
Agnes first heard of Qhapaq Ñan while hiking in Huaraz in 2013.

Andean Road System

Meaning 'Royal Road,' Qhapaq Ñan radiated from Cusco in the four directions of the Tahuantinsuyo: Chinchaysuyu (north), Antisuyu (east), Qullasuyu (south) and Kuntisuyu (west). Stretching across deserts, mountains and tropical valleys, it was one of the largest and most ambitious road systems of the ancient world. Main 'highways' spawned into secondary and tertiary paths, enabling swift conquest and imperial control through administration, communication and ceremonial exchange across an empire that grew to encompass present-day Colombia, Ecuador, Bolivia, Chile, Argentina and Peru. Yet the road did more than consolidate power: along its stone corridors traveled stories, agricultural knowledge, textiles, music and ritual traditions, linking diverse ecosystems and cultures.

When 7000km of the network were inscribed as a UNESCO World Heritage Site in 2014, Qhapaq Ñan officially took the name Andean Road System, a decision that reflected both geography and politics. Other countries felt it would be unfair to call it the Inca road system since Peru has such a strong affiliation with the Inca 'brand.' Plus, the name 'Andean Road System' is more inclusive of the pre-Inca cultures that laid the foundations for many of these pathways.

As with many other aspects of Inca culture, the empire maximized and improved upon infrastructure created by earlier civilizations. But this inheritance was just the stepping stone for what the Incas would transform into one of the most extensive and sophisticated roadway systems in human history.

Adaptive by necessity, the Incas let the land dictate their design.

Engineering Feat

If its scope was monumental, the collective ingenuity behind the Qhapaq Ñan was equally so.

No single founding date can be attributed to the network, as it evolved gradually, reaching its greatest expansion under Pachacutec, the empire's most visionary ruler. To perfect pre-existing routes and link them through new stretches of terrain, the Incas relied on the *m'ita*, a rotational labor system in which communities contributed workers instead of taxes, as the Incas did not use money. Through this collective effort, the empire achieved what no other pre-Columbian civilization could: a web of roads – sometimes reaching mountain passes as high as 5000m – without wheels, iron or paid labor.

Adaptive by necessity, the Incas let the land dictate their design. Roads curved with the contours of rivers and hugged the flanks of mountains, blending seamlessly into their surroundings. In remote highland sections, perfectly fitted flagstones still support the occasional hikers' boots. In the valleys, packed earth and gravel fade into the landscape, while in the arid coastal plains, compacted sand tracks were marked by low boundary stones to guide llama caravans. Suspended bridges of woven ichu grass spanned roaring gorges and, along near-vertical slopes, retaining walls of interlocked rock lean away from paths, making it difficult to determine if the trails are clinging to the cliffs or vice versa.

Every few leagues stood a *tambo,* a way station serving travelers, soldiers and the empire's famed *chasquis* – the relay runners who carried messages across the Andes. These trained athletes covered roughly five to 14km (depending on the terrain) before handing off a *quipu* (a coded knot string) to the next runner. Scattered among *tambos* or tucked into small settlements along the way were *qolqas*, or storage houses, where the true riches of the empire – maize, tubers, coca leaves, dried fish and woven textiles – were preserved until needed elsewhere.

Qhapaq Ñan may not have reached the scale of the ancient Roman road system, but it surpassed it in audacity. Where Roman roads connected cities across gentle terrain, the Inca roads ventured into the impossible. Threading through deserts, glaciers and jungles, it's little wonder that many stretches remain hidden or have been lost over time.

The Great Inca Trail

The main corridor of the Qhapaq Ñan network, the Great Inca Trail reaches northwest from Cusco's Huacaypata (now the Plaza de Armas) into Chinchaysuyo, the largest of the empire's four regions. Beginning in the former capital, this resource-rich route extends through the Andes for nearly 2900km, reaching as far as Cuenca, Ecuador.

The trail rises across high Andean plains where herders still guide their llamas along wind-carved ridges, then dips into valleys marked by ancient terraces and adobe villages. Further north, its stone pathways cross open puna and into the shadows of ravines, threading together sparse communities.

At the halfway mark of this stretch lies Huánuco Pampa – the capital of Chinchaysuyo and once the largest administrative center outside the Cusco region. The main intersection connecting transversal roads, Huánuco Pampa was the foremost entryway of the Andes to the Amazon and coast. Honoring the site's legacy and using it as their main axis, travel companies ExplorAndes and QN Travel, in partnership with the Patronato Cultural del Perú, are leading a pioneering project to restore and promote sections both north and south of Huánuco Pampa. The initiative aims to develop sustainable tourism and benefit nearby communities while protecting the integrity of the original trail.

General Manager of ExplorAndes, Martin Romero, explains: 'The Great Inca Trail has the potential to become South America's first long-distance trek. Spending more time and thus money in rural communities while preserving history, these treks can become tools for development – just as we've seen happen in other countries around the world, where entire local economies have flourished around responsible trekking.'

As of now, no permits are required to walk the Great Inca Trail, though only certain portions are clearly marked. Navigating lesser-known stretches unguided demands not only physical preparation and logistical skills, but also familiarity with local communities. And while Tambo del Soledad is one of the most accessible entry points for adventurous hikers looking to navigate Inca pathways on their own, 'accessible' is relative: an hour flight from Lima to Huaraz is followed by a 2½-hour drive to Chavin de Huantar, followed by another 45-minute drive to the trailhead where a 3km hike along stone pathways leads to the archaeological site.

'And in Peru, we've got the greatest long-distance trail that already exists and is packed with historical and cultural context. So why wouldn't we work to preserve and promote it?'

JOLYN CHUA/SHUTTERSTOCK

Huánuco Pampa

Roads, Not Ruins

Though it might seem Qhapaq Ñan belongs to the annals of archaeology, in many places it continues to serve as a living pathway connecting Andean communities. People still walk segments of it daily – herders moving livestock, farmers accessing distant fields and neighbors visiting one another across ridgelines.

Paradoxically, as much as these local communities keep the spirit of the road alive, they also pose one of its biggest threats. Unauthorized roads built atop the historical pathways, motorcycles displacing stones from their home of half a millennia, and even the unintentionally harmful act of 'repurposing' roadway material for construction of private fences and walls are all too common. Match that with illegal and legal mining, erosion and neglect, and the battle to preserve these living links becomes all the more challenging.

Just ask Nick Stanziano, founder of QN Travel and one of the loudest contemporary voices in the revival of Qhapaq Ñan. Stanziano, a California native and longtime resident of Peru, doesn't just talk the talk, he has also walked the nearly 3200km from Tumebamba (near Cuenca, Ecuador) to Cusco, Peru.

'We are at risk of losing the remnants of the largest and most advanced road system from pre-industrial times. And we're also losing what, in my opinion, is potentially the most abundant cultural resource for tourism, and thus development, in the country that exists today.' Stanziano's passion for this cultural heritage is evident, 'I see it as a vein of gold down the spine of the Andes, but not the type of gold that conquistadores and explorers were searching for.'

Restoring sections can strengthen local economies without sacrificing authenticity, turning forgotten paths into sustainable tourism routes that directly benefit families that live along the paths, as well as larger communities in the vicinity. The logistics for coordinating transportation, llamas, cooks, guides and food is complex and expensive in these remote areas, but it's also an opportunity for economic stimulus in often overlooked pockets of Peru – and to diversify tourism in Peru away from the unsustainable bottleneck that leads to Machu Picchu.

'There's all these long-distance trails around the world, such as the Pacific Crest Trail in California, which I grew up near, and Jordan's 700km trail from Petra to the Red Sea that was only developed in this century,' observes Stanziano. 'And in Peru, we've got the greatest long-distance trail that already exists and is packed with historical and cultural context. So why wouldn't we work to preserve and promote it?'

The First Step

With thousands of miles still winding through mountains, valleys and cloud forests, no single path along the Qhapaq Ñan is greater than the next. Each trail walked is another chapter in the story of an empire that once united the Andes, and every step an invitation for a deeper understanding of the Inca civilization's extraordinary prowess.

'Unlike the Classic Inca Trail to Machu Picchu, which was a secondary route with more spiritual and ceremonial context, the Great Inca Trail was practical in innumerable ways,' explains Romero. 'But it's not to take away from one or the other: I believe they are complementary to each other. Machu Picchu may be the so-called crown jewel, but you don't truly grasp how vast the empire was until you're in the remote northern Andes, days or maybe even weeks away from seeing any other tourists.'

Preserving this network is not the task of any one institution but a shared commitment among governments, travel operators and travelers alike – which is no small feat. Then again, if ever there were a road capable of connecting worlds and generations, it's the Qhapaq Ñan. Count your eventual arrival at Machu Picchu not as your last step along the Classic Inca Trail, but your first upon the vast Andean Road System.

Qhapaq Ñan, Ollantaytambo (p53)

ANDREAS WOLOCHOW/SHUTTERSTOCK

Patallaqta

By the end of this stretch, you'll have reached the highest point along the Inca Trail. As you plant one hiking pole in front of the other, debating whether to reach into your daypack for something sweet to revive your energy, don't forget to look around and soak up the surrounding landscape: herds of llamas, enchanting forests and magnetizing peaks.

Agnes Rivera

Patallaqta ruins (p66)

E MARTINEZ/SHUTTERSTOCK

Warmiwañusqa

11.4KM
8 HOURS' WALK

THIS LEG:

- Patallaqta Ushnu
- Hatunchaca
- Wayllabamba
- Ayapata
- Llulluchapampa
- Warmiwañusqa Climb
- Abra Warmiwañusqa

Walking Notes

Leave the fertile Quechua zone behind as you climb the ecological tier to enter a unique Andean forest in Llulluchapampa. Nearing the windswept puna of Warmiwañusqa during the dry season means pristine views of the oncoming peaks, while the rainy season makes up for slippery stone steps with shrubs in bloom and drifting clouds that add mystique to peripatetic meditations. Your path becomes increasingly steep as you near the highest point on the trail, Abra Warmiwañusqa (Dead Woman's Pass)

Breaking Your Journey

Those on the five-day itinerary may spend their first night at Hatunchaca, while those following the Classic four-day trail usually camp overnight at Wayllabamba (p76). A constant incline moving towards the highest pass, day two is broken up into increments and rest stops.

Agnes' Tips

BEST VIEW Forest of endemic unca trees.

FAVORITE STOP From Abra Warmiwañusqa, look back and see how far you've come.

TIP Wayllabamba is your last chance to buy a sugary snack for a quick energy boost to get you up the pass or a roll of toilet paper.

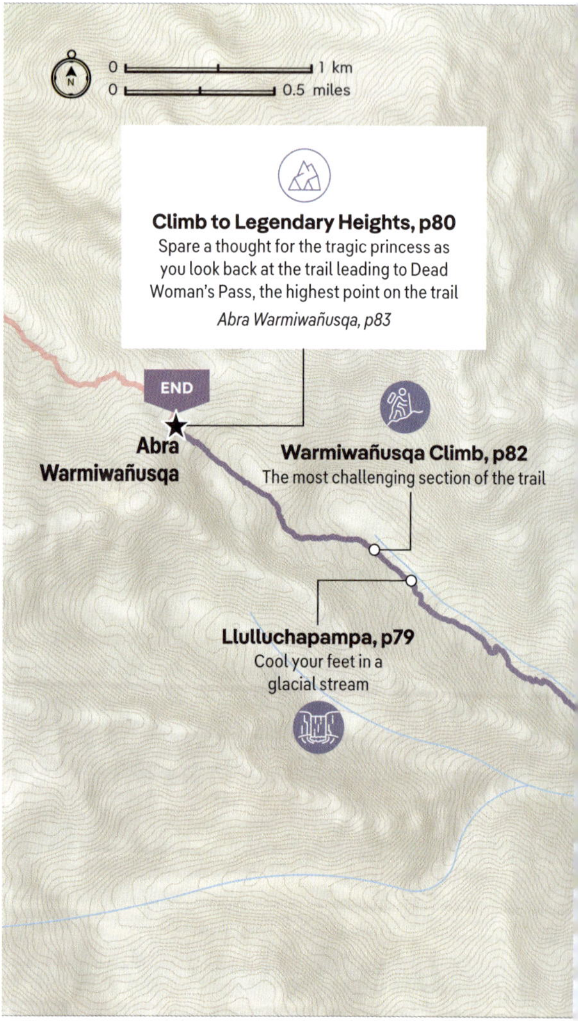

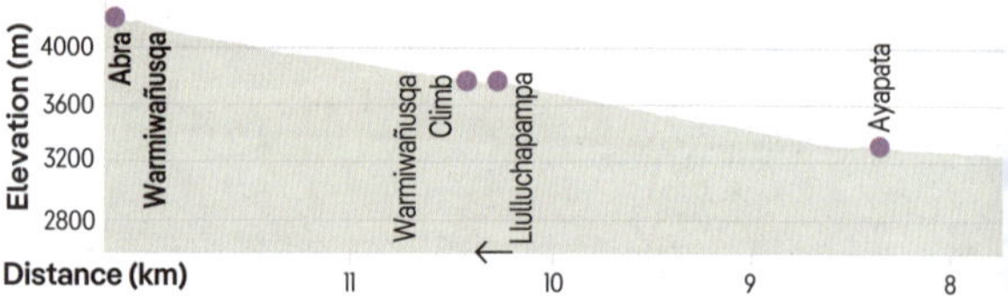

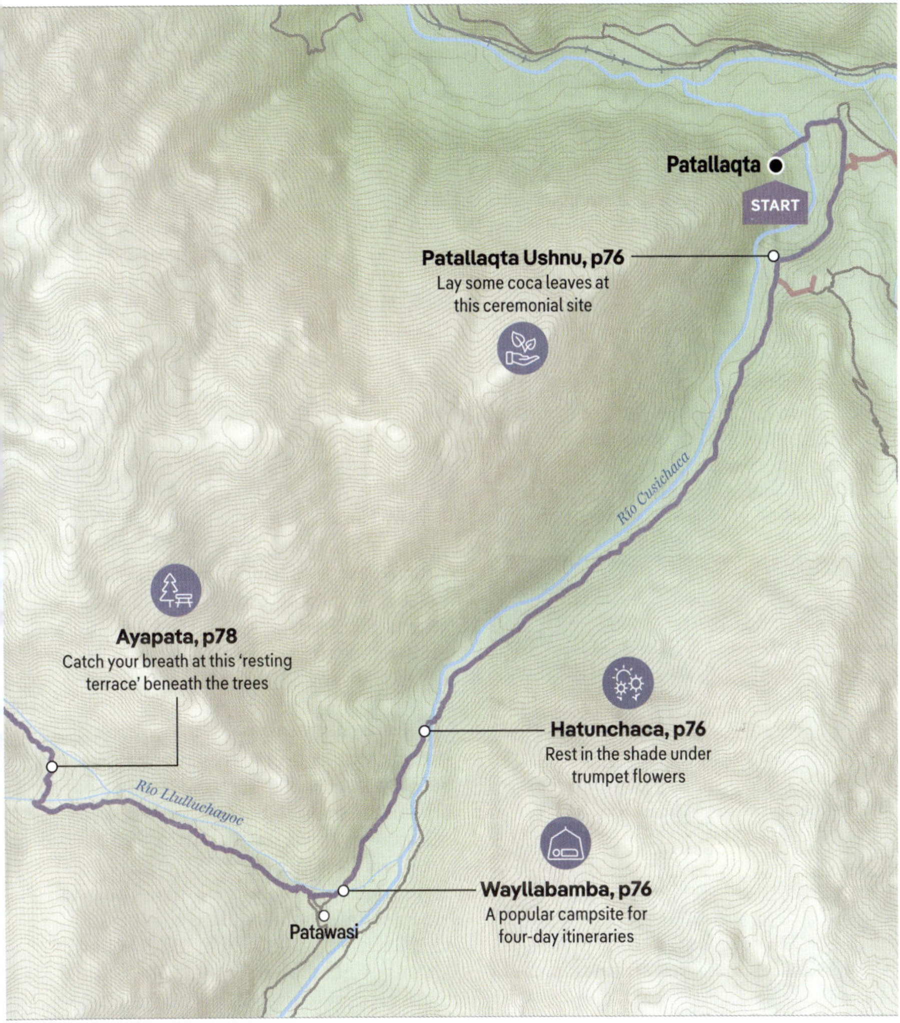
Patallaqta
START
Patallaqta Ushnu, p76
Lay some coca leaves at this ceremonial site
Río Cusichaca
Ayapata, p78
Catch your breath at this 'resting terrace' beneath the trees
Hatunchaca, p76
Rest in the shade under trumpet flowers
Río Llulluchayoc
Wayllabamba, p76
A popular campsite for four-day itineraries
Patawasi

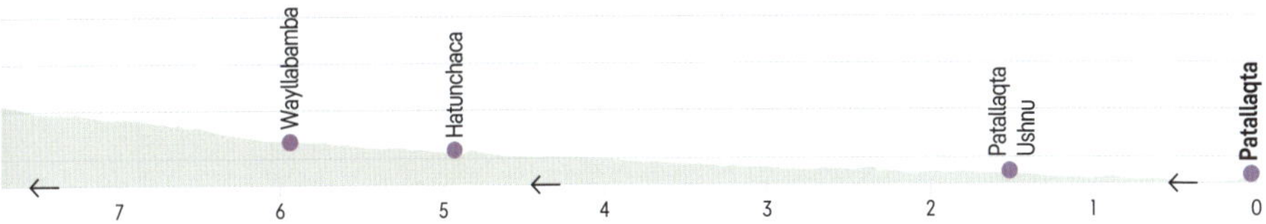
Wayllabamba
Hatunchaca
Patallaqta Ushnu
Patallaqta
7
6
5
4
3
2
1
0

PREVIOUS STOP Cross back over the Río Cusichaca and retrace your steps from Patallaqta back to the main Inca Trail.

Patallaqta Ushnu

On your way out of Patallaqta (if you were able to visit) and back towards the classic Inca Trail, don't miss the opportunity to walk up a steep narrow path to an *ushnu,* a raised stone altar used for ceremonial offerings or ritual communication with surrounding *apus* (mountain deities). Sometimes they were used for astronomical observation as well. In this case the altar overlooks the Patallaqta archaeological site, worn like a skirt around the base of the mountain, and the rushing Río Cusichaca. Perhaps the Patallaqta *ushnu* played stage to offerings made to ensure abundant agricultural output. Lay some coca leaves and say goodbye to the Río Urubamba and the faint sounds of the occasional Aguas Calientes-bound train – you are now turning south, to be enveloped by canyons clung to by bromeliads and rising mountain passes.

Río Cusichaca

FROM LEFT: KEVIN NICOL/ALAMY, PHIL CREAN A/ALAMY

Hatunchaca

A 3.5km (around two-hour) hike along fairly flat dirt paths brings you to a footbridge crossing a small tributary of the Río Urubamba leading you into Hatunchaca (meaning 'grand bridge'), a compact farming community. Near the entrance, a roofed seating area framed by pendulous angel's trumpet flowers *(Brugmansia)* offers welcome respite from the climate and an opportunity to quench your thirst. Basic toilets maintained by local families and camp sites are available, though this camp is typically used by agencies offering the slowed-down five-day Inca Trail. Groups on the four-day itinerary will wait until the next town 1.5km over to call it a day.

Wayllabamba

At the mouth of the Llulluchayoc Canyon lies Wayllabamba (2974m), the largest settlement on the trail. On the other side of the Río Llulluchayoc you will spot **Patawasi**, an Inca-era administrative site of truncated terraces. From where you stand, there is a fork in the path, demonstrating the web that is the Inca Trail: one branch descends south in the direction of Salkantay, while the other – your path – steadily climbs northwest towards Machu Picchu.

Patallaqta Ushnu

3.5km

Leave some coca leaves as an offering

Wayllabamba

Meaning 'grassy plain' in Quechua, Wayllabamba's riverside forests consist mainly of Andean alders *(Alnus acuminata)*, deciduous trees that thrive in challenging ecosystems – perhaps a metaphor for your own acclimatization journey.

This popular campsite will give your legs time to recharge in preparation for the following day's climb. When you wake, do as the locals do and gulp down a steaming cup of *mate de coca* (coca-leaf tea) with breakfast, a mild stimulant and traditional remedy for *soroche* (altitude sickness). As you hold the warm brew, don't be surprised to observe your hands shaking ever so slightly: a mix of morning shivers in the brisk Andes, and surely a bit of nerves about tackling the biggest climb of the trail.

LOOK FOR HUMMINGBIRDS

Though not part of the Andean three-world animal triad – serpent (underworld), puma (land), condor (sky) – hummingbirds (*q'enti* in Quechua) nevertheless seem to cross all three realms. A common yet never tiring sight as you climb, hummingbirds appear from humid cloud forest around 1500m above sea level to open puna above 4000m above sea level, with the giant hummingbird reaching up to a heavenly 5000m above sea level. A connector of worlds and certainly landscapes, the speedy flier will greet you at the start and the end of the up-and-over of Warmiwañusqa.

Hatunchaca — *1km* — **Wayllabamba**

Stop here for the bathroom and a rest

MARK EVELEIGH/ALAMY

LLULLUCHAPAMPA

Llulluchapampa takes its name from *llullucha (Nostoc sphaericum)*, a gelatinous alga that appears in high Andean wetlands. Reminiscent of boba pearls, the tiny green spheres are added to Andean soups for a boost of protein. While you won't be seeing *llullucha* (also referred to as *cushuro*) for yourself on the trail, you can find them for sale in the San Pedro (p38) or Urubamba (p51) markets. Just something to take your mind off the challenging ascent that begins as soon as you exit Llulluchapampa.

Before leaving Wayllabamba, pass a medical post and proceed through a **checkpoint** (keep your passport on hand). Consider if you need any snacks or drinks, as these are the last shops along the Inca Trail.

Ayapata

As leg muscles stir awake, a steady yet gentle climb out of Wayllabamba brings Abra Warmiwañusqa (Dead Woman's Pass) into view – distant but daunting.

Step beneath a forest of *queuñas (Polylepis)*, trees uniquely adapted to cold, thin air and high-altitude extremes. Their trunks peel away in miniature scrolls of paper, helping trap moisture in these wind-scoured slopes. Cross a tiny wooden footbridge and the path veers at a steep incline.

Wayllabamba

2.4km

This is where you'll see a fork in the path, one side leading on toward Salkantay

Llama, Llulluchapampa

Less than half a kilometer later you've arrived at Ayapata, a many-tiered campsite for some and a tree-filled rest stop for others. Native *chachacomas (Escallonia resinosa)* abound, releasing much needed oxygen and gracing the view with their white blossoms. Take the name Ayapata, meaning 'resting terrace' or 'place of rest,' to heart before the climb to the pending pass transitions to steep terrain.

Llulluchapampa

As you crank your legs up a constant slope, an enchanting forest of *unca* trees will beg you to slow down – if the climb in altitude hasn't forced you to already. Endemic to Peru and Bolivia, the *unca* tree *(Myrcianthes oreophila)* is a sign of a humid environment, and here it thrives among dangling moss and silent hummingbirds. Just beyond the forest's edge, a slender waterfall spills to your right, while a creek rushes downhill at your feet, teasing you with how much easier it would be to turn around and drift with the current.

Llulluchapampa (3760m) lies directly beneath a looming Warmiwañusqa and marks the transition into a rare patch of high Andean cloud forest. Though technically the last inhabited area you will pass through until you reach Machu Picchu Pueblo (also known as Aguas Calientes), it's more likely that you'll run into a herd of alpacas than a group of people, unless they are other trekkers. A stream of glacier water runs in front of some tucked-away bathrooms.

Continues on p82

Ayapata

Llulluchapampa

1.9km

Your last chance to buy snacks and first view of Warmiwañusqa

Prepare yourself for the upcoming 500m gain in elevation

Climb to Legendary Heights

Though most *apus* (mountain deities) were seen as male, Abra Warmiwañusqa embodies the fierce, protective energy of a woman who risked everything for love and was eternally claimed by the Andes. As you climb Dead Woman's Pass, the most challenging stretch of the Inca Trail, use the legend as your motor.

GOOD TO KNOW

Name: Abra Warmiwañusqa is Quechua for 'Dead Woman's Pass'. This startling name is often attributed to the shape of the surrounding peaks, which – when viewed on a clear day from the valley and with some imagination – trace the silhouette of a reclining woman: her face, chest and knees outlined against the sky.

Altitude: 4215m

Elevation gain: 500m

Trekker fatalities: Zero

The Andes are a land shrouded with spirituality and mysticism, so there are, unsurprisingly, variations of a legend inspired by the shapely pass. As you climb hundreds of steps and over 500m to reach the pass, you may feel the presence of a woman who rests eternally in the mountains, watching over travelers like yourself, as they enter her domain.

A Tragic Princess

One version tells of a young Inca princess who defied her family's wishes and fled to the mountains to be with her lover, a *chasqui* (relay-runner messenger) on the royal road. Exhausted by the altitude and cold, she died before reaching him, and Pachamama (Mother Earth) transformed her body into the mountains so her spirit could remain close to the road frequented by her beloved messenger. Some say her presence is felt in the thin air and gusts of winds that breathe across the pass – though you will have to interpret for yourself if she exhales gentle guidance or is huffily testing each passerby.

Body & Soul

If you can't determine her mood, think of her as an observant female guardian spirit, offering protection to those who walk with respect and humility, but challenging those who approach her with competition-based arrogance.

MARK EVELEIGH

LEGENDS ABOUND

In the Sacred Valley town of Calca, the snowcapped *apu* Pitusiray holds another tale of a woman transformed by love. According to local folklore, a princess defied her family to be with her beloved Sawasiray. Pursued and forbidden to unite, the pair fled into the high mountains, where the gods turned them into twin peaks - perhaps as tragic punishment or as a gift of grace, forever linking the lovers. Today, Pitusiray and Sawasiray face each other, eternal sentinels over the valley below.

Left: Trail up Abra Warmiwañusqa
Below: Mt Pitusiray

The moment you reach the top - where oxygen thins and an inner silence takes over - is not purely a physical feat but a kind of spiritual initiation. From this point on, the trek becomes a mindful pilgrimage. Even if you don't buy the spiritual framing, something has undeniably shifted and loosened, with the hardest stretch behind you.

Even today, you may see porters or guides silently honor the summit with a quiet offering of a *quintu* of coca leaves, a splash of water or a piece of fruit in honor of Warmiwañusqa, the mountain woman now immortalized in stone.

BETO SANTILLAN/SHUTTERSTOCK

Along the Way We Met...

MARÍA PREVATTE Hiking the Inca Trail was one of the most meaningful experiences of my life – beautiful, challenging and something I had dreamed of doing for a long time. There were moments, such as climbing Dead Woman's Pass, that truly tested me, but our group's encouragement, along with the supportive and attentive porters, helped me keep going. Our guide, Fisher, was patient, encouraging and always seemed to know exactly when I needed a push or a kind word. What made this journey especially meaningful was sharing the experience with our daughter. Even though we hiked at our own paces, simply knowing we were on this adventure together – each of us facing the same mountains and celebrating the same milestones – meant so much to me. It's a memory I will treasure forever.

María Prevatte is from Colombia. She hiked the five-day Inca Trail with her daughter Jen and her husband Ed.

Continued from p79

If you have a moment, remove your boots and peel off your socks to give your feet a refreshing ice bath in the stream.

Warmiwañusqa Climb

As Abra Warmiwañusqa (Dead Woman's Pass) comes into view, hikers often start to joke about the inevitable destiny the name of the pass implies – a bit of laughter therapy to cover honest doubts about their leg and lung stamina. In reality, though, there haven't been any fatalities of trekkers recorded.

Nevertheless, the stretch between Llulluchapampa to Abra Warmiwañusqa is considered to be the most challenging section of the entire trek with an elevation gain of nearly 500m as patches of original Inca stonework guide you upwards of 4000m above sea level. Original Inca engineering has been married with modern restoration as you near the jagged silhouette of a resting woman.

Intermittent stone steps in groups of twos and threes, many laid before the turn of the 21st century to prevent erosion, become steeper and more frequent as you near the pass, testing legs as well as lungs. Conversations that quickly dropped off after leaving Llulluchapampa have been replaced with the crunch of gravel beneath your boots and an inner monologue. Perhaps

Llulluchapampa

Abra Warmiwañusqa

1.6km

Rest as needed to stabilize breathing or any lightheadedness

Look back to see how far you've come

it's a soothing mantra to recalibrate breathing patterns ('inhale, exhale') or something to blow off the low-oxygen steam as you stop every 20 seconds ('c'mon, we're not there yet?!'). Both are valid.

Scattered at the base of the route are woody shrubs and vibrant blooms like *arete de Inca (Brachyotum ledifolium),* alongside low, hardy ground cover. Signaling an increasingly harsh climate, the path becomes exposed as you near the top. It's one of those rare sections where you'll peel off your wide-brimmed hat to slather on sunscreen, only to pull on gloves minutes later as the wind becomes chilly near the summit.

Abra Warmiwañusqa

When the remaining stone steps feel impossible, turn around. The valley below tells the story of how much ground you've already covered. Even if you are feeling comfortable with the altitude, hold back from racing to the Warmiwañusqa 'finish line' so as not to deplete all of your energy – you'll want steady feet and focus for the descent.

Grueling yet rewarding, conquering Dead Woman's Pass (4215m) is the Andean concept of duality in experienced form. A signpost with the altitude reminds you why your breathing has become syncopated, though your elation at having overcome the physical and mental challenge leaves you momentarily unaware. In a shared high of accomplishment and camaraderie with your other group members, soak in a panoramic – and slightly toppling – view of valleys and mountains on either side of the pass.

Don't linger too long while waiting for the rest of your group to reach Dead Woman's Pass though, as gusts at this altitude can quickly chill you to the bone. Rehydrate and, if approved by your guide, begin the descent toward Paqamayu Alto.

Hikers ascend Abra Warmiwañusqa (Dead Woman's Pass)

MARK EVELEIGH

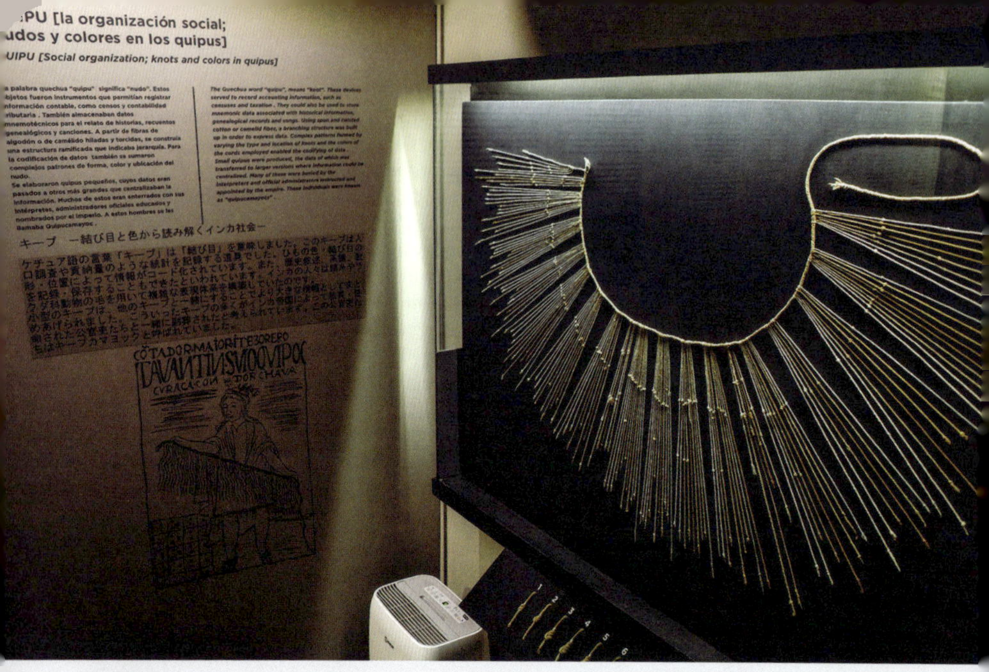

Quipu
MARK GREEN/SHUTTERSTOCK

INSIGHT

Chasquis: Inca Messaging System

As the trail rises and the air thins, it's difficult to imagine overcoming mountain passes at the speed and tenacity of the *chasquis*, foot messengers who pounded these paths centuries ago.

WORDS BY **AGNES RIVERA**
A runner, Agnes has never used her pair of ojotas *for sport.*

Relays & Way Stations

Zooming past caravans of llamas, soldiers and the Inca Sapa himself, were *chasquis*. The elite runners bound the Inca Empire together through their message delivery service, beating the paths of the Qhapaq Ñan beneath their sandal-clad feet. Woven from plant or animal fibers, *ojota* sandals are often associated with *chasquis* and are commonly seen to this day in the Andes, though they are now made of recycled tires. While long distances were covered between sender and receiver, the messengers themselves only ran a portion of the route before relaying the communication duties to the next *chasqui* in line.

The Andean Road System was meticulously organized with *tambos* – roadside rest stops where messengers would make the hand off, refuel, then surely collapse for the night. Depending on the terrain, the runner rest shelters were placed every five to 12km. On flatter ground the distances between *tambos* stretched longer; in steep, oxygen-thin passes, the distance was thoughtfully tighter.

Tambos dot the Inca Trail, such as the Runquraqay archaeological site (p93), strategically (and mercifully) placed halfway up its namesake mountain. Perched on a slumped shoulder en route to the second-highest mountain pass climbed during the Inca Trail, the first glimpse of cloud forest lingering nearby, the site is a semi-circular portal into the world of chasquis.

Trained to be Trusted

More than just speedy young men, those chosen to become foot messengers were a specialized caste. Trained for speed and endurance since childhood, *chasquis* were chosen for their athleticism, memory, trustworthiness and sense of geography.

Messengers relayed valuable information at astonishing speed, passing along memorized oral messages or quipus (a system of knotted cords). *Chasquis* would not have been able to decipher the encrypted message of a quipu, as they could only be interpreted by specialists, or *quipucamayocs*. This deliberate separation between transmission and interpretation was not a reflection of the runners' limitations. Rather, as argued by anthropologist and leading scholar of Inca recordkeeping Gary Urton, it was an admirable communication system by which structured records were carried by many and read by few.

Sure, their rank was nowhere near the Sapa Inca, but the work of the *chasquis* literally kept the empire connected, enabling Cusco to respond swiftly to events far from the capital. It is said that a message carried by the *chasquis* could travel from Quito, Ecuador, to Cusco in two weeks (some estimate one). And perhaps more impressive than the speed itself was its reliability. The Inca state knew roughly how long it would take for information to move between two places because the relay system was standardized, allowing the empire to plan and respond accordingly.

> Messengers relayed valuable information at astonishing speed

Signals & Spies

If running a night shift, *chasquis* are said to have announced their approach by blowing a *pututu* (conch shell), alerting the follow-up messenger to stuff their cheeks with coca and loosen weary ankles. By day, sunlight may have darted from a reflective object held in fatigued hands. Even with rest stops and handoffs, the work was punishing and the life of a *chasqui* could end abruptly – like a racehorse collapsing at the finish line.

Messengers circulating through the trails day and night was added security for the empire. Highly structured, it shouldn't come as a surprise that the Incas had dedicated spies. Beyond the runners, the *tambos* were frequented by the *tokoyrikoq,* royal inspectors whose name translates as 'he who sees all.' Traveling unannounced and often disguised as locals, the *tokoyrikoq* assessed provincial loyalty, labor obligations and any hint of rebellion within the four *suyus* (quarters). They were the eyes and ears of the Sapa Inca and would send their reports through the network of *chasquis,* who were themselves policed and reported upon.

As you stand upon the balcony of Runquraqay, the steep backside of Warmiwañusqa in view, you feel incredibly safe in the cradle of Pachamama's undulating landscape. Free from watchful eyes and the demand for speed, *tambos* like these cultivate a deeper respect in modern trekkers for the role of the *chasquis,* the runners who once kept the empire connected.

Warmiwañusqa

What goes up must come down – and you'll walk the walk of the physical law of gravity more than once on this leg. Trace the highs and lows of the mountains while maintaining a northwestern direction, and keep your knees guessing (and possibly aching) as you drop nearly 700m in altitude only to climb 400m more – and descend 700m again. Use the numerous *chasqui* posts as well-earned rest stops as you traverse what is perhaps the most diverse trail section of ecological tiers.

Agnes Rivera

Sayaqmarca (p96)
JAMES WAGSTAFF/SHUTTERSTOCK

Sayaqmarca

THIS LEG:

- Descending Warmiwañusqa
- Paqaymayu Alto
- Runquraqay Archaeological Site
- Runquraqay Pass
- Sayaqmarca

Walking Notes

A natural transformation takes place with each step: descending the high-altitude puna of Warmiwañusqa, where dry brush leads to a river-fed resting spot. Ascend a sloping forest, racking up those step counts and climb the second-highest pass, Runquraqay. Perhaps more than anywhere else on the trail, you'll embody muscle empathy for the Inca foot messengers as you commute from one archaeological site to another.

Breaking Your Journey

Positioned between the two highest passes on the trail, Paqamayu Alto is a popular campsite for day two of the four-day Inca Trail. After a night's rest or brief respite, shorten your poles to help produce a propulsive force up to the basket-shaped Runquraqay and a tucked-away 'inaccessible town.'

Agnes' Tips

BEST VIEW A shameless look back at how far you've come as you near the Runquraqay Pass, and the bonus of catching the halfmoon-shaped archaeological site from above.

FAVORITE STOP Paqaymayu, after having overcome Warmiwañusqa – but the pending Runquraqay pass stirs up some adrenaline.

TIP Stretch the knees and quads when you can to avoid next-day stiffness.

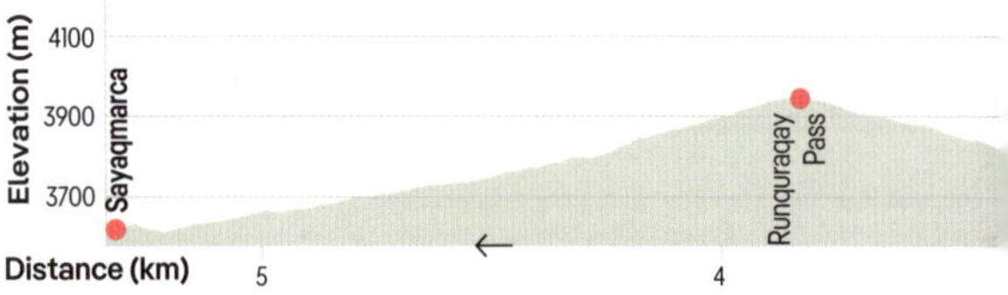

Río Paqamayu
Rest at Runquraqay, p93
Follow in the footsteps of *chasquis* (relay-runner messenger) and rest at this *tambo* (rest house) in the folds of Runquraqay
Runquraqay Archaeological Site, p91
Descending Warmiwañusqa, p90
Use hiking poles as you descend over 600m
Paqaymayu Alto, p90
Common campsite for day two
Abra Warmiwañusqa
START

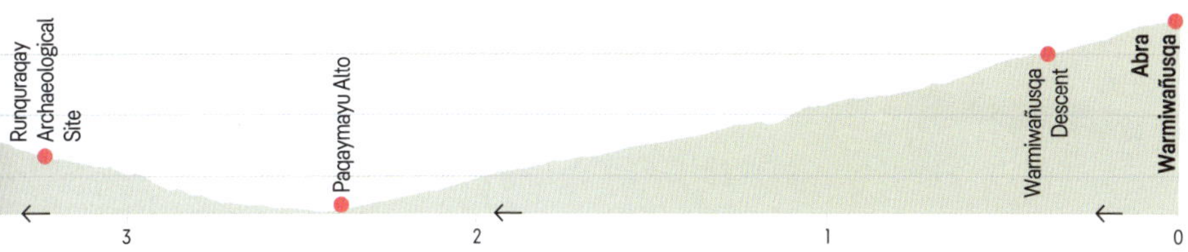
Runquraqay Archaeological Site
Paqaymayu Alto
Warmiwañusqa Descent
Abra Warmiwañusqa
3
2
1
0

PREVIOUS STOP If you hadn't had prior experience using trekking poles, this stair-packed stretch will make you the wiser: stabilize your footing down the stone steps scaling the backside of Dead Woman's Pass.

Descending Warmiwañusqa

As the altitude lowers with each step down the backside of Warmiwañusqa, the surrounding flora leaves no doubt in your mind that you've entered the high-altitude puna. Stiff ichu grass, traditionally used for Andean rooftops, bursts on either side of the sloping path.

Walking down a mountain is typically faster than going up – however, descending Warmiwañusqa may be an exception to the rule. Making your way down a relentless staircase to drop over 600m in altitude in a little over 2km is hard enough on the knees. Add to that the challenge of maneuvering a slick stone surface and it requires extra focus on your footing.

Put your hiking sticks to use to brace your weight upon the slick stairs, which begin with a wide girth then slowly narrow as you make your way down. Don't mind the experienced porters, bounding down with elastic ease as if the load on their backs didn't weigh up to 20kg, but do take their relaxed disposition as a reminder that patience is key.

Hiker descends Abra Warmiwañusqa

FROM LEFT: MATTHEW WILLIAMS-ELLIS TRAVEL PHOTOGRAPHY/ALAMY, MARTIN GRACE/ALAMY

Paqaymayu Alto

After the exposed ascent to the Warmiwañusqa Pass, the cool, shaded and sheltered valley of Paqaymayu (3596m) can feel like an oasis. Strategically positioned between the first and second passes, it is a common campsite for day two. Quechua for 'hidden river,' Río Paqamayu is tucked in a deep, narrow gorge below the campsite.

During the Inca Empire, *chasquis* may have also caught their breath in this enclosed and watered area. They would have arrived from a trail leading up from the Río Urubamba, on their way to Runquraqay. Honor the area's legacy and rest your possibly locked knees before the next ascent.

Coincidentally, Paqaymayu is the halfway mark – well, 56% to be exact, according to government signage – of your Inca Trail journey. This area also marks the transition between humid

View from Paqaymayu Alto

shrubby grassland and montane forest, and species of flora and fauna from both ecosystems coexist. *Papa silvestre* (wild potato), with its light purple petals and yellow yolk center, peer out from tree limbs, having snaked their way up. While it's not impossible to see four-legged wildlife such as vizcacha *(Lagidium viscacia)* scurrying about, don't hold your breath – unless you can convince all 499 other trekkers to do so in order not to startle the furry creatures.

Runquraqay Archaeological Site

Back on the original (and refurbished) imperial road, the elevation gain from Paqay-mayu to Runquraqay Pass is a comparatively

LOOK FOR THE UNORIGINAL INCA TRAIL

Curiously enough, the stretch of thoughtfully laid stone steps from Dead Woman's Pass to Paqaymayu Alto is not the original Inca Trail; rather, it was introduced before the turn of the century as a way to connect hikers to Paqaymayu Alto (a campsite for some, a rest area for others). The contemporary, v-shaped path offers hikers a brief respite from the altitude between the highest passes of the trek while the original path continues at the level of Dead Woman's Pass, nearing Quinsacocha Lake. Though you won't be able to see the high-altitude lake, a waterfall gushes down from its direction on your left-hand side.

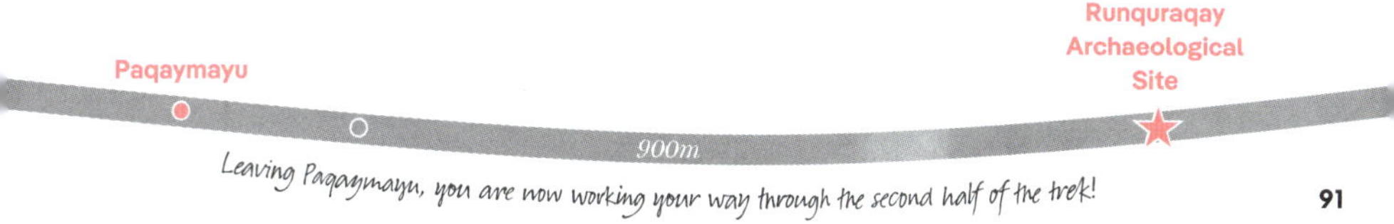

MARK EVELEIGH

Climb to Runquraqay

modest 374m (versus the roughly 1250m climbed from Wayllabamba to Warmiwañusqa), though the climb is sharper. Thankfully, this second effort comes with the confidence of knowing what your body (and mind) can achieve – and the added bonus of a pit stop in between at Runquraqay archaeological site.

Working your way up step after step, give in to the urge to pause and l ook back throughout this stretch – you'll be rewarded with views of a waterfall spilling down the backside of Dead Woman's Pass, with Paqaymayu suddenly revealed as a long drop below. On the Inca Trail, the past is never something to ignore.

Clusters of red trumpet flowers from the Bomarea vine peek above tall tufts of Andean grass, waving you along as the click of hiking

Continues on p94

Along the Way We Saw...

URUBAMBA ANTPITTA On my way down the slope towards Sayaqmarca, the clouds embraced the stone pathway, making me utterly present to what was only a few meters in front of me. Suddenly a small rusty orange body stepped in front of me, bopping its plump torso which appeared cartoonishly large upon its stick-like legs. Endemic to Peru and native to the high Andes, the Urubamba antpitta *(Grallaria occabambae)* is a rare and cherished sight, according to my guide who was a birder himself. I stopped in my tracks to observe the self-assured creature, not daring to take out my phone and risk startling it away. How curious that this little fellow, with eyes ringed in white, seemed to be welcoming me along the trail, in no rush to carry on with its day and fly away. In a flash, it dipped into the bushes without a sound. I interpreted the appearance of the Urubamba antpitta, a mainly terrestrial bird, as a guardian of the ecosystem, permitting me to enter.

Agnes Rivera

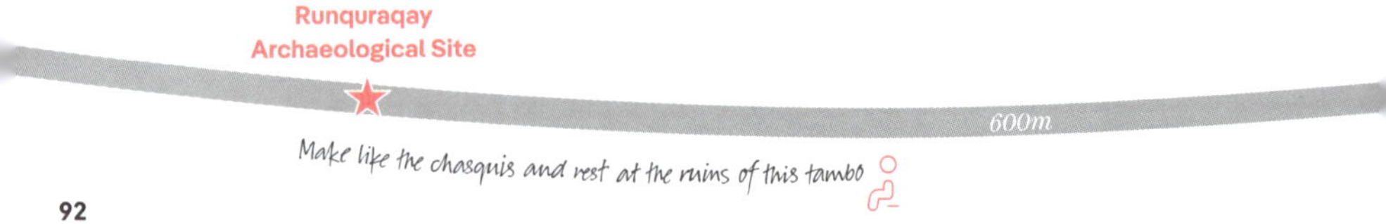

Rest at Runquraqay

Perched on a slumped shoulder of the second-highest mountain pass along the Inca Trail, with the first glimpse of cloud forest lingering nearby, Runquraqay is a semi-circular portal into the world of *chasquis*.

GOOD TO KNOW

Name: Often translated as 'rounded enclosure,' the literal translation of *runqu* is 'basket' – a reference to the site's unique shape which is best appreciated near the pass above.

Elevation: 3760m

Camouflaged into the folds of the mountain, the Runquraqay *tambo* (rest stop) was strategically and (mercifully) placed halfway up the mountain of the same name.

Step into the discreet and compact archaeological site through a narrow doorway set between two concentric walls of irregular stone, carefully bound with mortar. A magnetic view of lush mountainsides pulls you through a circular plaza and toward the rounded balcony that peers over the Paqaymayu campsite and the knee-shattering backside of Warmiwañusqa.

Stationed at the lower left of the site is a modest *chasqui wasi,* an inn for foot messengers. It was likely shared by a few messengers: one who had recently completed their delivery service and at least one other waiting to receive a message to relay.

A portion of the main complex, a *tambo* for pilgrims making their way along the spiritual path as well as a checkpoint for security, would have served as a *qolqa* (food storage house), maintained by an on-site resident so travelers had no need to weigh themselves down with food.

Above: Runquraqay
Right: View from Runquraqay

FROM LEFT: KBRIMAGER-BOWLES/SHUTTERSTOCK, SHARPTOYOU/SHUTTERSTOCK

Continued from p92

poles against winding stone stairs provides the soundtrack to your imminent arrival at the Runquraqay archaeological site. As you near, steep steps alternate with sloped, paved sections, triggering sore muscle memory from the recent ascent of Warmiwañusqa. Hummingbirds flickering overhead and *qera qera* – an Andean lupine bursting in purple bloom – often mark the approach to the *chasqui wasi* (a rest stop for Inca foot messengers).

Runquraqay Pass

As you leave the Runquraqay site, continuing your way up the second-highest climb of the entire trek (3970m), patches of the path become narrow, wedged between stone, and completely uneven. Be careful with your footing.

Along the Way We Met...

FISHER CHAVEZ I've been guiding the Inca Trail for nearly 20 years, and became interested in birding about seven years ago. Across the four days of hiking, you'll see hundreds of bird species reflecting the change in ecosystems. However, I'd say one of the best places to see birds is from Paqaymayu to Runquraqay, as you'll see a great variety of bird species as you enter the cloud forest. Ten minutes down from the Runquraqay Pass, heading towards Chakiqocha, you'll see a lot of interesting species, including endemics such as the Urubamba antpitta, Cusco brushfinch, rusty-fronted *canastero* and Inca wren. One of my most memorable bird-watching moments was near the Phuyupatamarka campsite when, suddenly, a royal *cinclotes* was just 1m in front of me. Very rare and critically endangered, it felt extremely special to see this high-altitude bird so close.

Fisher Chavez, a guide on the Inca Trail, is a passionate birder at Perú Nature Photography.

FISHER'S TIP: *Don't forget key equipment such as your binoculars, and stay enthusiastic. The best hours to see birds are from 5:30am to 11am and 3pm to 6pm.*

Don't forget to take a moment to look back and down toward the exquisitely shaped archaeological site you just left behind – some say it looks like a *tumi,* the Inca ceremonial knife. At a false summit, surrounded by boggy ground, there is a small lake to your left, which looks more like a swamp during dry season.

A rather large clearing laid with stone welcomes you at the actual pass, where you can steady your breath. Upon arriving you'll be facing west, in the direction of the next-in-line archaeological site, Sayaqmarca, with your starting point, Km 82, nearly a direct shot east.

Nearly as soon as you begin stepping down the steep backside of Runquraqay mountain, a large boulder looms over the trail like an embracing limb, creating a brief tunnel that swallows you in a mere preview of a longer Inca tunnel that will appear later that day.

Cusco brushfinch

Sayaqmarca

A series of steep switchbacks (yes, knees, we hear you!) followed by a gentler undulation winds you down a 700m drop towards the next archaeological site, Sayaqmarca (p96). Early on, a finger-shaped lake comes into view on your right (north), while the flora to the left thickens and rises, an early hint that climate and altitude are once again becoming more forgiving.

Just before a sharp right is offered to lead you northwest, a narrow stone stairway crawls up a precipice to the other side. You (or someone in your group) may grumble about 'more stairs,' but the 50m climb to the cliff-hugging Sayaqmarca site (3245m) is well worth the elevated detour.

In Quechua, Sayaqmarca can be translated to 'perched village' though it is sometimes translated a bit more dramatically as 'inaccessible town.' Protected on three sides by sheer cliffs, steady yourself as you eye the slightly dizzying layout of multiple levels and stairways facing this way and that.

Much remains to be revealed about this Inca site, as little research or excavation has taken place, but it is theorized as having been an administrative center and checkpoint.

Accessing Sayaqmarca

Take a slight detour from the Inca Trail to wander the labyrinthine Sayaqmarca site. Believed to have served as an administrative center and checkpoint, the 'inaccessible town' extends little more than 50m toward the Ahobamba Valley.

GOOD TO KNOW

Getting here: Follow the trail 2.1km downhill from Runquraqay Pass. Just before the sharp right, climb 50m up the stairs to Sayaqmarca.

Elevation: 3245m

Name: Sayaqmarca can be translated from Quechua as 'perched village' or 'inaccessible town.'

Guided by the Land

Despite its name, Sayaqmarca has a secondary access point emerging from the forested Ahobamba Valley. The staircase is nearly hidden beneath overgrown vegetation, but a discerning eye can spot it tucked further north-west, behind the main entryway. With such narrow entryways, the sense that access was carefully controlled here is reinforced. It leaves one wondering how many other stairways still lie buried – and what hidden paths and ruins these mountains may yet hold.

A curved tower stands upon the upper section, overlooking a midsection sliced by rectangular rooms of all sizes. In fact, the site layout feels unusually spontaneous compared to other Inca Trail sites. Adapting to the mountain's contours or perhaps prizing the outstanding vistas, the plaza sits at the end of the site, in lieu of a central courtyard.

The crown of the entryway wall, the highest point of the site, is trimmed with a U-shaped aqueduct, eager to catch the rain. Follow the high-sitting channel to a set of fountains or ceremonial baths set at staggered levels. Set above the lowest fountains sit stones carved with beam sockets (pictured left), once used to anchor wooden elements. They are similar in form (though not function) to the bar holes seen at Pulpituyuq in Patallaqta (p66).

The Perfect Photo Op

Continue toward the mountain edge, where the site flares out wide into a triangular plaza.

JAMES WAGSTAFF/SHUTTERSTOCK

CEDROBAMBA

In 1915, Hiram Bingham visited this site and reportedly referred to it as 'Cedrobamba' in reference to cedar trees. It wasn't until 1941 when Hungarian-American anthropologist (and early explorer of Inca Trail sites) Paul Fejos visited the site on an expedition that it was renamed Sayaqmarca, a wink to its outlying nature.

Left: Sayaqmarca
Below: Trail to Sayaqmarca

From here you'll see how stairways and walls have been collecting the thirst-quenching fog, resulting in a soft green armor. During the rainy season, the clouds will hover close to the site, giving it a dream-like feeling. On a clear, dry day, you'll want to soak in the views of the sweeping Ahobamba Valley below, painted in thick brushstrokes of rainforest, with the snowcapped Pumasillo peak to the far west. Take a photo as you reflect on the opportunity to visit a lesser-known Inca site that only those with the audacity to walk the Inca Trail can access.

FROM LEFT: LMTAYLOR/SHUTTERSTOCK, CKCHIU/SHUTTERSTOCK

Alfredo Ferreyros on an early expedition
EXPLORANDES

INSIGHT

Making the Inca Trail Famous

US explorer Hiram Bingham III may have brought Machu Picchu to the world's attention, but Alfredo Ferreyros helped shape the site's footpath, what is now known as the Classic Inca Trail, into a global invitation to adventure travel in Peru.

WORDS BY **AGNES RIVERA**
Agnes's first Inca Trail experience was with ExplorAndes.

THE INCA TRAIL has never been a forgotten road – but for much of modern history, it was a quiet one. After sections of the Inca highway were fractured to prevent Spanish conquerors from reaching sacred sites, remnants of stone steps continued to climb through rambling cloud forest, and mountain passes still stitched valleys to remote summits. Paths along the valley floor continued to be used by local farmers, herders and *chasquis* of another era.

A Modern Reawakening

It wasn't until the mid-20th century, however, that outsiders began to grasp the significance of approaching Machu Picchu on foot, following the same mountain- and river-defined paths constructed centuries earlier by imperial engineers. Today, the Inca Trail stands among the world's most sought-after multiday hikes, shared by nature lovers and bucket-listers alike. Alfredo Ferreyros was a first-hand observer of the trail before fame.

'I'm supposedly officially retired,' laughs the entrepreneur, feeling at home in a Sacred Valley cafe. It's been over 50 years since he founded ExplorAndes, the premier Peruvian adventure operator on the Inca Trail. Since then, the company has become a voice for sustainable tourism – winning the World's Leading Green Tour Operator consecutively from 2018 to 2025, in fact – as intense global demand brushes past fragile archaeology.

Born in Lima, Alfredo went to boarding school in Europe where he would venture to the Alps on vacation instead of making the long return home. In 1973, he graduated from Cornell University with a degree in Social Sciences focusing on rural development and memories of long weekends trekking in the White Mountains along the US East Coast. That same year he made a 3½-month road trip from New York down to Peru's capital. But after living nearly a decade abroad, his homecoming was brief.

> Today, the Inca Trail stands among the world's most sought-after multiday hikes, shared by nature lovers and bucket-listers alike.

Rediscovering the Classic Inca Trail

'I got to Lima and didn't like it so I decided to go to Cusco, where I had never been,' reminisces Alfredo. 'I invested in a printing press with the idea to print information for tourists, but that quickly turned to operating as a guide because customers would begin asking me questions about their upcoming trips. On the weekends I'd go out hiking to remote sites that weren't yet studied profusely by archaeologists, such as Huchuy Qosqo or ruins around Chinchero.'

Visiting remote sites and reading up on Inca archaeology, Alfredo could see the potential for Peru as an adventure travel destination. Every now and then, within those first two years of living in Cusco, a hiker would ask about the Inca Trail. It was still relatively unknown at the time, as there were only a few US or European companies that would bring groups, led by a foreign tour leader. Alfredo decided to see it for himself.

'In 1974, I stepped foot for the first time on sections of what would become the Classic Inca Trail. I was with the son of the archaeologist in charge of Machu Picchu at the time, Manuel Chavez Farfan, so I got the inside scoop on what was going on. I'd say we rediscovered the original route, which has since been cut and rerouted,' divulges Alfredo, referring to the backside of Warmiwañusqa. 'Some trail sections were completely covered in plants. At the time, the whole sanctuary and trail belonged to a hacienda of a family called Zavaleta. They had cattle all over. The round structure of Runquraqay was used as a coral for example, and we came across all sorts of vestiges.'

Preserving the Old, Birthing the New

After his first encounter with the trail, culminating with a camp out within the citadel itself, Alfredo saw organized trekking as a means to preserve a historical route while generating new opportunities for growth and development.

'I didn't do a market study, I just decided to go for it: developing itineraries, putting out information about altitude for safety reasons, documenting as best I could the hiking experience,' he recounts. In 1975, after printing a catalog with itineraries, ExplorAndes was launched and the founder guided travelers himself. 'Little by little, we trained members of communities in the Ollantaytambo area as kitchen assistants, mule drivers, and taught them how to properly pack and set up camp. We encouraged local guides to continue training and studying to be on par with the foreign guides. Our philosophy has always been to provide work opportunities for local people if they want it.'

Rather than 'experimental,' Alfredo prefers to refer to the initial years working the Inca Trail as 'inspirational' – a time when the learning curve was as long and steep as the climb up Dead Woman's Pass. The main challenges were external factors, such as seasonal mudslides, quality of roads – 'there was only one asphalted road leading out of Cusco at the time' – and, throughout the 1980s and '90s, the terrorist activities of the Sendero Luminoso (Shining Path). Not to mention the work that needed to be done on the trail itself.

EXPLORANDES

Alfredo Ferreyros

'Finally in 1983 we got the first official exploration party together with the government, with the Ministry of Tourism and Culture, and did a two-week exploration. We needed to improve infrastructure. Runquraqay and Sayaqmarca were completely overgrown with vegetation, as was the section leading up to Phuyupatamarka, for example. And once bushwacked and cleared, we were able to do some more research on these sites,' recalls Alfredo. 'This is when the government began to see the trail as a potential tourism product and, soon after, the boom of tourism along the Inca Trail began.'

Rather than 'experimental,' Alfredo prefers to refer to the initial years working the Inca Trail as 'inspirational' – a time when the learning curve was as long and steep as the climb up Dead Woman's Pass.

Too Much of a Good Thing

Before significant regulations were established in 2001–02 – which prohibit independent hiking and set a daily limit of 500 entries, including porters – Alfredo recalls there'd be days with a thousand hikers setting off on the trails, with the ascent to passes looking from afar like an anthill swarmed by its colony.

'I've seen the Inca Trail pass through some bad moments, but we've come a long way and are learning, as an industry and as a country, to take care of a pivotal piece of Peru's anchor site, which is Machu Picchu,' reflects Alfredo, pointing to the fact that weight needs to be taken off the Classic route. 'There are pristine alternative treks that lead to Machu Picchu, but they haven't gained the attention of travelers because they think there is only one true 'Inca Trail' – but actually, the authentic imperial roads are in remote areas,' he says, referring to impressive sites like Huaco Pampa along the Qhapaq Ñan (p68).

Beyond the Inca Trail

Half a century after having helped establish the Inca Trail as an accessible tourist draw, it may be surprising to hear the entrepreneur direct travelers otherwise. Yet Alfredo's intention, since the early days as a guide and eventual tour operator, has always been to share the beauty and diversity of Peru with the world in a conscious manner.

'The experience on the Inca Trail is a good baptism to that end in that, in those stretch of days, you go through a handful of ecosystems, wildlife habitats,' Alfredo says, describing the fern and orchid-filled section between Runquraqay and Phuyupatamarka as his favorite. 'And many people who join the five-day trek, which has less participants and is spaced away from other groups, go through a transformational experience on the Inca Trail: questioning what they've lived through, how they live and contemplating their future. It's a mystical experience.'

He notes that none of it would have been possible without teamwork: charismatic guides that know their stuff, porters that supply the services that often surprise guests – from the food to just a smile along the way. Now in his seventies, it's been years since Alfredo walked the Inca Trail, a trek that he's done upwards of 50 times. Even so, he's an adventurer at heart and believes in the power of an industry he helped develop in Peru.

'Adventure travel can be an integrational experience, bringing together different cultures,' he says. 'And the Inca Trail, even though it's no longer just for adventurists, is a microcosm of Peru's incredible diversity.'

ExplorAndes campsite
EXPLORANDES

Sayaqmarca

Compared to earlier climbs, the gain of less than 400m on this leg feels almost like a walk in the Andean park as you crest the third pass of the trek – your last hurrah at an archaeological site and high-altitude camp above 3000m. Now suspended in the warm and humid embrace of the cloud forest, contour-tracing Inca paths stay true to airy views over the Ahobamba Valley and the well-postured peaks beyond (assuming the clouds cooperate).

Agnes Rivera

View over Phuyupatamarka from Phuyupatamarka camp (p108)

40 STEPS BEYOND/SHUTTERSTOCK

Phuyupatamarka

5.9KM

3 HOURS' WALK

THIS LEG:

- Q'onchamarka
- Chakiqocha
- Inca Tunnel
- Phuyupatamarka Camp

Walking Notes

With minimal altitude gain ahead, your legs will rejoice in the near absence of stairs as you glide gently up slopes of grey stone sometimes streaked with hints of green or blue. After passing through a dank Inca tunnel, the trail delivers you just above the Phuyupatamarka archaeological site to its namesake campsite.

Breaking Your Journey

Cross your fingers for clear skies as you traverse this scenic stretch. You may even want to ask your guide about waiting out lingering cloud cover, as both Sayaqmarca and the Phuyupatamarka campsite (a possible overnight camp, particularly for those on the five-day itinerary) offer panoramic views of multiple *apus* (mountain spirits) when visibility improves. Many four-day trekkers will break at Chakiqocha or continue on to Wiñay Wayna Camp (p132) for the night.

Agnes' Tips

FAVOURITE VIEW Standing atop Phuyupatamarka campsite, in the cradle of *apus*

ESSENTIAL STOP Wandering around Sayaqmarca (p96)

TIP The shortest of the legs so far is also one of the most picturesque. Slow down to appreciate the details: wide paths, valley views and diverse flora.

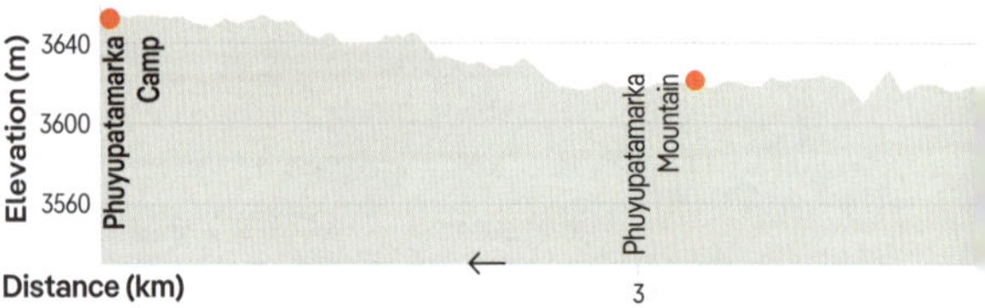

Go Apu-Bathing in the Clouds, p110
Make like the Inca and stand in awe of the mountains that surround you
Phuyupatamarka Mountain
Q'onchamarka, p106
Exposed highlands give way to cloud forest
Chakiqocha, p106
Apply insect repellent at this popular camp and rest stop
Sayaqmarca
START

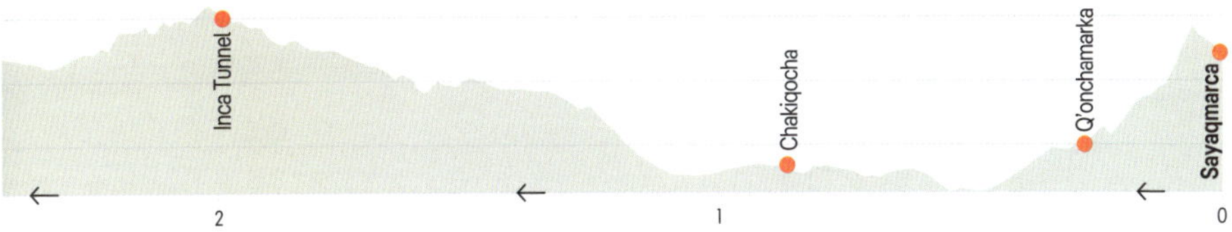
Inca Tunnel
Chakiqocha
Q'onchamarka
Sayaqmarca
2
1
0

PREVIOUS STOP Exit the 'inaccessible' Sayaqmarca through the same set of narrow stairs you used to enter and veer left (northwest), back onto the Inca Trail.

Q'onchamarka

Shortly after exiting Sayaqmarca, a finely paved section of the trail winds past and through a modest set of agricultural terraces. The uncovered platforms are nothing in scale like those spotted at Patallaqta, though they likely helped supply those residing at Sayaqmarca or nearby Runquraqay, where agricultural terraces are nearly non-existent.

Just above the terraces sits a small cluster of curved ruins known as Q'onchamarka. Researchers posit that *chasquis* and other travelers on foot may once have paused here, using the site as a *tambo* (resting place). That said, Q'onchamarka was only documented in the late 20th century and the site remains largely enigmatic.

As you continue northwest, rounding the curved terraces, the air grows heavier with moisture. You'll be wicking more sweat away than when you climbed Warmiwañusqa. For trekkers along the Inca Trail, Q'onchamarka is less a destination and more a mark of transition: an in-between place where the exposed highland of mountain passes climbed kilometers behind give to the cloud forest ahead.

Inca tunnel

FROM LEFT: AGNES RIVERA, HANNAH RUSSELL/ALAMY

Chakiqocha

Trace the contours of the mountainside along twisting paths shaded by ferns and limber trees. Mostly of Inca origin, the craggy trail here is dotted with green-blue stones known as serpentine, their unexpected color catching the eye like diamonds in the rough. Fifteen minutes from Q'onchamarka lies Chakiqocha (3454m).

The name can be translated as 'lake of the tired feet,' though, as is the way with Quechua ambiguities, it may also be referred to as 'dry lake.' Either way, both definitions are fitting for this resting place with seasonally diminished boggy lands that lay to its west.

This is a popular second-night campsite for groups on the four-day trek, while those on the five-day itinerary typically stop here for lunch or a rest on day three. Either way, keep in mind the swamp-like conditions attract mosquitoes.

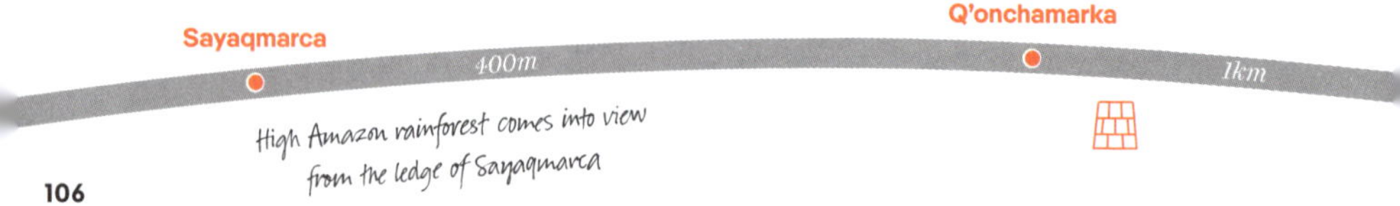

View over Q'onchamarka

If you haven't already, now's the time to apply insect repellent.

Inca Tunnel

From Chakiqocha, the third pass is marked by a gentle 150m climb toward Phuyupatamarka. The trail winds through 'dwarf forest,' where tiny, enchanting trees and plants glow in effervescent reds and greens until the path delivers a hollow surprise.

When you arrive at the entrance to the longest Inca tunnel on the Classic Inca Trail, don't rush through. You may find yourself quietly asking Pachamama (Mother Earth) for permission to enter, or pausing in momentary awe at this deceptively simple feat of Inca engineering.

LOOK FOR SERPENTINE

Recognizable by its greenish sheen, serpentine appears along several stretches of the Inca Trail, where its smooth, waxy surface makes it noticeably slippier than other stones. The Latin root is *serpentinus,* meaning 'of or relating to a serpent,' which, in the Andes, could be associated with the Inca *amaru,* the sacred serpent linked to water and the underworld. While spotting the stone out on the trail can feel like coming across a gem, artisans today commonly use the (comparatively) soft stone for carvings and jewelry.

Most trees near this area don't surpass 10m in height

Inca subterranean tunnels have been discovered throughout the Andes. Archaeologists have found that Inca engineers generally opted for a hand-hewn option in the face of a rock spur. Abrasion techniques using hammers or chisels made of stone or bronze may have been used in this particular case.

Stretching longer than 15m, the stone corridor found on this leg is just wide enough for loaded travelers in single file. Enough light seeps in that you won't find yourself at a loss of how to proceed, though be aware of its initial downturned slope.

Upon exiting the carved passageway you'll emerge to once again begin a soft ascent towards the third and final pass of the trek.

Phuyupatamarka Camp

Meaning 'town above the clouds,' you've now reached the high-mountain campsite of Phuyupatamarka (3601m). A restroom maintained by park rangers lies at the bottom of what is perhaps the most scenic sleeping spot along the Inca Trail. Multilevel decks for pitching tents crawl up a slopeside, each with sweeping views of valleys below and peaks looming on the horizon in every direction.

The site name doesn't include the word 'cloud' for nothing. With luck, the veil will part and stars made visible will glitter impossibly close by night. Almost completely exposed, this could be one of the coldest nights spent on the trail. With another 13km until Machu Picchu, this is the last time you'll stand at over 3000m above sea level on the Inca Trail.

Before you head down to explore the Phuyupatamarka archaeological site (p127), use your hands and keep your legs bent to scramble to the highest point of the campsite. A 360-degree panorama of the who's who of Andean peaks includes some of the most important Inca *apus* (p110).

Porters rest, Phuyupatamarka Camp

MARK EVELEIGH

Along the Way We Met...

FLOR ZUÑIGA I was born two hours from Machu Picchu, in Kuquipata, Quillabamba, but soon after moved to Huancacalle, Vilcabamba, the last Inca city, where I lived until I was nine years old. I've always had a deep connection to nature. One of my favorite sections along the trail is from Sayaqmarca to Chakiqocha. In that section, where the trails follow the shape of the mountain, you see an incredible range of vegetation – it's just full of life. We are above Pachamama – walking on her trails, eating food grown from her soil – but she is what makes our life possible, and it's in this section, where the oxygen is pure and free from pollution, that her importance and beauty is undeniable. My ancestors didn't destroy their ecosystems, like how we are doing in modern civilizations. Instead, the crops grown on the terraces were of more value than gold, because it was essential to life. I believe walking the Inca Trail has the power to rebuild the connection to nature that so many of us have lost over time – and reminds us of our responsibility to take care of Pachamama as well.

Flor Zuñiga is a freelance tour guide based in Cusco. She began working on the Inca Trail in 2013.

As you scan the ridgelines, your eye may catch a small raised platform to the right of the camp's apex. What is believed to be an *ushnu* (altar) adds a ceremonial element to this high-rising site. Set on a knife-edge ridge, it is linked to the campground by a narrow, vertiginous path. Often shrouded in clouds, trekkers are deterred from crossing the teetering path, though just observing its thin passage hints at the significance it must have held centuries ago. Across the Inca world, *ushnus* are thought to have been used for rituals and offerings to the *apus* or to Pachamama. This particular sacred platform may have played an astronomical role, possibly linked to observations of the Chakana (Southern Cross) – an important constellation in Inca cosmology – though, like many Inca sites, its precise role remains open to interpretation.

Go Apu-Bathing in the Clouds

A climb up narrow stairways or exploring sloping paths is never in vain on the Inca Trail. High-elevation sites and platforms, such as Sayaqmarca and the Phuyupatamarka campsite, offered security through surveillance and obscurity, but also rewarded with panoramic views of watchful *apus*.

GOOD TO KNOW

Mountain peak elevations:

Machu Picchu Mountain: 3082m

Nevado Salkantay: 6271m

Pumasillo: 5991m

Wakay Willka: 5893m

The Inca Empire went to great lengths – and heights – in order to access and build upon improbable terrain that offered security. A *tambo* camouflaged within the mountainside, such as Runquraqay, would go unnoticed should there be unwelcome passersby. While at the triangular perch of Sayaqmarca, jutting out like a sharp chin, the two steep and narrow stairways would have been impossible to access without someone taking notice well in advance.

But as you look over the edge of Sayaqmarca's wide plaza (vertigo sufferers may want to hang back), gazing upon Pumasillo, you wouldn't be far off in thinking that Inca sites were also selected to appease their mountain-loving sensibilities. Sweeping views like these were their version of hanging up a framed canvas from a master painter.

More than Mountains

Heaven-reaching guardians and protectors – but also providers of water and, thus, life-sustaining – mountains in the Inca world-view were sacred entities known as *apus*. These revered peaks fell beneath the wider umbrella of *huacas*, or sacred places, and were honored with ceremonies, offerings and ritual acts.

Considered living beings, *apus* keep watch over every side of the Inca Trail. This becomes astonishingly clear as you stand above the clouds from the highest point of the Phuyupatamarka campsite, coming face-to-mountain-face with an

OFFERINGS

During a traditional Andean coca ceremony, the strength and protection of nearby *apus* is called upon. First, three green leaves are selected (no tears or holes) and formed into a *quintu*. Then, into each cardinal direction, a respective *apu* is named and an intentional breath is blown into the leaves. It's a respectful way of asking for good health and safe passage from the mountains as you move through a new chapter in life.

Left: Mt Salkantay and Mt Humantay from Phuyupatamarka
Below: Wakay Willka (Mt Veronica)

assembly line of powerful peaks cascading across the horizon.

From here, make a full revolution to get acquainted with the peaks before you: Nevado Salkantay, the highest peak in the Vilcabamba Cordillera, to the south; the jagged crest of Pumasillo to the west; protecting premature views of the citadel is the backside of Machu Picchu Mountain to the north and Wakay Willka, better known now as Mt Veronica, sitting pretty northeast.

Standing in the middle of this mountainous orbit, far above the tree line, a sense of calm washes over you. *Apu*-bathing might just be the new forest bathing.

Man performs ritual with coca leaves
WIRESTOCK CREATORS/SHUTTERSTOCK

INSIGHT

Coca Leaf: Sacred Blessing of the Incas

Coca leaves have been used as a herbal remedy, energy booster and ritual offering since well before the time of the Incas and continue to be a lasting component of many Andean traditional beliefs.

WORDS BY **MARK EVELEIGH**
Throughout two decades traveling in Peru, Mark Eveleigh has seen changing attitudes to the coca leaf.

A PORTER SHRUGS his pack onto his back and stares staunchly toward the winding trail that leads up to Abra Warmiwañusqa. His left hand brings a trio of little green leaves close to his mouth and he blows gently towards the fearsome summit that his international clients know as Dead Woman's Pass.

The scene is timeless. For countless generations, Andean highlanders have sought blessing from the *apus* (mountain deities) with the little cluster of three coca leaves that are known as *quintu*.

Coca Use on the Inca Trail

Aside from helping the body adapt to lower levels of oxygen in the thin Andean air, coca leaf extract was believed to ease hunger and exhaustion, whether consumed in tea or directly by chewing. Two decades ago it was so ubiquitous among Inca Trail porters as to be considered almost crucial to their harsh working life. These days it's only the older generation of porters who continue to chew the leaves. The waning use of the leaves on the trail is perhaps a hopeful sign that more recent legislation has eased the brutally tough working conditions that older porters still recall.

Coca Tea & Other Specialties

Apart from the ubiquitous coca tea, which continues to be served as 'welcome drinks' in the lobbies of high-end Cusco hotels, you'll see coca as an ingredient in a mind-boggling range of items in restaurants and markets. Coca chocolate is a favorite souvenir, along with coca sweets, toffees and *gominolas* (chewy coca-flavored jellies). Cafes serve coca lattes and some bars in tourist areas serve pisco shots infused with coca.

> For countless generations, Andean highlanders have sought blessing from the *apus* (mountain deities) with the little cluster of three coca leaves that are known as *quintu.*

Sacred Plant of the Incas

Cocaine, the active ingredient in coca, was not discovered by international scientists until the 1860s but *mamakuka* (Mother Coca) was known to the forefathers of the Incas as long as 8000 years ago. There have been numerous discoveries of pre-Inca sculptures of human faces with the cheek bulging, portraying the act of chewing coca leaves.

At the time of the Incas, coca was considered a divine plant and a crucial part of the religion. Its use was prohibited and only the Sapa Inca (emperor) and other royalty were allowed to chew the leaves or drink the infused tea at ceremonial occasions. Inka Garcilaso de la Vega, often said to be Peru's first indigenous writer, described the use of coca during this period in his *Comentarios Reales de los Incas,* first published in 1609: 'The use of coca was nothing like so widespread then as it is today, but was the exclusive privilege of the king who, occasionally, offered a few leaves, as a mark of favor, to this or that prince...'

It's believed that special dispensation was made also for the *chasqui* (relay-runner messengers) who were allowed to chew coca leaves as an aid to their endurance.

Coca Use in Ritual Sacrifices

There's a theory that Machu Picchu and nearby agricultural centers like Intipata and Wiñay Wayna – built at a significantly lower altitude than most Inca cities prior to the arrival of the Spanish – were considered favorable locations in part because they had prime conditions for growing the all-important coca.

Coca leaves were offered to Pachamama (Mother Earth) during planting season in the hope that she would reward her devotees with bountiful harvests. A more disturbing form of offering known as *capacocha* (sometimes written as *qhapaq hucha*) were human sacrifices. Specially selected and often groomed children and women were killed by strangulation, burial or simply be being left to freeze on the mountains. Experts believe that coca leaves were given to the victims, presumably as a sedative but also very likely as ritualistic sustenance for what would have been considered an extremely long journey to the spirit world and the realm of the ancestors.

Hiram Bingham's second expedition in 1912 uncovered 104 grave sites near Machu Picchu, the last resting place for a total of 174 men, women and children. Some of the mummies were also provisioned for their journey with packages of coca leaves. Some guides hypothesize that the Incas were well aware of the high calcium content of coca leaves and so deliberately gave 'double doses' to pregnant women who were mummified, but it seems more likely that they included doses for both mother and baby.

Coca in Inca Medicine

The Incas had a medical tradition of trephination, in which a hole was opened through the bone of the skull with gold or silver knives to relieve pressure from head injuries. The skull was then enveloped with a sheet of gold. Experts believe that coca may have been used as a sedative before the operation. According to a study that examined 109 cases of trephination in 66 skulls found in this part of Peru, the operation was 83% successful.

Some of the mummies – or, as archaeologists prefer to call them, ancestral bundles – at Machu Picchu also had strangely elongated skulls that displayed intentional 'artificial cranial deformation' (ACD), in which the skulls of young children were bound with belts, straps, boards or molds depending on the desired effect. The idea was to create a skull shape that clearly marked the individual as a member of a 'privileged' class.

Such ancestral bundles would have been an important feature of the Inca Trail during the time of the Inca Empire. Many of the buildings you see along the route are believed to be *tambos* (resting places), where the mummies would be housed during the pilgrimage. The conquistador Pedro Pizarro (Francisco's cousin) wrote in 1571 that 'the people brought mummies when visiting the homes of others...they brought the mummies to festivities of dancing and drinking, the dead would visit the living and the living would visit the dead.'

LECKER STUDIO/SHUTTERSTOCK

Coca leaves

Spanish Attitudes to Coca

The Spanish conquistadors – and, even more so, the priests who followed them – were notoriously unforgiving with anything that seemed to them to be paganism. In the words of 17th-century missionary Francisco de Ávila, they devoted themselves to 'stamping out and ripping from the hearts of the Indians that empty and false religion of idols and demons.'

> Many hacienda landlords and mine owners quickly realized its value as a tool of oppression – making workers toil harder, for longer, in harsher conditions.

The ritualistic use of coca particularly attracted their anger. Officially, the Spanish viewed this 'Devil's leaf' as an 'instrument of Satan,' but privately, many hacienda landlords and mine owners quickly realized its value as a tool of oppression – making workers toil harder, for longer, in harsher conditions (just as more recently it was used widely by overworked Inca Trail porters).

A Jesuit by the name of José de Acosta cautioned against destroying the crops: 'I believe that it produces strength and spirit in the Indians,' he wrote in *Natural and Moral History of the Indies* (1589), '...such as doubling the workload with a handful of coca without ingesting anything else and other similar feats.'

By then, though, the Potosí silver mines had been discovered about 1000km south of Cusco and within a short time the Bishop of Cusco himself was selling baskets of coca by the thousands to overworked miners who would pay well over the usual market price.

A Living Legacy

When an offering is being made to Pachamama, coca leaves and other objects – traditionally gold, silver, *chicha* (fermented corn beer), feathers, aromatic palo santo wood and, bizarrely, hair from the eyebrows – are laid on a rock, known as a *huaca,* considered sacred as it's part of the earth itself. If, however, the offering is being made to the *apus,* then it is usually raised on the wind in the form of smoke or simply blown aloft with the breath of the worshiper. Today coca leaves continue to form an important part of most *pagos a la tierra* (offerings to Pachamama).

Many traditional healers, known as *yachaqs* in Quechua or *curanderos* in Spanish, claim to be able to tell the future by reading the random patterns of dropped coca leaves, while a *huirapirico* specialized in burning coca leaves in a fire of llama fat and reading the future in the flames. You'll sometimes find *yachaqs* telling the future with coca leaves, much as they did centuries ago, on the outskirts of Cusco's Mercado San Pedro (p38), and at Cusco's **Museo de Plantas Sagradas** *(@museo_de_plantas_sagradas),* there's always an expert on hand to tell your fortune with coca leaf or coffee.

Woman making offering of coca leaves
CARLOS DUARTE/GETTY IMAGES

PHOTO ESSAY

Wildlife & Flora of the Inca Trail

AMONG THE JOYS of hiking the Inca Trail is the always present possibility of encountering one of the many fascinating birds, animals and plants that call the high altitudes of the Andes home. From sacred animals like the condor and the puma to avian jewels like the hummingbirds, here are some of the highlights of the Inca Trail.

Right: The puma *(Puma concolor)* is a sacred animal to the Incas, thanks to its almost ubiquitous presence as an Andean super-predator.

IMAGEBROKER.COM/SHUTTERSTOCK

Below left: Synonymous with the world-famous Paddington, there are now around 44 spectacled bears *(Tremarctos ornatus)* inhabiting the Historic Sanctuary of Machu Picchu.

Below right: Believed to be a natural manifestation of the *apus* (mountain spirits), the majestic Andean condor *(Vultur gryphus)* is occasionally spotted soaring high above the Inca Trail.

ADILSON SOCHODOLAK/SHUTTERSTOCK

BUENAVENTURA/SHUTTERSTOCK

TOP LEFT: ELEN MARLEN/SHUTTERSTOCK

Above: Families of South American coati *(Nasua nasua)* are sometimes seen on the slopes around Wiñay Wayna ruins.

Right: White-tailed deer *(Odocoileus virginianus peruvianus)* are frequently seen by Inca Trail hikers on the slopes below Dead Woman's Pass.

WIRESTOCK CREATORS/SHUTTERSTOCK

Left: Commonly seen near the archaeological site that inherited its name, the 'Forever Young' Wiñay Wayna orchid *(Epidendrum secundum)* was so called for the frequency and duration of its bloom.

Below: Recognized in 2024 as a separate species, the robin-sized northern giant hummingbird *(Patagona chaski)* is a common, yet spectacular, sighting.

FROM TOP: ELEN MARLEN/SHUTTERSTOCK, CHRISSY MCCLARREN AND ANDY REAGO, CC0, VIA WIKIMEDIA COMMONS

Left: A rare sighting, the sword-billed hummingbird *(Ensifera ensifera)* has the longest bill-to-body size of any bird in the world.

Below: The first evidence of the presence of the Andean cock-of-the-rock *(Rupicola peruvianus)* might be its strange pig-like call or a gorgeous flash of scarlet.

Right: Domesticated long before the arrival of the Incas, the llama *(Lama glama)* remains a permanent fixture of some of the Inca Trail's iconic sites.

TOP: MILAN ZYGMUNT/SHUTTERSTOCK, BOTTOM: AGAMI PHOTO AGENCY/SHUTTERSTOCK, RIGHT: DENNIS JACOBSEN/SHUTTERSTOCK

Phuyupatamarka

Welcome to the cloud forest. The landscapes have changed dramatically throughout the hike, but beyond Phuyupatamarka campsite you enter a new world where bamboo forms a tunnel over the trail and trees drip with moss. For those drawn to the Inca Trail for its natural diversity, this leg is a real highlight, and for history buffs, Intipata and Wiñay Wayna ruins are among the most spectacular Inca relics on the trail.

Mark Eveleigh

Phuyupatamarka ruins (p127)

DAMIAN BASANTE/GETTY IMAGES

Wiñay Wayna

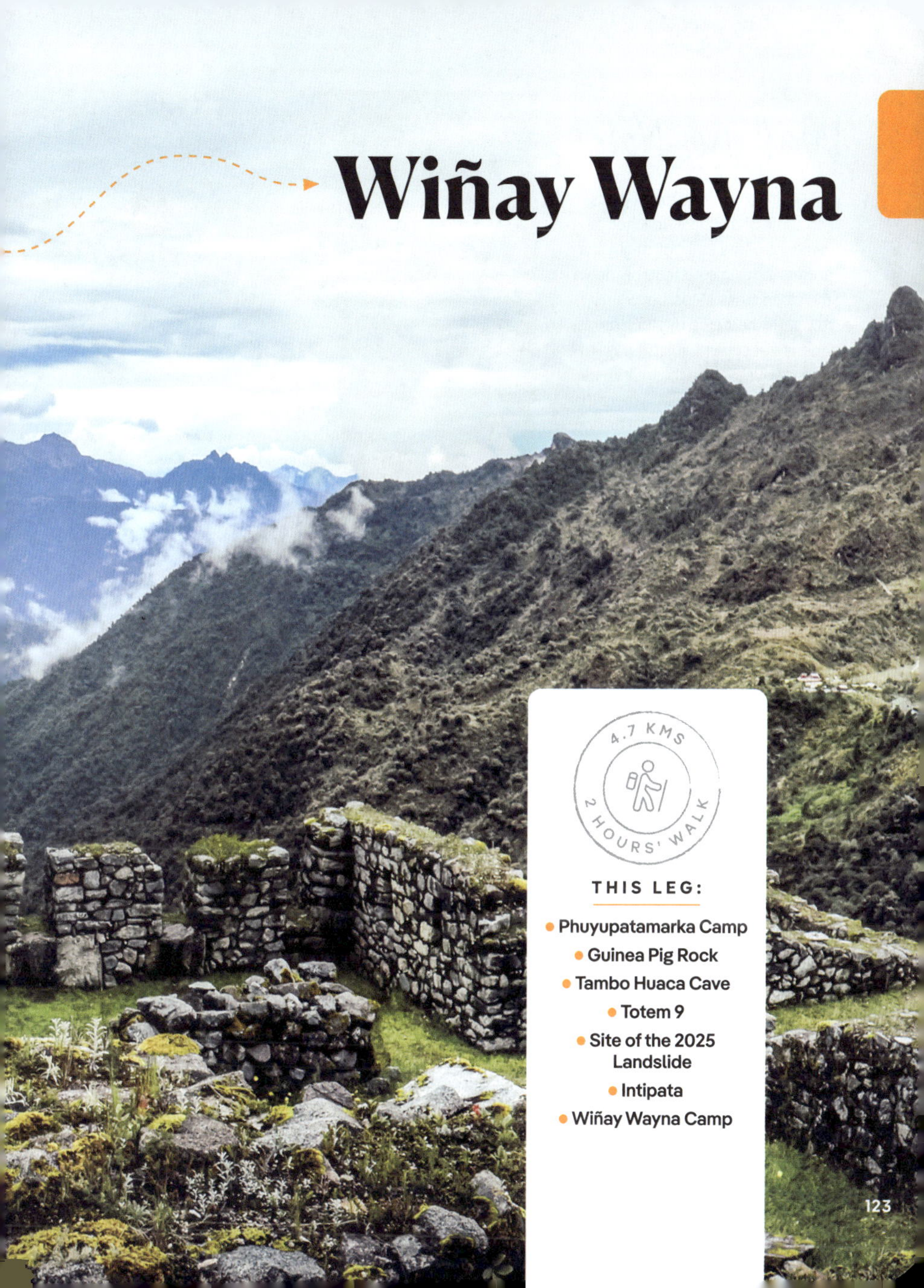

4.7 KMS

2 HOURS' WALK

THIS LEG:

- Phuyupatamarka Camp
- Guinea Pig Rock
- Tambo Huaca Cave
- Totem 9
- Site of the 2025 Landslide
- Intipata
- Wiñay Wayna Camp

Walking Notes

The dripping cloud forest leads to some of the most treacherous sections of the trail. You might see porters jogging sure-footedly down the steep stone steps, but with narrow paths bordered by steep drops, this is a section in which it pays to focus your eyes on the trail. There are numerous viewpoints where the forest opens and forces you to stop and stare.

Breaking Your Journey

Some itineraries (especially the five-day) have an overnight stop at Phuyupatamarka Camp. It's a privilege to stay in such a beautiful – often uncrowded – spot. Wiñay Wayna Camp is more popular. With tents pitched side-by-side on narrow terraces it can feel cramped but the trail's busiest camp is just 10 minutes from the official entrance to Machu Picchu.

Mark's Tips

BEST VIEW On the upper terraces at Intipata you'll share breathtaking views with the llamas as you gaze toward Wiñay Wayna Camp and along the Urubamba Valley.

FAVORITE STOP Phuyupatamarka Camp (p108) is a favorite Inca Trail resting place.

TIP Trekking sticks can be helpful on the twisting stone steps.

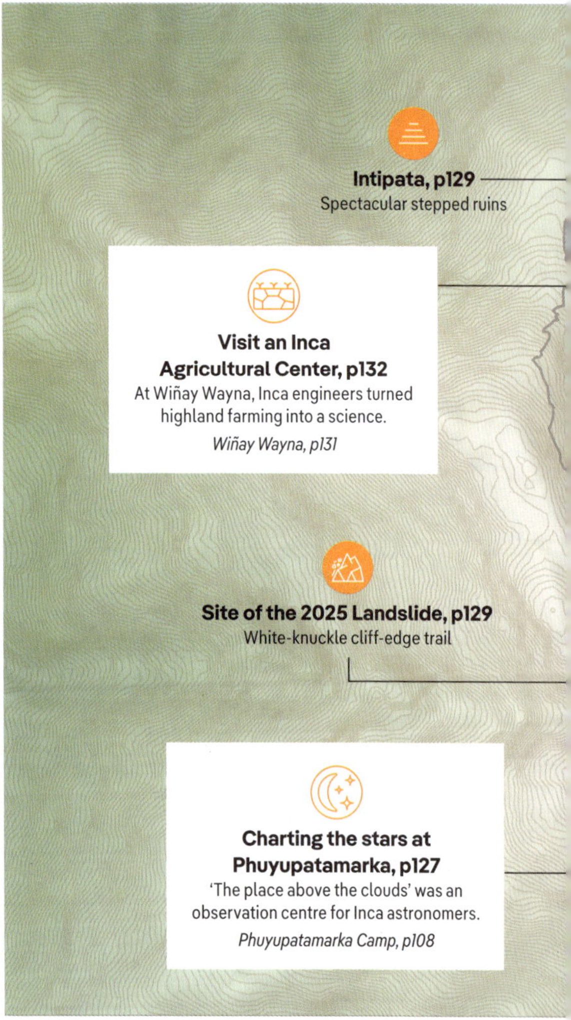

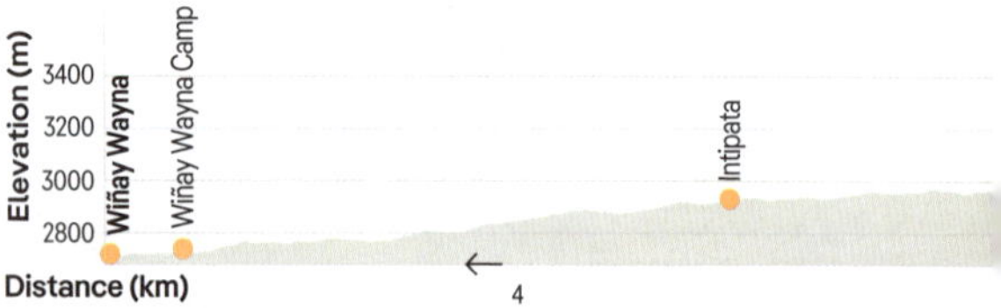

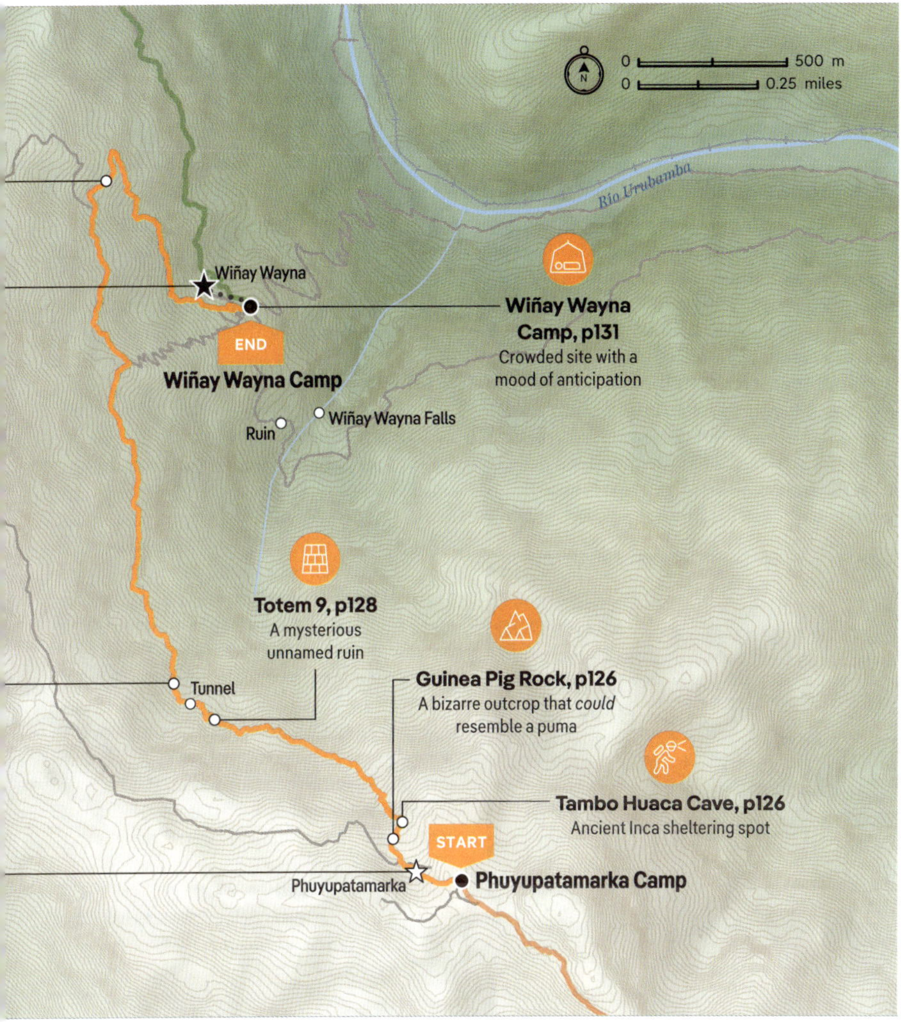
0 500 m
0 0.25 miles
N
Río Urubamba
Wiñay Wayna
Wiñay Wayna Camp, p131
Crowded site with a mood of anticipation
END
Wiñay Wayna Camp
Ruin
Wiñay Wayna Falls
Totem 9, p128
A mysterious unnamed ruin
Tunnel
Guinea Pig Rock, p126
A bizarre outcrop that *could* resemble a puma
Tambo Huaca Cave, p126
Ancient Inca sheltering spot
START
Phuyupatamarka
Phuyupatamarka Camp

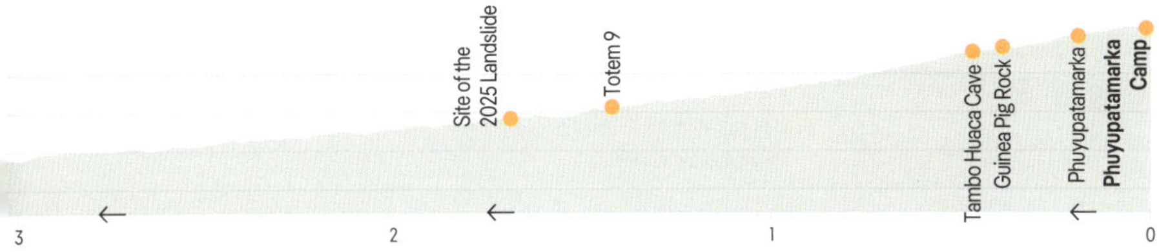
Site of the 2025 Landslide
Totem 9
Tambo Huaca Cave
Guinea Pig Rock
Phuyupatamarka
Phuyupatamarka Camp
3
2
1
0

PREVIOUS STOP At 3601m Phuyupatamarka Camp (p108) is a popular lunch stop. If your tour is scheduled to camp here enjoy the privilege because it might be the most beautiful camp on the entire trail (and worth the extra high-altitude chill). Just 150m west of the camp you'll find the ruins of the same name (right).

From Phuyupatamarka Camp

Within minutes of leaving Phuyupatamarka Camp, you'll have the impression that you've walked into an immense tropical greenhouse. The stunted trees that have become familiar over the high passes are suddenly – seemingly in moments – replaced with 30m-tall monsters. You'll pass monumental *intimpa (Podocarpus glomeratus)*, quina *(Cinchona pubescens)* and ancient cedar *(Cedrela angustifolia)* trees, all of them draped heavily with the moss known as 'old man's beard' and heavily loaded with bromeliads and vibrant orchids. This *bosque nublado* (as the cloud forest is known in Spanish) is also home to spectacular fauna. Look out for the colorful flash of a grey-breasted mountain toucan *(Andigena hypoglauca)* or, with a lot more luck, a fleeting sighting of the timid *tigrillo (Leopardus tigrinus)* – a slightly larger, more leopard-like cousin of the ocelot.

MARK EVELEIGH

Tambo Huaca cave

Guinea Pig Rock

You get your first sight of the whitewashed walls of Machu Picchu Pueblo (p180), in the shadowy depths of Urubamba Valley, but don't let it hog all your attention: turn around and look back uphill to see the bizarre **natural rock formation** on the hilltop. The more romantic among the guides might try to convince you that it's a puma's head but it actually looks more like a giant rodent – a guinea pig or a capybara perhaps. It's hard to believe that the Guinea Pig Rock shape – complete with staring eye and dented nostril – isn't artificial. It's certainly easier to recognize than the far more obscure (but infinitely more famous) silhouette of the reclining woman on Dead Woman's Pass.

Tambo Huaca Cave

Continue through bamboo stands, where the spindly *curcur (Chusquea delicatula)* cane arcs over your head; deeper in the forest, the

Continues on p128

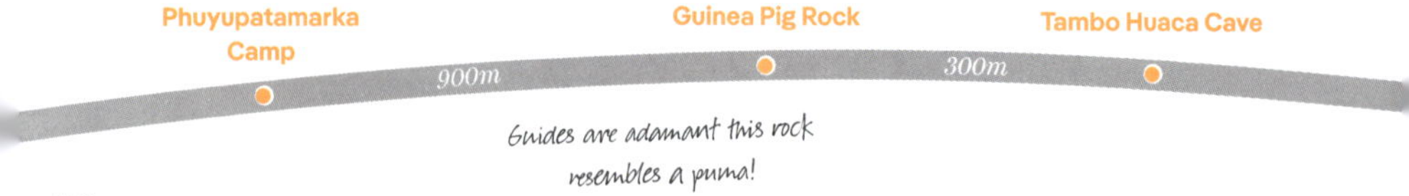

Charting the Stars at Phuyupatamarka

Meaning 'place above the clouds,' Phuyupatamarka has a series of towers from which Inca astronomers were able to watch the movement of the night skies.

GOOD TO KNOW

Population: The population here was unlikely to have been much over a dozen people, including students who came to study astronomy and the guards whose job it was to oversee the movement of pilgrims on the sacred Inca Trail.

Location: It's a mark of the isolated location that these ruins were not even mapped or recorded until 1915, four years after Hiram Bingham III took the first photos of Machu Picchu.

As well as being a *tambo* (resting place), experts believe that Phuyupatamarka was probably also an astronomical observatory. At an altitude of 3580m, it offered clear night skies (hence its name), perfect for observation. From its sturdy towers experts believe Inca astronomers were able to map and predict the passage of seasons through the movements of constellations and the Milky Way. Its location overlooking the valley also offered the perfect vantage point from which to view the Río Urubamba, sacred to the Incas in part because its route runs inline with the passage of the Milky Way.

The first thing you're likely to notice on arrival is the row of five fountains surrounded by almost intact stone walls. Similar fountains, believed to have been used for ceremonial purposes rather than irrigation, are found at Machu Picchu. At the lower end of the site are some buildings that may have provided overnight accommodation for pilgrims and a permanent resting place for their 'ancestral bundles' (the archaeologist's term for mummies).

FROM LEFT: DANIEL TOH/SHUTTERSTOCK, MARK EVELEIGH

Above: Stone walls, Phuyupatamarka; Right: Hikers descend to Phuyupatamarka

Along the Way We Saw...

WIÑAY WAYNA FALLS From the typically trapezoidal eastern windows of Wiñay Wayna archaeological site (p132), it's possible to see the crashing veil of white water plummeting from the cascade a little farther down the track. It just takes a few minutes to walk down to the point where a sturdy timber bridge crosses the stream at the foot of Wiñay Wayna Falls, so it's well worth the detour if you can make time. The falls only become busy around midday when hikers on the two-day Inca Trail begin to arrive as it's a popular rest spot on their route. At other times it will be very peaceful. Keep an eye out for the semi-aquatic rodent known as the 'river puma' *(Incanomys mayopuma)* that was discovered in this area in 2025. The icy water is bracing and only the toughest or most foolhardy hikers take the opportunity for a dip. It's a wonderful place to take your boots off and to (literally) cool your heels for a while, though.

Mark Eveleigh

Continued from p126

Incas once harvested sturdier *caña brava* to roof their houses. Less than 10 minutes after leaving the Guinea Pig Rock view behind, you pass a deep **cave** with an Inca-built wall on one side. Archaeologists claim that because the three niches are elevated above waist level (the floor of the cave would have been lower 500 years ago) this was used as a *huaca* (religious site), as well as a *tambo* (resting place).

Totem 9

The trail meanders onwards across the flank of Intipata Hill. It's estimated that the flagstones and steps you're walking on now are about 80% authentic Inca-built. Wear-and-tear on this perpetually moist section of the trail, trodden often by 1000 boots each day is intense. In the 1980s and 1990s the army took on the job of making the trail passable. While they did a thorough job, they were somewhat less diligent about recording the extent of their work so in many places it's largely guesswork as to exactly what was original and what's been 'improved upon'. Nevertheless, there's there's a sense of excitement knowing you're traversing a path that was built half a millennia ago.

Descending a series of often slippery slopes brings you to another mysterious **ruin**. The single entrance opening onto the relatively sheltered flank of the hillside suggests this was a dwelling – perhaps a guardhouse – rather than a ceremonial site. Officially it has no name, though it's marked on some maps simply as 'Totem 9'. It is a poignant reminder of the historic richness of this area that this 500-year-old stone building, which would be prized as a national treasure in other countries, is not even given a name in Peru.

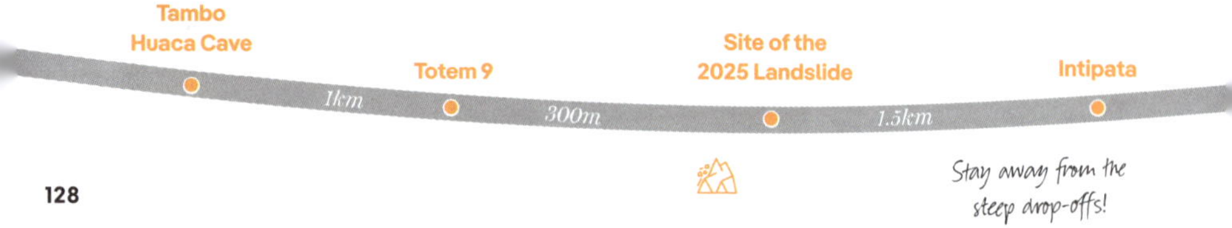

Site of the 2025 Landslide

A narrow **tunnel** that lies just a few minutes walk below 'Totem 9' is exactly as it was when the last Inca passed through after abandoning Machu Picchu. The **site of a recent landslide**, coming almost immediately after the tunnel, is memorable too, but for entirely different reasons. In March 2025, within days of the Inca Trail reopening after the February maintenance period, a landslide carried away a large section of the trail. It was several weeks before the route could be reopened and the rough-hewn logs that replaced the Inca stonework are best hurried across without looking down.

Intipata

The first really extensive view of the **Río Urubamba** – sacred to the Incas, so it's said, because it flows in the precise direction of the Milky Way – comes about 2km before you reach **Intipata** (literally 'Sun Steps') at 2930m above

LOOK FORICONIC CLOUD-FOREST BIRDS

Queztals

The golden-headed quetzal *(Pharomachrus auriceps)* is a living jewel, and the even more vibrant crested quetzal *(Pharomachrus antisianus)* is a privileged sighting.

Toucans

Despite their lurid colors the grey-breasted mountain toucan *(Andigena hypoglauca)* and the blue-banded toucanet *(Aulacorhynchus coeruleicinctis)* are more often heard than seen.

Motmots

The Andean motmot *(Momotus aequatorialis)* is a permanent resident of these forests. Inconspicuous but common, it's an avian gem with a spectacular racket-shaped tail.

Andean cock-of-the-rock

The first sign of its presence might be the pig-like squeal that gives this beautiful scarlet bird its unflattering Quechua name: *cuchi pishku* ('pig bird'; *Rupicola peruvianus*).

Grey-breasted mountain toucan

FOTOREQUEST/SHUTTERSTOCK

Intipata

REOPENING THE INCA TRAIL

'We heard from one of the Indians that there were ruins in the impenetrable jungle south of Machu Picchu Mountain,' Hiram Bingham III wrote in *Lost City of the Incas*. Over the centuries the jungle had reclaimed most of the trails and there had been countless landslides and rockfalls. After weeks of jungle-bashing – trying to approach from both ends – Clarence Maynard (an engineer on Bingham's 1915 expedition) finally opened the route we now know as the 'Inca Trail' to enter Machu Picchu through the Sun Gate. It would be almost three decades before archaeologists came across Wiñay Wayna.

sea level. The spectacular terraced ruins lie a little further along the hillside than Wiñay Wayna Camp, but there's no detour involved because the Inca Trail route passes directly through the ruins before dropping back down to the camp.

Sometimes known as Yunkapata, Intipata was an agricultural outpost supplying food and coca leaves to Machu Picchu. Its 30 or more steep terraces – some more than 70m long – were farmed mostly by the inhabitants of Wiñay Wayna, which is about an hour's walk down the valley from here. Before you exit the bottom corner of the archaeological site in the direction of Wiñay Wayna Camp, be sure to detour into the iconic triangular-shaped temple that points directly (whether by coincidence or intention) toward the peak of Mt Veronica.

Wiñay Wayna Camp

Situated less than 3km (as the condor flies) south of Machu Picchu, Wiñay Wayna is the logical final campsite on almost all Inca Trail itineraries. After the wide-open spaces of the mountains it can feel very cramped here, even on a relatively quiet day. At the height of the season there's sometimes barely room to drive a tent peg between the nylon walls that are pitched shoulder-to-shoulder. There are shower blocks, but the icy water means that few are brave enough to try them out.

This is the spot where you'll say goodbye to the porters who have made the whole thing possible. Many porters have never seen the trail to Intipunku or even had the wherewithal to visit Machu Picchu. Tips (p241) are usually handed out during a small 'ceremony' after dinner.

Along the Way We Met...

MARITZA CHACACANTA Most trekkers have overcome the worst of the negative effects of the altitude by this stage so it tends to be a cheerful camp. While chewing coca leaves or drinking *mate de coca* (coca-leaf tea) has become famous as a remedy, it is possible to overdo it. If you've been chewing it all morning, you might want to ease off as it gets to late afternoon since it can inhibit sleep. Altitude sickness also inhibits digestion so it's best to avoid heavy, meaty meals and alcohol and it's crucial to keep hydrated. Rehydration salts in drinking water help a lot. If things get worse you can buy Oxishot (small cans of oxygen) in pharmacies and there is a very effective drug called Diamox (acetazolamide), but it should only be prescribed by doctors since it can have serious side-effects.

Maritza Chacacanta, operations manager at Intrepid, has walked the Inca Trail as a guide more than 500 times.

MARITZA'S TIP: *I recommend* muña *(Minthostachys mollis) tea. Sometimes known as Andean mint, it helps with altitude but also has the benefit of easing stomach problems.*

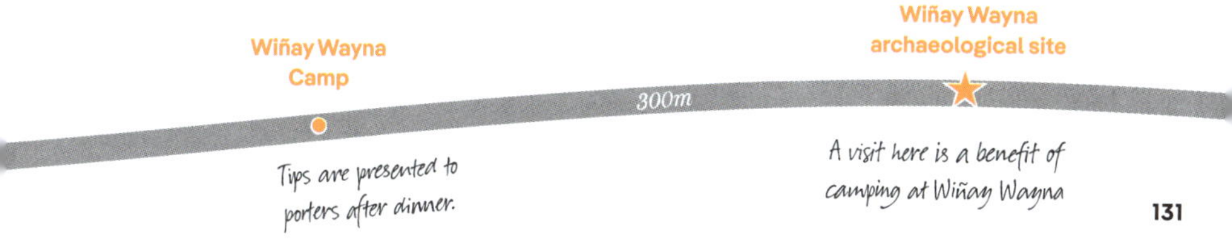

EXPERIENCE ★

Visit an Inca Agricultural Center

Wiñay Wayna, one of the most spectacularly picturesque archaeological sites on the Inca Trail, is a highlight of the hike to Machu Picchu. Predominantly an agricultural center, it testifies to how Inca engineers were able to take Andean farming to levels that are hard to match even today.

HOW TO

Getting here: A stop at Wiñay Wayna is not necessarily included as part of every Inca Trail itinerary; usually though, groups will visit if there is time. The site is well-signed and easy to access from the trail.

Camping nearby: One of the benefits of camping at Wiñay Wayna Camp (p131) is the chance to visit the archaeological site independently. Those who camp at Phuyupatamarka – and those who arrive at Wiñay Wayna Camp too late lose out.

Elevation: 2666m

Upon arriving at Wiñay Wayna Camp, it can be tempting to lay down and rest your weary body for the 'main event,' but that would be a mistake. If at all possible, summon the extra energy to visit these nearby terraced ruins because Wiñay Wayna is one of the most enchantingly beautiful pre-Colombian sites in South America.

The 'Lost Terraces' of Wiñay Wayna

During the three years in which Hiram Bingham III visited the area, Wiñay Wayna was so overgrown that his entire team completely overlooked it. In fact, this complex of spectacular terraces and almost 20 majestic buildings remained hidden until Peruvian archaeologist Julio C Tello documented the site in 1942. Sometimes known as Rucrepata, Tello bestowed the now more familiar name on the ruins after noticing that the area flourished with the orchids that local people know as Wiñay Wayna (meaning 'forever young').

The serried ranks of 50 terraces are stepped down the hill, with the longest stretching over 100m, and are protected between sturdy walls that rise more than 2m.

Feeding the Citadel

It was here and at nearby Intipata that much of the produce that fed the 600 or so people who lived at Machu Picchu was grown. Crops of potatoes, yucca, corn, quinoa, beans, peanuts, tomatoes, avocados, cucumbers,

MARK EVELEIGH

HOME OF THE HUMBLE SPUD

Today around 4000 varieties of potato grow in Peru. It's believed that tubers were first domesticated around 8000 years ago in the area close to Lake Titicaca, and the Incas perfected the art of dehydrating potatoes through successive nights of frost and days of sun to make freeze-dried potatoes now known as *moraya* or *chuño*. *Chasqui* (relay-runner messengers) carried small bags filled with these dehydrated potatoes for sustenance, along with the little pouches of coca leaves that, with special dispensation from the Sapa Inca (emperor), were a privilege of their office.

Left: Wiñay Wayna terraces
Below: Hiker, Wiñay Wayna

peppers, cotton and especially coca (see p112) were farmed on these deep terraces oriented to harness the heat of the sun. The attentively nurtured topsoil was laid over carefully regulated layers of sand, gravel and stones that acted like radiators so that the roots of the crops were protected from frost.

This in-depth engineering know-how was cultivated during the incredibly brief span of around 150 years of the Inca Empire; it's interesting to imagine just how much the Incas might have achieved had they been left to progress without Spanish interference.

MARK EVELEIGH

Hilda Mayta, founder of Andean Colors, with alpaca

MARK EVELEIGH

INSIGHT

Peru's Iconic Camelids

The ancestors of modern-day llamas and alpacas have played a part in Andean life for thousands of years. Today, four distinct species of Andean camelid continue to be an iconic feature of Peruvian journeys.

WORDS BY **MARK EVELEIGH**

Mark first walked the Inca Trail in 2001.

LLAMAS AND ALPACAS were domesticated by pre-Colombian civilizations long before the arrival of the Incas and have served as pack animals and sources of wool and protein for thousands of years, as a depiction of a vicuña hunter in rock art dating to 5000 BCE found in Virginniyoq Cave attests. Today, these domestic camelids are ubiquitous, their presence felt in almost every aspect of the traveler's experience.

You're unlikely to get through an hour wandering Cusco's old town without seeing a baby alpaca being paraded around the streets by a vibrantly dressed Quechua women who makes her living posing for photos. On the lawns at Sacsaywaman ruins (p39) and Cusco's Campo de Artesanos, delightfully haughty-looking llamas pause momentarily in their grazing to gaze at you with unperturbed curiosity in their huge eyes.

You'll see countless high-end outlets on the streets of Cusco advertising fashion items made from 100% baby alpaca wool. Alpaca wool is still sought after for weaving in Quechua communities, and many villages (notably Chinchero) specialize in turning raw wool into gorgeous ponchos, scarves and wraps.

You will also see alpaca steaks and brochettes on the menu all over the region. The more lithe llama is less coveted for its meat (with the exception of *chalonade* jerky, see p137) and is therefore used more as a beast of burden.

Unlike their intimidating and bad-tempered cousin the camel, the domestic camelids of the Peruvian Andes are good-natured to the point of being affectionate. You'll often see them nuzzling their owners and sometimes almost appearing to kiss them.

> Domestic camelids of the Peruvian Andes are good-natured to the point of being affectionate.

Close Encounters

'Peru's greatest wealth is the livestock, which the natives call llamas. It is the animal of greatest profit and least expense that we know of,' wrote the Spanish chronicler José de Acosta in 1550.

There was a time when convoys of llamas plied the Qhapaq Ñan (Inca highways) all over the empire distributing provisions and trade goods, but the Classic Inca Trail is now off-limits to pack animals. If you want to interact with these charming and characterful creatures, head to the little highland hamlet of **Racchi Ayllu**, near Chinchero, where llama-breeder Marco Zuniga Sihuin from the **Andean Colors** *(andeancolors.com)* weaving community leads visitors on unique walking tours near the pre-Incan ruins of Machu Colca.

Marco will lend you a hand-woven alpaca-wool poncho – perfectly suited to this area, where the cooling properties of the highland wind was harnessed almost 1000 years ago by Machu Colca's builders to preserve provisions stored in what was effectively a massive granary. These provisions were kept here as a form of 'disaster relief' by a civilization that was far ahead of its time in such things.

Marco explains that a llama can carry around 20kg, but the moment they feel that they've been overloaded they will – in characteristic camelid style – simply lie down and refuse to get up until the load has been reassessed to their satisfaction. While Andean Colors' herd of llamas are decked in traditional hand-woven saddle-bags, they are not used as pack-animals; instead, you carry your own gear.

It's a walk of less than 3km from **Machu Colca** with its more than 20 ancient stone granaries (some measuring over 65m long) across the valley to Marcos' weaving workshop. The walk allows just enough time to glean some intriguing insights into the complexities of llama and alpaca husbandry, such as how, despite their apparent mild manners, the dominant males will sometimes fight, rearing like horses on their back legs. You'll learn about the timing of coordinated births, occurring after 10 months of gestation, and how, in times of hardship, female llamas will often self-abort the fetus. And that a llama fetus is among the most powerful offerings to Pachamama (Mother Earth) that can be made.

Wild Cousins

Peru's two wild camelid species were also prized for their wool. The guanaco, the largest of the Andean camelids at 140kg, lives at lower elevations of up to 4000m and has soft wool that is considered second only to the similarly wild vicuña.

In the 1960s, there were only an estimated 6000 vicuña left in the wild. In 1979, the species, which features on Peru's coat of arms, was protected by the Convention for the Conservation and Management of the Vicuña, signed by Peru, Bolivia,

Chile and Ecuador. Reinforced by Convention on International Trade in Endangered Species (CITES), this edict prohibited the trade and domestic exploitation of the species. Thanks to this, the wild population of vicuña is now believed to be higher than 350,000. While in remote highland areas herds of up to 15 are sometimes seen, they're extremely timid and you're very unlikely to see any in the Sacred Valley.

Although DNA examination is yet to conclusively prove their origins, many naturalists believe that the domestic llama descended from guanaco, while the alpaca descended from vicuña. It's said that during the time of the Incas only royalty could wear garments made from vicuña wool. Textiles were more valuable to the Incas than gold or silver and the finest pieces, known as *cumbi,* were prepared by *aclla,* the 'chosen women' who were the most skilled weavers in the empire. Today vicuña wool, which has fibers that are considerably finer than that of the prized cashmere goat, can sell for as much as US$400 per kg.

Textiles were more valuable to the Incas than gold or silver and the finest pieces, known as *cumbi,* were prepared by *aclla,* the 'chosen women' who were the most skilled weavers in the empire.

'Some companies have permits that allow them to capture vicuña for the wool since it commands a much higher price than alpaca wool, which is only about US$100 per kg,' explains Marco. 'I don't like this practice – it's a wild animal after all and should be left to roam free, rather than face the stress of periodic capture for shearing.'

Preparation of Alpaca Wool

While vicuña can only be sheared every two to three years, domestic alpacas are sheared once a year, usually around November, and the complex series of processes that turn the dirty, matted wool into a vibrant work of woven art is typically the domain of women in the Quechua community. Hilda Mayta founded Andean Colors in 2015 and now spearheads a group of 38 women – many of whom are single mothers or, like Hilda herself, have heart-rending stories to tell of domestic violence. A day spent with Hilda and Andean Colors' other 'chosen women' is a poignant and unforgettable experience.

Visitors can enjoy a class with Paulita Quispe, the first of these inspiring women to teach herself English, who will lead you through the entire process. First, you'll try your hand at cleaning the wool with a root called *sachaparacay,* which is grated to create a sort of soap. Then you'll try spinning the yarn by hand with a bobbin that's somewhat like a spinning top. Paulita will even show you how to create a minimalist form of backstrap loom – an impressive party piece that you can take with you to create handwoven friendship bracelets at home.

Even more fascinating are the processes by which the dyes are prepared using traditional plants. To create yellows of varying intensity, you pound 'rock beard,' a type of moss, to a paste and then simmer it in hot water on the wood-fired earthen stove. A type of leaf known locally as *chillq'a* is boiled intensively in another cauldron to create light green dye, which magically transforms into dark green with the inclusion of just a pinch of sulfur. Brown comes from *nogal* (walnut) and a vibrant blue is created using fermented *anil* (wild indigo). But most spectacular are the magical processes that produce red alpaca wool fabrics.

The cochineal bug is a miracle dye ingredient that was known to pre-Colombian civilizations from the Aztecs of Mexico down to the early inhabitants of what became Peru and Bolivia. The female bug feeds on the leaves of certain cacti so textile workshops need only keep some of these leaves in stock to have a constant supply of the spectacularly useful and versatile dye.

While it's a natural dye, the squeamish might balk at crushing the live bugs in the palm of their hand. The resulting mash of intensely scarlet fluid is spectacular, but this is only the beginning of the magic of cochineal: add a little lemon juice and the citric acid will transform the scarlet into orange; a tiny smear of vinegar will create purple; ammonia instantly creates shocking pink. With the addition of various other ingredients, even in the most minute quantities, you can create nine other colors.

And this is just the first step – simply mix any of those 12 shades with a little human urine to create 12 brand new colors! Human urine – stored in big jars, preferably kept in the open air – also comes in handy later as the fixing agent that prevents the colors from fading.

Cochineal dye is produced for export but the product comes at a price as it takes around 140,000 tiny bugs to make 1kg of cochineal dye.

Other By-Products

Lunch served at Andean Colors is often chicken, sometimes guinea pig, but never alpaca. However, the meat of alpaca is commonly served all over the region, and both alpaca and llama meat is dried to make *chalonade* (jerky). While alpaca makes the best steaks, many people say that the best *chalonade* is prepared from the tougher llama.

Camelids of all species have particularly tough skin on their necks. In the case of the Andean species, it's believed that this was an evolutionary response to attacks by pumas. In some Andean communities the neck skin of the guanaco in particular was traditionally used for the soles for shoes and sandals.

To learn even more about these iconic species, visit the **Mundo Alpaca museum** *(mundoalpaca.com.pe)* in Cusco.

Alpaca wool colored with natural dye
MARK EVELEIGH

Wiñay Wayna

With an early start, the beginning of the day's trek will be blessed by Mama Killa (Mother Moon) rather than Papa Inti (Sun God). It's with a feeling of reluctance that you say goodbye to the porters who have made the whole thing possible, as they descend directly to Machu Picchu Pueblo. While the vegetation thickens until it seems you can almost taste the jungle humidity, sunrise reveals landscapes that are as dramatic as ever.

Mark Eveleigh

Machu Picchu viewed from Intipunku (p147)
RALF BROSKVAR/SHUTTERSTOCK

Intipunku

3.6KM
2 HOURS' WALK

THIS LEG:

- Wiñay Wayna Checkpoint
- Chachabamba Viewpoint
- Chasqui Wasi
- Choquesuysuy Viewpoint
- 'Gringo Killers'
- Intipunku (Sun Gate)

Walking Notes

With the absence of the up to 200 porters during the high season, the trail becomes less crowded. Be aware that some hikers labor under the misapprehension that they need to race to Intipunku (the Sun Gate) in time for sunrise. Let them overtake, but stick to the mountain side of the trail rather than the side with the steep drop-off.

Breaking Your Journey

Most itineraries involve camping the last night at Wiñay Wayna (p131), the most crowded camp on the entire route. Even after the pre-dawn exodus has departed, hikers on the two-day Inca Trail (p148) begin to drift through. Chasqui Wasi is one of several appealing rest stops along the route and considering the periodic flights of stone steps, it's invariably appreciated.

Mark's Tips

BEST VIEW Wiñay Wayna's ancient Inca terraces (p132) ripple like the fabled 'fingerprints of the gods' around a graceful curve that sweeps over the spectacular Urubamba Valley.

FAVORITE STOP Chasqui Wasi is where *chasquis* (relay-runner messengers) rested.

TIP Don't rush to Intipunku – enjoy the morning's walk as the view actually tends to improve later in the morning.

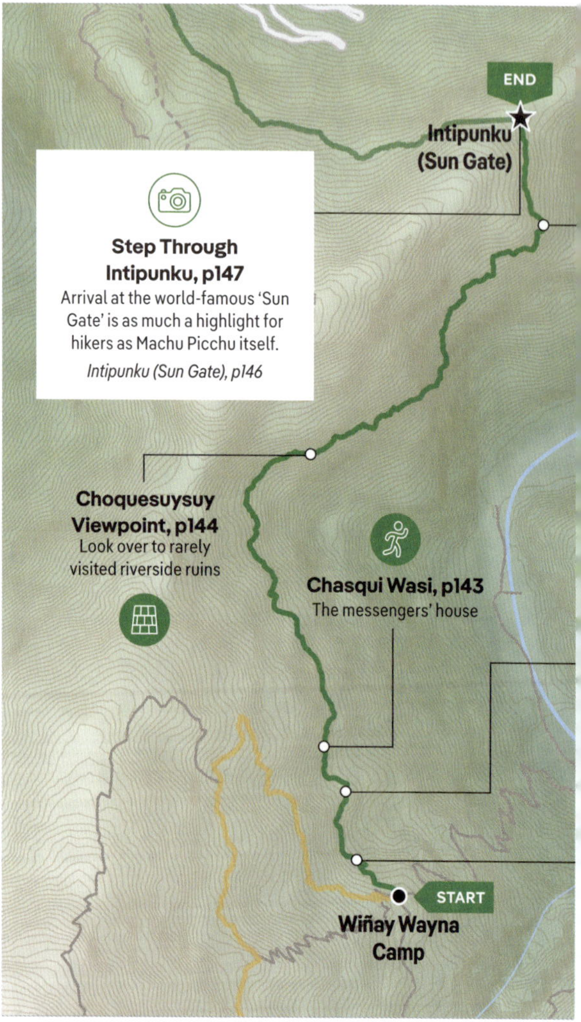

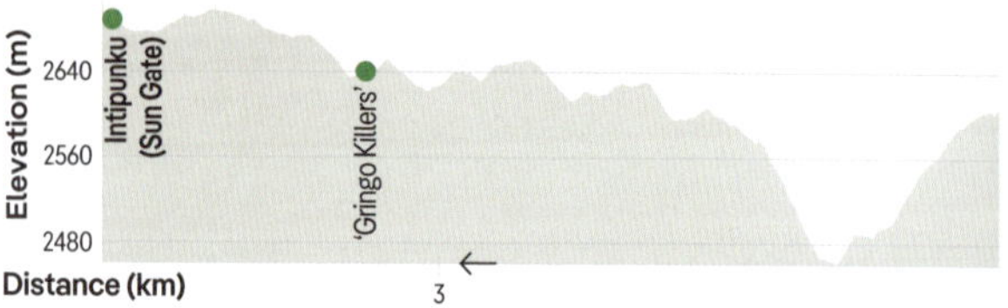

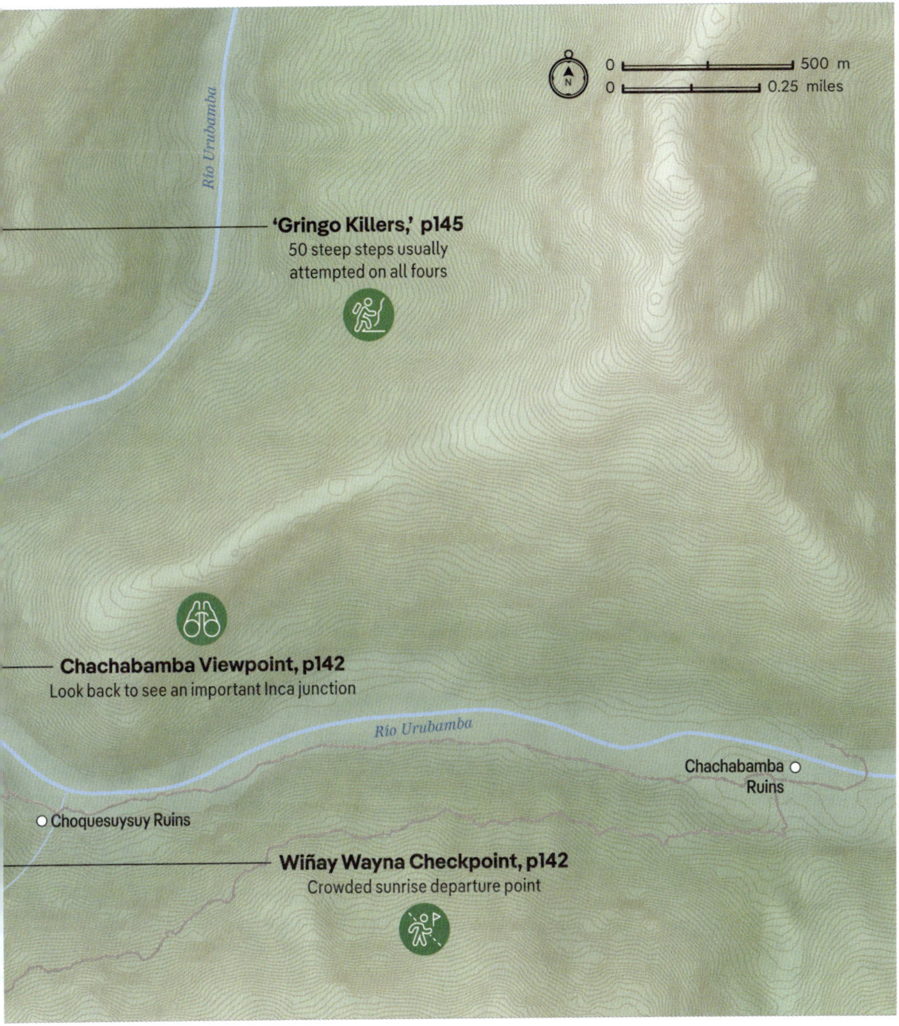
0 500 m
0 0.25 miles
N
Río Urubamba
'Gringo Killers,' p145
50 steep steps usually attempted on all fours
Chachabamba Viewpoint, p142
Look back to see an important Inca junction
Río Urubamba
Chachabamba Ruins
Choquesuysuy Ruins
Wiñay Wayna Checkpoint, p142
Crowded sunrise departure point

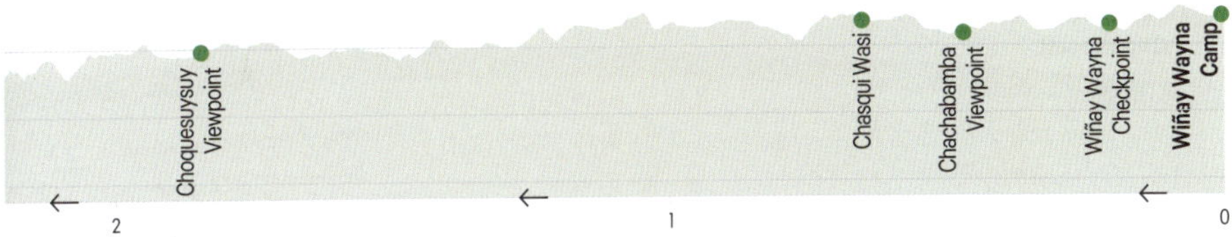
Choquesuysuy Viewpoint
Chasqui Wasi
Chachabamba Viewpoint
Wiñay Wayna Checkpoint
Wiñay Wayna Camp
2
1
0

PREVIOUS STOP You will be woken at Wiñay Wayna Camp (p131) long before first light, typically around 3:30am. You'll sip your coca tea and be issued with a packed breakfast while the porters break camp around you. At around 4am, you will set out on the 10-minute walk from the camp to the Wiñay Wayna Checkpoint.

Wiñay Wayna Checkpoint

The Wiñay Wayna Checkpoint security personnel open the gate at 5:30am, so you will normally wait for around 1½ hours in the dark – the lights are not switched on until the gates open, which is perhaps a blessing given the voracious jungle mosquitoes. The reason for the seemingly incomprehensible rush to get to the closed checkpoint is that there is only enough shelter and bench space for about 100 people. Those who arrive late often have only their ponchos to protect them from the morning mist/drizzle/downpour.

Chachabamba ruins

FROM LEFT: IVO ANTONIE DE ROOIJ/SHUTTERSTOCK, PIEMAGS/NATURE/ALAMY

Take note: once you leave Wiñay Wayna Camp and pass through the checkpoint there are no toilets until you exit Machu Picchu in about two to three hours. Machu Picchu regulations stipulate that there is no re-admittance, so any visitor who leaves the site to go to the toilet effectively forfeits their once-in-a-lifetime visit to this Wonder of the World!

Chachabamba Viewpoint

As the path sweeps left around the valley edge, be sure to turn and look backwards. From here you can see the meandering sweep of another Inca Trail: this is the route that hikers on the two-day Inca Trail follow from the 104km mark on the railway line. Allow your eye to follow the trail down to the bank of the Río Urubamba and you'll see the cluster of well-preserved stone buildings that's known to archaeologists as **Chachabamba**. Nobody can be sure of the original name for the site, but the new name comes from its profusion of chachacoma trees.

The Inca Trail that we know today was not traditionally the only access route to Machu Picchu. The railway line below follows a mule road built in 1898, which in turn followed an Inca Trail that was used primarily to resupply Machu Picchu with provisions. Chachabamba's buildings are certainly ceremonial in nature and it seems the site may have been an important junction between this trade route and the main

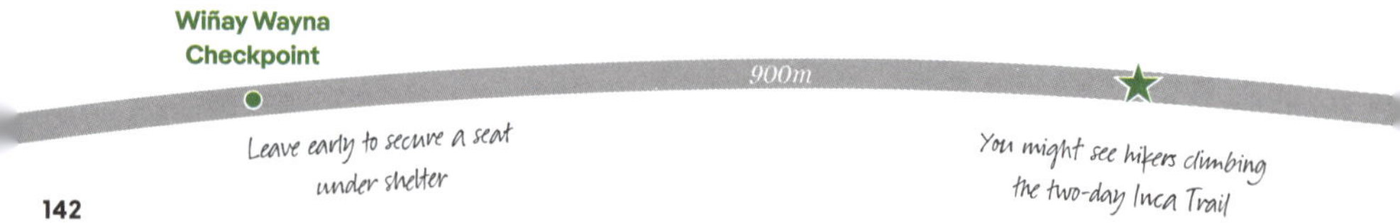

Andean bamboo

highland Inca Trail, which functioned primarily as a pilgrim route and royal road.

Chasqui Wasi

About 30 minutes after leaving Wiñay Wayna Checkpoint you'll reach a ruined stone building, known as Chasqui Wasi (Messengers' Hut). Rather than being permanently occupied, it is believed that *chasqui* who were resident at nearby Wiñay Wayna or Intipata would be summoned by the wailing call of the conch shell (known onomatopoeically in Quechua as *pututu*) and would hurry to this meeting point to be ready to accept the message, then run the next section of the trail. Sometimes the message was passed

LOOK FOR ICONIC TREES OF THE JUNGLE

Chachacoma *(Escallonia resinosa)*
Used for roofing timbers, tea from the leaves was also traditionally used to combat altitude sickness.

Pisonay tree *(Erythrina falcata)*
Once prized by the Incas, this tree is still considered sacred in villages along the Sacred Valley.

Andean bamboo *(Chusquea delicatula)*
Known locally as *curcur*, this slender bamboo was useful for making baskets and for lightweight roofing.

Tree ferns *(Pteridophyta)*
A spectacular aspect of the Inca Trail's cloud-forest stage, tree ferns date back about 300 million years.

Along the Way We Met...

FRANCISCO CRUZ QUISPE In my village there are scores of men – and these days also women – who make a living as porters on the Inca Trail. It's a hard life but these days we have regulations and a strong union, so it's a huge improvement from the situation back when I started out as a junior porter. As a head porter I lead a team of 16 men and I get to see firsthand how life has improved not only for them but for all their families. I've been able to afford an education for my children that would have been impossible a generation ago. These days we're only supposed to carry 20kg (15kg for female porters), but even now there are still a few unscrupulous operators that bend the rules.

Francisco Cruz Quispe has been a porter on the Inca Trail for more than two decades.

FRANCISCO'S TIP: *It's understandable that people look for the best deal for their holidays but please remember that when you book with the cheapest companies it's often the porters who pay.*

on by word of mouth but more often through coded *quipu* strings – a system of knotted cords fundamental to the Inca Empire administrative organization (see p85).

Notice that the several niches around the walls are set fairly high up: while it's not a fixed rule, most archaeologists agree that niches set low were used for storage while those set high on the walls were used for offerings or other religious purposes. The duty of the *chasquis* were sufficiently important that it is likely that some blessings would have been asked of Pachamama or the *apus* (mountain spirits). For obvious reasons, Chasqui Wasi makes for an irresistibly evocative place for a rest break.

Choquesuysuy Viewpoint

Your path now weaves through the tangled jungle over some particularly well-preserved Inca paving. Spare a thought for the porters who may never have seen this section of the trail – some have not even had the benefit of visiting Machu Picchu. The absence of heavy foot-traffic has certainly helped preserve this section of the trail but bear in mind that, along with the 200 or so hikers on the four-day Inca Trail, another

100 or so join on this section from the two-day Inca Trail.

About 10 minutes after Chasqui Wasi you are faced with a particularly spectacular view of the Río Urubamba meandering toward you and, on a clear day, the snow-capped peak of Mt Veronica on the horizon. The agricultural terraces and crumbling residential buildings of **Choquesuysuy** archaeological site can be seen far down on the riverbank, but few foreigners ever visit the site that was said to be named in Quechua for a 'gold panning' spot.

'Gringo Killers'

By this stage you've probably got into the rhythm. As with the high passes, slow and steady is the best way, with plenty of rest stops during which you breathe deeply, filling your lungs down to your diaphragm. The final 50 steep steps are sometimes known as the 'Monkey Steps' because most people tackle them on all fours, but they also go by more dramatic names: some guides

CHASQUIS & THEIR QUIPUS

It's believed that the legendary Inca runners, known as *chasquis* (p84), were chosen for stamina and strength and were even tested for their memory. Occasionally the messages they carried were conveyed via word of mouth, but more often they were relayed in the form of coded *quipu* (knotted strings). What seems fairly certain is that the messengers' training did not include learning how to read the *quipu*, which could only be decoded by trained experts known as *quipucamayocs*. Far more than simple accounting devices, some experts claim the *quipus* may have relayed detailed reports and crucial news across the empire.

'Gringo Killers' steps

WILLIAM MULLINS/ALAMY

refer to them as the 'oh my God steps,' while others jokingly call them the 'gringo-killer steps.'

While the steps themselves are not as dramatic as their names imply, it's not a good idea to crowd onto them. Allow plenty of space before and behind you and, if you're using trekking poles, consider strapping them to your pack so that you have your hands free. The platform at the top of the 'Gringo Killers' is – unsurprisingly – a popular place for hikers to pause and catch their breath before continuing, but be sure to move to one side rather than block the exit.

Intipunku (Sun Gate)

The arrival at Intipunku is the moment that many have been waiting for and, whatever the weather, it never disappoints. Despite the frequent lack of a view (or perhaps because of it), there's something truly powerful and iconic about stepping through the 500-year-old gateway and knowing that the great city might appear at any moment. Regardless of whether it does or not, all that faces you now is a 'simple' 45-minute descent to your final destination and the climax of your hike.

Along the Way We Met...

REUBEN PFOCCO PFURO Among the codes of living that have been handed down to Quechua people from the Incas are the principles that stress the importance of *ayni*, *mit'a* and *minka*. *Ayni* is the community support system whereby one family will help another in the assurance that one day that help will be reciprocated. We sum it up with the phrase 'today for you, tomorrow for me.' *Mit'a* was the system by which the Inca state would convince entire communities to work for a set period in return for gifts or privileges from the emperor. *Minka* is when an individual or family invite members of their community to a feast or fiesta in return for donations which can help a specific cause – in modern times maybe hospital expenses or educational costs.

Reuben Pfocco Pfuro was raised in a traditional Quechua family and now works as an assistant guide for Salkantay Trekking (salkantaytrekking.com).

REUBEN'S TIP: *Take an opportunity to learn from Quechua guides not only about ancient history but also how Inca beliefs have been passed down to modern times.*

Step Through Intipunku

Intipunku (Sun Gate) is one of South America's most emblematic spots, yet most modern travelers misunderstand its importance. Here's our Intipunku myth buster.

GOOD TO KNOW

Early mornings: Most itineraries involve a 4am start on the last morning because the only train that has cargo space leaves Machu Picchu Pueblo at 5:45am, so the porters need to leave Wiñay Wayna Camp by about 4am in time to catch it. It is primarily for this, rather than for any sunrise photo opportunity, that guests are hurried on their way before sunrise.

If you've ever seen a photo that was taken from Intipunku (Sun Gate) showing sunrise over Machu Picchu then you can be sure of one thing: it was an AI-generated image. Intipunku was so-named because it lies southeast of Machu Picchu and is roughly where the sun appears to rise if you're looking at it from the city – not the other way around.

If you've been expecting an epiphanous, life-changing moment as you step though the stone gateway to see Machu Picchu picturesquely bathed in golden sunlight below, don't hold your breath: more often than not, Machu Picchu is shrouded in mist in the hours around sunrise.

Since the weather is more likely to clear later in the morning, resist the temptation to treat the walk from Wiñay Wayna Checkpoint as a race. Instead, take your time and allow yourself to savor the last evocative cloud-forest section. This way, you stand a better-than-average chance of seeing Machu Picchu below you as you stand in triumph at the Sun Gate.

BETO SANTILLAN/SHUTTERSTOCK (2)

Above: Intipunku
Right: Hiker en route to Intipunku

Walk the Two-Day Inca Trail

Rather than being a shorter version of the 'main event', the two-day Inca Trail includes some unexpected experiences. Moreover, in many cases it offers what might be considered a more memorable and hassle-free arrival at Intipunku and Machu Picchu.

GOOD TO KNOW

Guided Tours: Like the four-day Classic Inca Trail, the two-day Inca Trail can only be undertaken with certified guides from a registered trekking company. Intrepid, Salkantay Trekking, Llama Path, Peru North and Inca Trail Reservations are all recommended companies.

Why the two-day Inca Trail: This option is particularly worth considering if:

- You are nervous about the high altitude, or have limited time to acclimatize.
- The four-day 'Classic' hike is beyond your budget.
- You're traveling with younger children.
- Time is short.
- You've left it too late to book and your dates are filled.

Known as the 'two-day Inca Trail,' this itinerary traditionally involved one night at Wiñay Wayna Camp. That option is no longer allowed (to cut down on crowding at the campsite), so hikers on the two-day route now walk the entire 11km from the **104km point** on the railway line to **Machu Picchu** on day one, which usually involves six to eight hours of walking. They then descend to **Machu Picchu Pueblo** by bus, spend a night in a hotel/hostel there, then return the following day for a guided tour of Machu Picchu itself.

As there's no camping porters are not needed on this trail. You are usually supplied with a packed lunch and walk with guides: for nine or more guests there should be two guides.

Along the River

One fascinating aspect of opting for the two-day hike comes almost immediately after crossing

the bridge and passing through the **Inca Trail Checkpoint**: a visit to the well-preserved **Chachabamba** ruins, an Inca religious, agricultural and reprovisioning center.

Starting at river level also means there is a possibility you will see lower altitude wildlife such as otters, agouti and the torrent ducks that courageously tackle even the most brutal cascades.

Into the Mountains

The path winds steadily up the mountainside, occasionally alongside very steep drops that might be a challenge for

MARK EVELEIGH

INTIPUNKU BY AFTERNOON

It takes about 45 minutes without stops to reach Intipunku, your maximum elevation of the hike at 2720m. Hikers on the Two-day Inca Trail might initially feel disappointment that their itinerary doesn't include stepping through the Gateway of the Sun at dawn but in reality, by arriving in early afternoon they are actually more likely to see Machu Picchu without its habitual veil of dawn mist. From here it's a further 45 minutes to Machu Picchu.

Left: Hikers begin the two-day Inca Trail

those who suffer from vertigo. However, the three-hour climb is not overly taxing as there are frequent rest stops – at **Wiñay Wayna Waterfall** (p128) for example, and at the **ruins** of the same name (p132). The route onward falls just short of Intipata and, after eating lunch at the **campsite** (p131), you should expect to breeze through the **Wiñay Wayna Checkpoint** (p142) with none of the drawn-out waiting suffered by the four-day Inca Trail crowd and then head onward to a similarly uncrowded **Intipunku** (Sun Gate; p147).

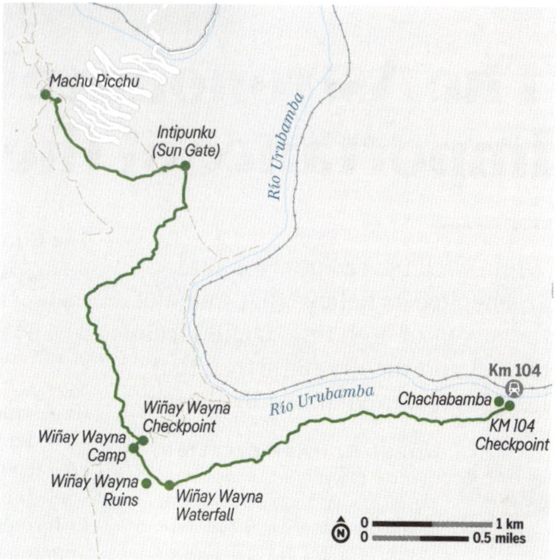

Milky Way over Mt Salkantay (p199)
FLAVIO HUAMANI/SHUTTERSTOCK

INSIGHT

The Astronomical Importance of the Inca Trail

While we'll never know for sure, archaeologists believe that much of the layout of both the Machu Picchu citadel and the dramatic trail that leads to it were dictated by the sky.

WORDS BY **MARK EVELEIGH**
Over the course of seven visits to Machu Picchu, Mark has struggled to untangle scores of conflicting theories on why the Incas did what they did.

The Sun, Moon & Stars

Archaeoastronomy has been described as the study of the astronomical practices, celestial lore, mythologies, religions and worldviews of ancient cultures. Archaeoastronomers have worked hard to untangle the intricacies of the Incas' study of the sun, moon and stars.

The Temple of the Moon is the most important archaeological site on Wayna Picchu (p175), while the Temple of the Sun (sometimes called El Torreon; p169) at Machu Picchu was of paramount importance as a solar observatory, particularly as the Inca Sapa (emperor) was considered to be the 'son of the sun.' Experts believe that a cord hanging in the east-facing window of the Temple of the Sun was used to predict the June (winter) solstice. Another structure called the Intimachay (Cave of the Sun) features a narrow window that was illuminated during the December (summer) solstice.

One of the windows in Temple of the Sun does indeed line up exactly with the position of the sun at first light on June 21.*

Hitching Post of the Sun

The Intihuatana stone (p168), one of the highest points in Machu Picchu's main citadel, is often called the 'hitching post of the sun' as it is believed that it was from here that Inca astrologers pinpointed the waning sun's trajectory and so ensured that its life-giving force would return. The beautifully sculpted granite slab is often said to be loaded with energy; you'll see guides inviting their guests to hold their hands close to feel the 'spiritual energy' emanating from the stone. The huge block of granite soaks up the sun's heat all day so few are disappointed. While you're there, look closely: in 2000, a film crew shooting a Cusqueña beer commercial lost control of a crane and chipped a corner off the 500-year-old Intihuatana.

Inca astronomers divided their calendar into 365 days and added an extra day every three years.

Somewhat inexplicably there is another *intihuatana* in a location deep in the valley near the confluence of the Ríos Urubamba and Ahobamba, about 2km southwest of Machu Picchu.

'Ungodly Arts'

Much of what has been written about such sites is, of course, mere conjecture, albeit on the part of some of the world's leading archaeoastronomy experts. After all, most of the written records that exist came from Spanish priests – men who were not unbiased reporters on aspects of what they considered to be pagan worship. Even the supposedly reliable chronicler Inka Garcilaso de la Vega, whose mother was an Inca princess, only published his *Comentarios Reales de los Incas* in 1609 after 40 years of living in Spain and so was likely influenced by Spanish worldviews.

Despite Spanish attempts to erase 'heretic' practices from their new dominion, some of the Inca festivals linked to the solstices continue to be celebrated to this day, including Qhapaq Raymi (in December) and Inti Raymi (in June; p44). Thanks to these observances and the way they were recorded (presumably on coded *quipu* strings), Inca astronomers divided their calendar into 365 days and added an extra day every three years. They worked from two separate calendars, however: an agricultural calendar for commoners and a religious calendar for noble people.

Mapping the Stars

It's said that the Chakana (or Yakana) – known as the Southern Cross in English – was important because it represented Tahuantinsuyo (the four nations that made up the Inca empire). The imaginary point where the lines bisect at the center of the constellation symbolized the position of Cusco city. One of the commonest Inca symbols that you'll see – a square-cornered star with a circle at the center – is also known as the *chakana* and represents this idea of the empire stretching out in four directions from Cusco.

Some experts claim that the Río Urubamba gained much of its prestige in the minds of Inca

* For a well-written and evocative insight into just what it's like to witness this phenomenon firsthand, read *Turn Right At Machu Picchu: Rediscovering the Lost City One Step at a Time* by Mark Adams.

astronomers from the fact that it mirrored the Milky Way, which Quechua speakers still know today as Hatun Mayu (Great River). While we tend to view the Milky Way in terms of its billions of stars, the Incas often focused instead on its dark spots. The shapes, as they viewed them, represented 10 celestial figures: the condor, the herdsman, the Andean fox, the black llama, the baby llama, the partridge, the toad, the snake, the bear and the deer.

Predicting the Seasons

The Mirador de Inkaraqay observatory is a well-preserved Inca building on the remote northern flank of Wayna Picchu Mountain – so remote in fact, that Peruvian anthropologist Fernando Astete Victoria only located it in 1982. It is said that this observatory was dedicated to the monitoring of the Pleiades star group and that the appearance of these 'Seven Sisters' in the night sky dictated the start of the harvest season. Some experts believe the blurred appearance of Pleiades would signify higher humidity in the sky over the Amazon and so the Inca astronomers could warn farmers of the probability of wetter weather.

The condor (*kuntur* in Quechua) was represented by part of the constellation that we call Scorpio. The llama constellation, meanwhile, featured the two Alpha and Beta Centauri stars, which represented the eyes of the llama that the Inca knew as Yaqana. When Yaqana, appearing to be drinking, almost touched the horizon, it would signify the start of the planting season. Having drank his fill, Yaqana would then return to the sky to begin a new rain cycle.

> While we tend to view the Milky Way in terms of its billions of stars, the Incas often focused instead on its dark spots.

It's believed that artificial hollows carved into rocks were filled with water and silver dust to create mirrors upon which these constellations could be mapped. Perfectly carved, shallow black-stone platters have been unearthed that were used as water mirrors. In this way, Inca astronomers also traced the passage of the red planet that we call Mars and some experts believe that the Incas thus discovered the existence of planets, which move on different trajectories to stars.

Above: Temple of the Moon, Machu Picchu
Right: Temple of the Sun (p169), Machu Picchu

The Mystery Continues

The full extent of Inca astronomical science was known only to the *amauta* (wise ones). The Spanish chroniclers never remotely grasped how advanced Inca civilization was and so did not record its details, leaving even the greatest minds in archaeoastronomy with little but educated guesswork to explain what all this means.

What seems to be clear is that, even after more than a century of studies and research, we're still only dimly aware of the vast depths of knowledge that the Inca 'wise ones' may have accrued through their observations.

Intipunku

The last leg and it's all downhill from here. If you've been lucky, you'll have had your first view of Machu Picchu from Intipunku (Sun Gate). Though it's not unusual for dawn mist to create a complete whiteout, don't fear – it's amazing how often the sun burns the haze off so that you arrive at the ruins under gleaming Andean sunshine. Although this is just a short walk, there are some astounding historical sites to take in along the way.

Mark Eveleigh

Machu Picchu (p166)
KELLY CHENG TRAVEL PHOTOGRAPHY/GETTY IMAGES

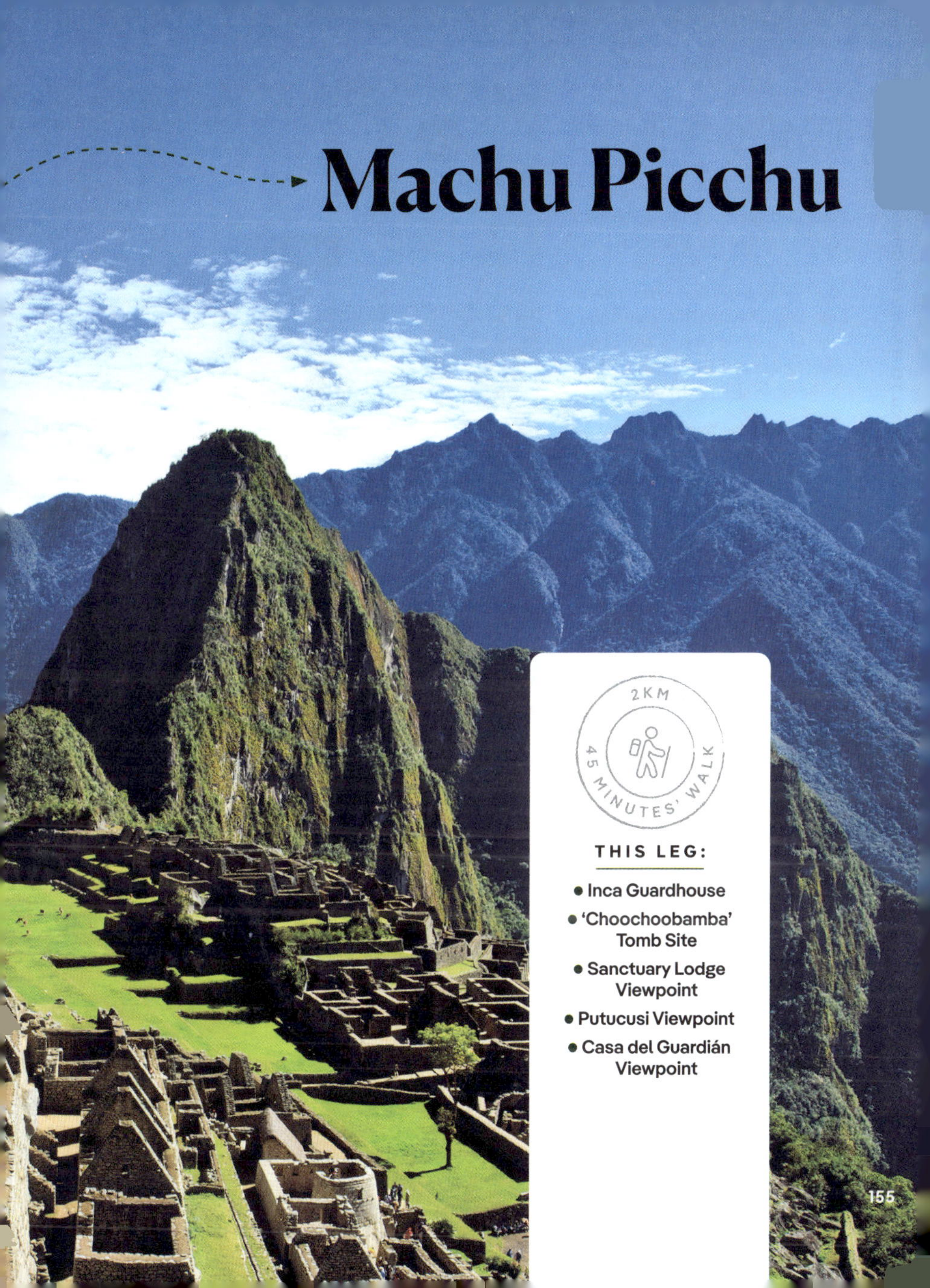

Machu Picchu

2KM
45 MINUTES' WALK

THIS LEG:

- Inca Guardhouse
- 'Choochoobamba' Tomb Site
- Sanctuary Lodge Viewpoint
- Putucusi Viewpoint
- Casa del Guardián Viewpoint

Walking Notes

Even those who have struggled over the highland passes will have a spring injected into their step on the last short jaunt down to the ruined city of Machu Picchu. Yet even within this short 2km stroll there are a couple of unnamed sites to visit. Don't get careless at this late stage, though – the stone slabs are often slippery.

Breaking Your Journey

There's no reason to break the journey on this section and pure adrenaline is likely to carry you the final 2km in any case. Try not to rush it, though, as there are several historic sites and a good guide will want to share with you as much as is known about these mysterious locations.

Mark's Tips

BEST VIEW
While the citadel is the undisputed show-stealer, be sure to spare a glance for the often unnoticed condor head on Putucusi Mountain.

FAVORITE STOP Choochoobamba is an evocative place to pause for a rest.

TIP You're approaching the most photogenic part of the trail – lower the camera to sit in silence and enjoy the moment.

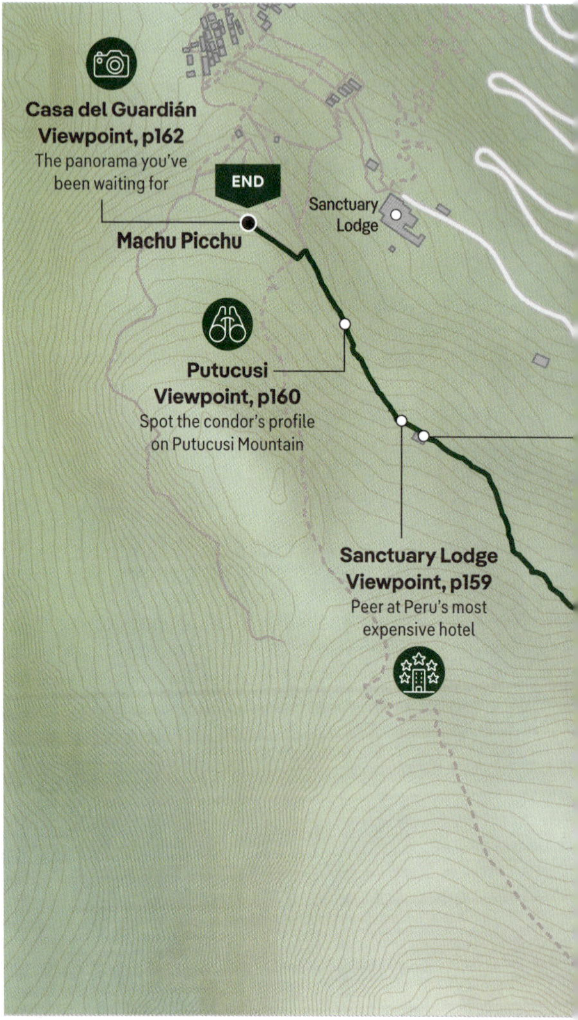

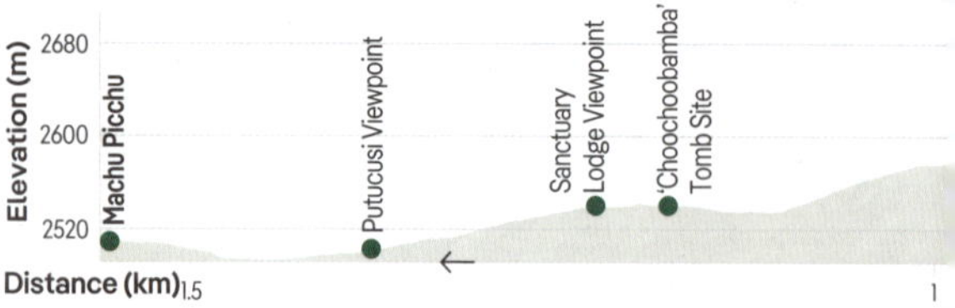

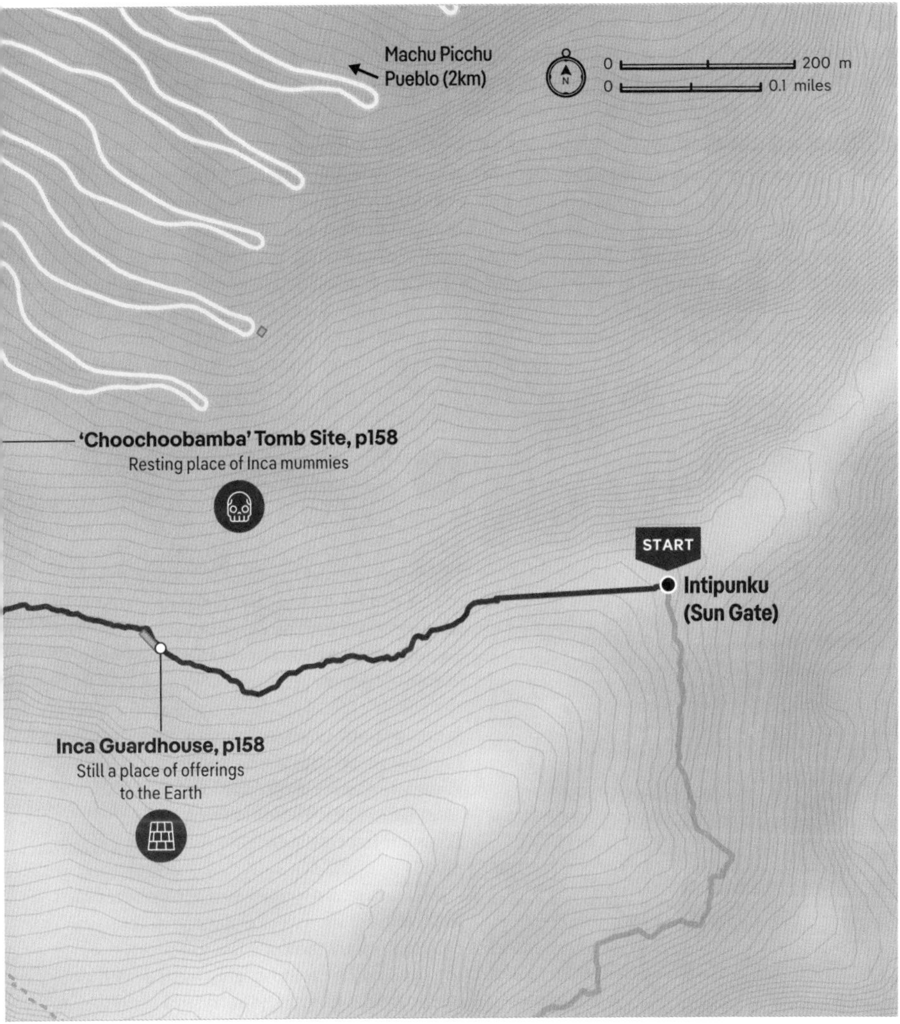
Machu Picchu Pueblo (2km)
N
0 200 m
0 0.1 miles
'Choochoobamba' Tomb Site, p158
Resting place of Inca mummies
START
Intipunku (Sun Gate)
Inca Guardhouse, p158
Still a place of offerings to the Earth

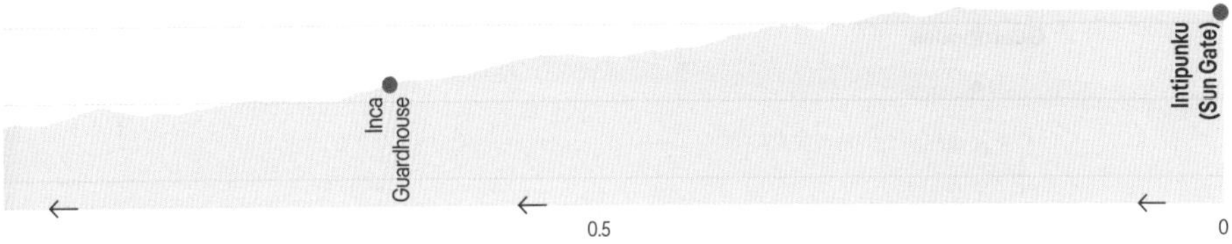
Inca Guardhouse
Intipunku (Sun Gate)
0.5
0

PREVIOUS STOP The famous section of Inca paving leading downhill and directly westwards from Intipunku is one of the most famous stretches of ancient highway on the planet.

Inca Guardhouse

It is extraordinary to think this section of well-preserved Inca paving wasn't noticed by archaeologists until 1915 – three years after Bingham first photographed Machu Picchu. It can only be taken as a sign of the incredible wealth of historic buildings in the actual city that this outlying trail – the most evocative way to reach the citadel these days – remained overlooked, despite the fact that there are several historic sites in the 2km stretch between Intipunku and Machu Picchu's ancient 'suburbs.'

The first of these sites, about 20 minutes from Intipunku, is known to guides simply as the Inca Guardhouse. While this site had a strategic purpose and must have served as a security post, it would certainly have played a ceremonial and religious role, too. The great granite boulder to the right of the path as you enter the complex was carefully sculpted by the Incas into steps. Experts agree that this was almost certainly a *huara* (a sort of altar) where offerings could be made to Pachamama. Even today, Quechua visitors will sometimes leave a small offering – what they call a *pago a la tierra* (offering to the Earth) – on what continues to be considered a sacred rock.

Inca guardhouse

FROM LEFT: MARK EVELEIGH, SERGI REBOREDO/ALAMY

'Choochoobamba' Tomb Site

Throughout the entire Machu Picchu complex you'll see countless examples of how rocks and boulders were deliberately incorporated into architecture. A spectacular example of this can be seen at the tomb site, around 10 minutes on from the Guardhouse, that some guides lightheartedly know as 'Choochoobamba' because, they point out, you can clearly hear the chug of the train rising up from the valley. A great granite slab leans at an angle towards the valley edge and it was under this rock that Hiram Bingham's team – verbosely known as the 'Yale University–National Geographic Society Peruvian Expedition of 1914–1915' – found two female mummies in 1915.

The team realized that caves and crevices such as these were the favorite place for tombs – rich pickings for archaeologists and collectors since the deceased were invariably buried with possessions such as tools, jewelry and ceramics.

Inca Guardhouse

1km

Still a site for offerings to the Earth

Sanctuary Lodge

Sanctuary Lodge Viewpoint

Ten minutes from 'Choochoobamba' you'll find yourself entering the suburbs of the great Inca citadel with the world-famous cityscape spread out before you. Turn to your right and you'll look down into the garden of Sanctuary Lodge: a Belmond Hotel, often billed as the 'most expensive hotel in Peru'. It's the only hotel located right at Machu Picchu's entrance – all other accommodation is a 25-minute bus ride away – and guests pay for the privilege of being among the first to enter the great Inca city each morning. It's also interesting that the hotel played a part in the history of the site: before the listed building

BEST BOOKS TO READ

Lost City of the Incas by Hiram Bingham
The classic story of Hiram Bingham's journeys to Machu Picchu, first published in 1948.

Turn Right at Machu Picchu: Rediscovering the Lost City One Step at a Time by Mark Adams
An enjoyable travelogue culminating in the Inca Trail and a solstice visit to Machu Picchu. Published in 2012.

Eight Feet in the Andes: Travels with a Mule in Unknown Peru by Dervla Murphy
Ireland's favorite adventuress never actually visited Machu Picchu but this entertaining yarn (ending in Cusco and published in 2003) offers all the inspiration you'll need for any Peruvian adventure.

'Choochoobamba' Tomb Site

Sanctuary Lodge Viewpoint

600m

A peaceful pause after the Intipunku selfie-frenzy

MACHU PICCHU'S 'CHOSEN WOMEN' MYTH

Based on the supposition that most of the skeletons found at Machu Picchu were women, it was long believed that the citadel was a haven where *acllas* (women chosen for their beauty and piety) were educated in weaving, textile production and the preparation of ritual foods. The 1915 expedition even unearthed a tomb that they believed belonged to the Mama Cuna (Head Matron) of the 'Virgins of the Sun', who, so they reported, unfortunately suffered from syphilis. While the citadel was apparently home to a large colony of weavers, traditionally women's work in the Andes, more accurate analysis in 2000 showed that half of the deceased were actually men.

became the Sanctuary Lodge it was the official residence for researchers and archaeologists. Pop in after you leave the archaeological complex if you're in need of a coffee or a hot meal because the walls of the restaurant – open to non-guests – are decorated with fascinating photos taken during early research trips.

Putucusi Viewpoint

Look to the northeast, across the valley over the tumbling waters of the Río Urubamba, and you'll see the soaring peak of **Putucusi Mountain**. Quechua people suggest there was a watchtower on the summit and that the mountain's name might have come from *cusi* (happy) and *putu* (which may derive from the trumpeting sound of the *pututu* conch shell).

Putucusi Mountain

FABIO IMHOFF/SHUTTERSTOCK

Few people notice – and most guides are not even aware – but if you look carefully at Putucusi's peak you'll see that the natural formation of the rock clearly shows the outline of a sitting condor, complete with eye, hooked beak and hunched wings. The light changes dramatically as shadows move across the peak but the condor's features are always visible. Little happened by coincidence in the design and layout of Machu Picchu and it's unlikely that the ancient Incas were unaware of the presence of their sacred bird watching over them from across the valley. It is said that the condor was believed to be the embodiment of the *apus* (mountain spirits) and so a mountain in the form of a condor must presumably have been an extremely powerful protective totem.

Until recently it was possible to climb Putucusi from Machu Picchu Pueblo, but the steep trail and sections of rickety wooden ladders have become so overgrown and dilapidated that, at the time of research, the peak was inaccessible.

Along the Way We Met...

TINA HEINRICKS I first walked the Inca Trail back in 2000, when I was teaching in Peru; the country is very special to me and I've returned a few times since then. Not long ago, at a point when life had become a bit messy, a close friend asked if I'd like to walk the Inca Trail again with her – and I knew that being on the trail might give me the space I needed to leave adulting responsibilities for a while, to reset and to return home as a steadier parent and therapist. The experience was perfect: I enjoyed the space I found on the trail, and forming connections with other hikers, too. Being out in nature, enjoying good food and company, and being surrounded by beautiful scenery was medicine for the soul.

The ancient citadel truly is a wonder and there couldn't be a more meaningful way to end the journey than arriving at Machu Picchu.

Tina Heinricks is a therapist from Calgary, Canada.

TINA'S TIP: *Pack lightly both for warm and cold conditions, and carry cash for tips and treats along the way.*

Few people notice the condor head

Along the Way We Met...

FABIAN COOK I'd wanted to hike the Inca trail for almost as long as I can remember. In fact, I tried to book on several occasions but couldn't get the dates I wanted because permits were sold out. I finally managed to book and it was worth all the effort. If you're a solo traveler, as I was, you can't go wrong joining one of the many organized trips since you're sure to meet some amazing, charismatic, friendly and interesting people. The hike up to Abra Warmiwañusqa (Dead Woman's Pass) on day two was more challenging than I'd expected because of the lack of oxygen, but the spectacular view from the top was ample reward. Reaching the Sun Gate, and ultimately Machu Picchu, is a memory that will always be with me. The sense of accomplishment exceeded all my expectations.

Fabian Cook, from Suffolk, England, has been planning his Inca Trail adventure for years. @demon_with_a_glass_hand

FABIAN'S TIP: *In hindsight, I'd advise using trekking poles. I decided to go without but feel they would have been a great help on the steepest sections.*

Casa del Guardián Viewpoint

Finally, you arrive on the wide terrace to find yourself gazing in awe at what is arguably one of the most photographed views on our planet. On an average day tens of thousands of images are captured from this point, with enough frantic activity to compel the Machu Picchu authorities to make jumping and sexual or acrobatic poses illegal (subject to expulsion without refund).

Machu Picchu is still considered a sacred place for the Quechua community and should be respected as such. The terraces, often with picturesquely grazing llamas, are a wonderful place to sit, gaze and ponder upon the once-in-a-lifetime pilgrimage that brought you here. You might even find yourself contemplating further hikes. If so, cast your eye to the southwest and you'll see distant Llactapata ruins (p186), still romantically covered in jungle.

Llama, Machu Picchu (p166)

INSIGHT

The Bingham Controversy

Lauded as a hero of exploration after his return to the US from Peru in 1911, Hiram Bingham III was celebrated for decades as the 'discoverer' of Machu Picchu. In fact, there were countless Peruvian people who knew of the site long before his arrival.

WORDS BY **MARK EVELEIGH**
Mark followed Bingham's trail from the lovely community of Mandor Pampa.

GRANGER - HISTORICAL PICTURE ARCHIVE/ALAMY

Hiram Bingham III, Machu Picchu, 1911

ON JULY 24, 1911, American explorer Hiram Bingham III climbed from his camp at Mandor Pampa to spend the afternoon photographing the site that would later become known as one the modern Wonders of the World. While the American explorer may be credited with bringing the site to the notice of the outside world, he was not, in fact, the 'discoverer' of Machu Picchu: there were many highland people who were well aware of its existence well before Bingham set foot in Peru.

'In the Wonderland of Peru'

In April 1913, National Geographic published a rare monographic issue on Hiram Bingham's earth-shattering excavations in what the explorer described as 'the most inaccessible part of the Andes.'

The image of a swashbuckling adventurer hacking the jungle foliage with his machete to reveal a 'lost city' caught the public imagination – and that of Hollywood producers who, much later, created Indiana Jones, supposedly inspired by Bingham's character.

In Peru it's often said today that Bingham was unduly arrogant in claiming credit for 'his discovery.' In fact, Bingham did mention a certain Melchor Arteaga who first told him about the ruins when Bingham and his colleagues were camped in the little settlement of Mandor Pampa.

As Bingham reported in his best-selling book *Lost City of the Incas* – written in 1948 when the explorer was in his seventies – there were two families, the Alvarezes and the Richartes, who had been farming the Inca-built terraces for four years. Both families welcomed the American warmly and Señor Richarte sent his young son to show the explorer around the neighboring ruins. This boy, who appeared in some of Bingham's celebrated photos but was never named by him, is popularly known among Machu Picchu guides as 'Pablito.' Recently, however, the young boy was named by the excellent Museo de Sitio Manuel Chávez Ballón (p174) as Melquiades Richarte.

Bingham also came across graffiti reading 'Lizarraga 1902.' Agustín Lizárraga turned out to be a local farmer and during that first visit Bingham scribbled into his notebook: 'Augustin Lizarraga is discoverer of Machu Picchu.'

HENRY CLAY GIPSON/FREDERIC LEWIS/GETTY IMAGES

Locals, Machu Picchu, 1911

What's in a Name?

As the Richarte boy led Bingham deeper into the wonders of what his family called Machu Picchu after the mountain that dominated it, the explorer jotted other names into his notebook: 'Temple of the Sun,' 'Temple of the Three Windows,' the mysterious cave that henceforth would became known as 'The Royal Tomb'...

Many of the names that Bingham scribbled that first afternoon are still used today. Although not a trained archaeologist, Bingham made full use of his pioneering position – 'by right of conquest' the Spanish would have called it – to freely hypothesize as to the purposes to which the buildings were put. The Royal Tomb is a major drawcard today, despite the fact that there has never been any evidence that it was used as a tomb and was more likely a temple to Pachamama.

For the National Geographic photo shoot, he had one of his laborers demonstrate how corn would have been ground in the carefully sculpted shallow depressions that archaeologists believe were actually water mirrors for studying the movement of the stars.

> The image of a swashbuckling adventurer hacking the jungle foliage with his machete to reveal a 'lost city' caught the public imagination

Melchor Arteaga & the Richarte Family

While Bingham has a luxury train and a highway named after him, Melchor Arteaga has almost been forgotten (although there's an alleyway named for him in Lima's Carabayllo quarter). Bingham and his researchers paid laborers 50c for each grave they could unearth and the farmer Richarte was, unsurprisingly, particularly successful at this. Then one of the other laborers became unexpectedly ill and Richarte began to fear 'the curse of the Incas.' He and his son left their farm, never to return.

It's a pity that among the great many people to whom Bingham showed gratitude in the acknowledgements of his book, there wasn't a single Peruvian named. There are those who say that the 'Hiram Bingham Hwy' should be renamed the 'Pablito Richarte Hwy' after Machu Picchu's first professional guide.

SITE GUIDE:

Machu Picchu

In 1953, Che Guevara wrote that Machu Picchu was one of those places that 'drives any dreamer to ecstasy'. Any excursion through the ancient staircases, temples and plazas is a mystery tour, but find a quiet corner to contemplate because it's still the perfect place for dreamers.

WORDS BY **MARK EVELEIGH**
Mark has visited Machu Picchu several times in the last 25 years.

BETO SANTILLAN/SHUTTERSTOCK

Visitors queue at the entrance to Machu Picchu

Arriving

Walking The most iconic way to arrive here is on foot along the Inca Trail. In this case, most of the headaches will be taken out of the planning thanks to the obligation to book through a registered Inca Trail tour operator.

Train The other option is to take a train to Machu Picchu Pueblo (see p180). A common misconception is that the train arrives at Machu Picchu archaeological site; instead, buses wait at the town's train station to shuttle visitors 25 minutes up the roller-coaster dirt track of the Hiram Bingham Hwy to the ruins. **Buses** *(comprar.caminoalamaravilla.com; one way S82)* must be booked in advance.

Getting Tickets

Booking entry tickets Be sure to book your tickets to **Machu Picchu** *(6am-5pm)* well in advance: six months or more during busy seasons. Prices vary but at the time of research they were around US$65 for a standard circuit ticket or US$75 for tickets with extra access, to Wayna Picchu (p175) or Machu Picchu Mountain (p172) for example. You will need your passport to enter the complex.

You can book online through tuboleto.cultura.pe but some international cards are not accepted. Many travelers find it more convenient to book through an agency who can source train, bus and entry tickets plus, if needed, book accommodations in Machu Picchu Pueblo (p180). If you book an Inca Trail package be sure to confirm that entrance to Machu Picchu is included.

Buying last-minute tickets in person Machu Picchu Pueblo Cultural Centre *(Plaza Manco Capac)* makes 1000 tickets available for the following day. They often sell very quickly so try to arrive at the center close to 6am to buy tickets for the following day. Real time availability is viewable online through tuboleto.cultura.pe/disponibilidad/llaqta_machupicchu.

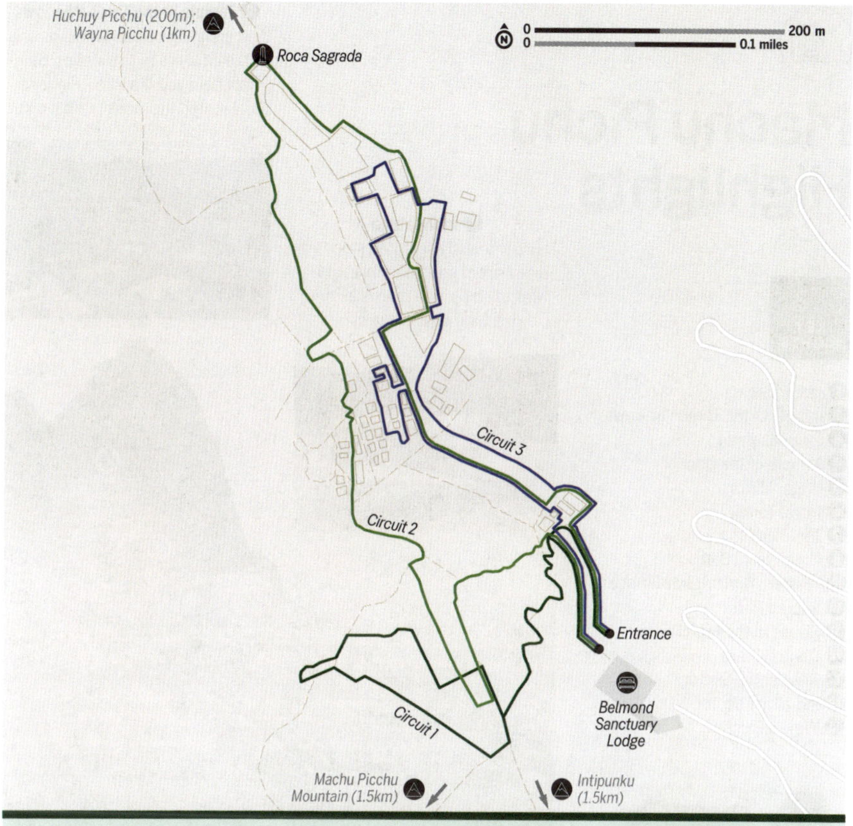

It's been said that Machu Picchu's ticketing system is as mysterious as the citadel itself. In 2021, authorities mapped out three circuits; in 2024, extensions were added so that you now have a choice of 10 routes.

'PANORAMIC' CIRCUIT 1

This is the circuit you'll usually experience if you arrive via the Inca Trail and it offers perhaps the best overall photo opportunity with the complex's Hanan (Upper Sector) to your left and the Hurin (Lower Sector) on your right. Ask for 'Route 1-A' to include Machu Picchu Mountain (p172).

'CLASSIC MACHU PICCHU' CIRCUIT 2

Circuit 2 covers the most ground but, at the time of writing, the whole part of the complex including the sacred Intihuatana ('hitching post of the sun') was off-limits due to erosion.

'CLASSIC MACHU PICCHU' CIRCUIT 3

Confusingly featuring the same name as Circuit 2, Circuit 3 offers more in-depth explorations of the sacred areas around Temple of the Sun and Temple of the Condor. Route 3-A includes Wayna Picchu Mountain.

Machu Pichu Highlights

KEY SIGHTS

1. Intihuatana
2. Temple of the Three Windows
3. Roca Sagrada
4. Temple of the Condor
5. Water Mirrors
6. Royal Tomb
7. Temple of the Sun
8. Ceremonial Baths
9. Western Agricultural Terraces
10. Sacred Plaza
11. House of the High Priest
12. Central Plaza
13. Residential Sector
14. Industrial Sector
15. Wayna Picchu

❷ Temple of the Three Windows

This stunning building remains one of the citadel's big mysteries. Bingham believed the three windows represented the Inca creation myth.

❶ Intihuatana

This gorgeously sculpted stone – a real work of pre-Colombian art – was used by Inca priests as the 'hitching post of the sun'.

❽ Ceremonial Baths

Originally assumed to have been bathing places, these cubicles near a weaving workshop may have been used for dying alpaca and vicuña wool.

❼ Temple of the Sun

Arguably the most perfect stone-masonry in the entire complex. The sun beams through the eastern window during the June (winter) equinox.

FROM LEFT: RUSSELL JOHNSON/SHUTTERSTOCK,BUTEO/SHUTTERSTOCK, MARKUS DANIEL/GETTY IMAGES, LU_SEA/SHUTTERSTOCK, IONUT DAVID/ALAMY, BETO SANTILLAN/SHUTTERSTOCK

❸ Roca Sagrada

The Sacred Rock is an 'echo stone,' mimicking the shape of the silhouette of Yanantin Mountain on the horizon.

❹ Temple of the Condor

The sculpted head and neck of a sacred condor is angled to compliment the soaring 'wings' formed by the natural rock backdrop.

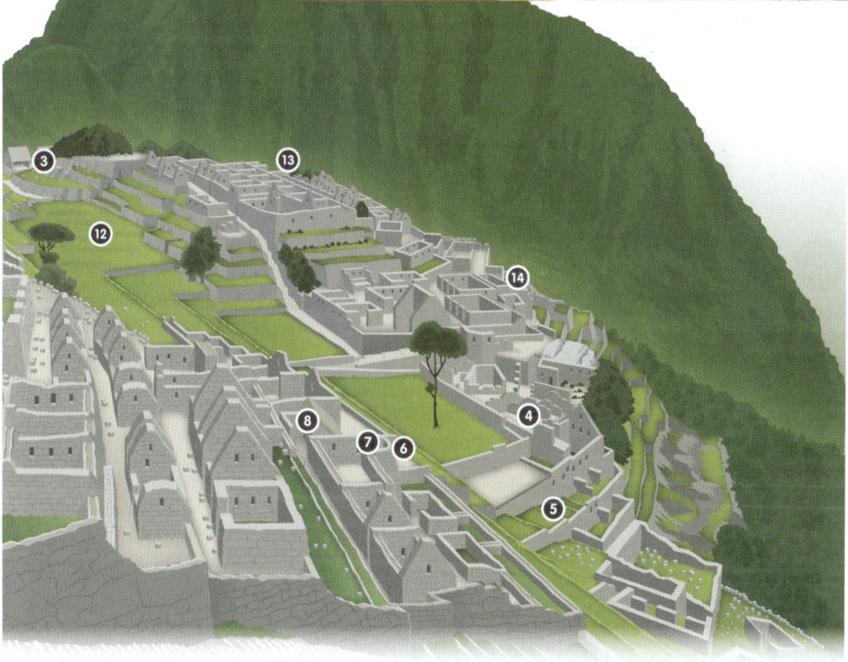

❻ Royal Tomb

No longer believed to have been the tomb of Pachacutec, the name has nevertheless stuck. The evocatively sculpted features are no less fascinating for their air of mystery.

❺ Water Mirrors

The *espejos de agua* (pictured right) are believed to have been used to measure the movement of stars so that Inca astronomers could anticipate the seasons.

Machu Picchu Mystique

No matter how you arrive, you're likely to be struck by the conviction that Machu Picchu was designed to be hidden. It's invisible from the Urubamba ravine until you're on its doorstep and even those arriving through the Sun Gate usually get the impression that the dawn mist is deliberately shrouding the sacred city.

Some of the most iconic outlying parts of the site were not rediscovered until many decades after Machu Picchu made headlines in 1911. In fact, it's part of the mystique of this location that unknown archaeological sites are almost certainly still waiting to be discovered in the surrounding mountains. Guides are knowledgeable and well-trained, but if you come away from this once-in-a-lifetime experience feeling that you have more questions than answers, don't be disappointed. Some of the best minds in archaeology feel the same way!

What Was Machu Picchu?

The short answer is that nobody really knows for sure. The widely accepted belief these days is that it was built around 1450 by the emperor Pachacutec as a sort of 'country retreat'. You might also hear a popular recent theory that Machu Picchu was a 'university' where men and women would come to study everything from metallurgy and astronomy to agriculture and weaving. Given the number of temples, sacred sites and complex astronomical observatories it is certain the citadel had an important ritualistic aspect. Machu Picchu was abandoned, supposedly before the Spanish conquest...but the reasons for this are also unknown.

FARMING AT ALTITUDE

From humble beginnings as alpaca farmers in the southern Andes, the Inca Empire grew to become a highly complex civilization that extended from present-day Colombia to Chile.

Yet even at the height of its powers, the majority of Inca society remained agrarian. It is thought that during the 1400s, terrace farms covered almost one million hectares in Peru. These terrace farms were carefully engineered to flatten the soil (reducing soil erosion), trap heat (protecting roots from frost) and facilitate the irrigation of crops, ensuring a consistent and varied supply of food for surrounding towns and villages year-round.

The Inca also practiced crop rotation, alternating crops each season to build up soil fertility and deter pests. Structurally supported by stone walls, terraces were cut into progressively steeper hillsides, creating microclimates that supported the growth of countless varieties of crops, including potatoes, squash, corn, peanuts, tomatoes, chili, quinoa and coca. Domesticated animals integrated into these farming systems included guinea pigs, ducks, dogs, alpaca and the iconic llama.

Following first contact with Spanish colonizers in 1528, introduced diseases quickly spread throughout the empire, decimating the population and weakening all areas of the empire, including farming. Today, the ghosts of Inca's extensive terraced farming system can be seen throughout the former empire, with extraordinary examples visible especially in Machu Picchu's western agricultural terraces (pictured below).

FROM LEFT: XOCHITL PILARTE/SHUTTERSTOCK, DON MAMMOSER/SHUTTERSTOCK

Photographing Machu Picchu

You've traveled a long way and will want to capture your time at one of the world's most photogenic spots. Here's how to make the most of Machu Picchu's ever-changing conditions.

HOW TO

Remain respectful: This is a sacred site and sexual images and/or nudity will get you ejected by security officers.

Avoid: Jumping, lying poses or dancing TikTok style. All are prohibited.

Equipment: Selfie sticks and drones are banned; tripods can only be used with advance written permission.

Traditionally the golden hours around sunrise and sunset are perceived to be the best for photography. In the High Andes, however, the light can change almost instantly and you can get lucky (or unlucky) at any time of the day. Early morning is the best time to see the ruins as there are fewer crowds and the swirling mists – a regular feature of this mountain landscape – often lead to the most spectacular images.

If you arrived via the Inca Trail you might have captured that sun-blessed cityscape scene from Intipunku (Sun Gate). The main agricultural terraces (part of the popular Circuit 1) also offer appealing wide-angle opportunities across the entire complex, frequently with a perfectly posed llama.

Be ready for anything but don't be blindly obsessed with the wide-angle panoramas: as the Inca stonemasons were aware, you can find incredible beauty even in the smallest details.

On a clear day it is worth hiking to the summit of Machu Picchu Mountain (p172) for views that are more spectacular than those from the often crowded summit of Wayna Picchu (p175).

Above: Camera; Right: Machu Picchu in the morning light

FROM LEFT: NEW AFRICA/SHUTTERSTOCK, JUDYTA JASTRZEBSKA/SHUTTERSTOCK

Climb Machu Picchu Mountain

Soaring almost 2½ times above the peak of Wayna Picchu, the mighty mountain that gave the citadel its modern-day name makes for an unexpected adventure...and offers some of the finest panoramas of the site.

HOW TO

Tickets: When you book your Machu Picchu ticket, be sure to request 'Route 1-A', which includes access to 'Montaña Machu Picchu'.

Getting there: The access point is inside Machu Picchu archaeological site, 150m south of Casa del Guardián.

When to go: Enter before 8:30am since you must be down by the time the security checkpoint closes at midday.

Difficulty: A guide is not needed as the route is well-marked and well-maintained but allow three to four hours to complete the 3.2km return hike to the summit.

Tallest of the three mountains surrounding the citadel, Machu Picchu offers the finest views of the city.

Until a few years ago the trail up Machu Picchu Mountain (3085m) was unknown to all but a few of the most determined travel photographers. While sightseers race at dawn to be the first to make it to the summit of relatively diminutive Wayna Picchu (p175), the slow and steady climb up Machu Picchu's 2670 steps is more of a marathon than a sprint. And, while visitors are sometimes disappointed by the crowds on Wayna Picchu, the solitude of Machu Picchu's summit makes it worth the effort.

Heading Up

There are three official viewpoints and even at the first (2680m) you're almost on eye-level with Wayna Picchu's summit. From here onward, the path – much of it original Inca paving since this too is an 'Inca Trail' – winds steadily past Viewpoint 2 (2730m) and Viewpoint 3 (2958m).

There's nothing technical about the climb but shoes with good grip and wet-weather clothes are advisable as the weather can change without warning. Those who suffer from vertigo might struggle on one steep rocky section and a narrow ledge that on a clear day has a vertical drop that can make your head spin. In general, though, it is a less dizzying climb than the one up the flank of Wayna Picchu.

FROM LEFT: JUCADIMA/SHUTTERSTOCK, IULIIA SEROVA/SHUTTERSTOCK

WHAT'S IN A NAME?

It's extremely unlikely that the real name of the site that we know as Machu Picchu will ever come to light, but when Hiram Bingham arrived here in 1911 local farmers referred to the citadel by the name of the mountain (literally 'Old Peak') that loomed over it. The first known written reference to the site is from a Spanish document from 1568 that shows a mysterious spot known only as 'Pichu' was registered to the clan of the Inca emperor Pachacutec.

Left: Machu Picchu from Machu Picchu Mountain
Below: Hiker descends Machu Picchu Mountain

At the Summit

Expect to take at least 1½ hours to reach the summit, where you'll be rewarded with condors'-eye views down on Intipunku and the Inca Trail, and right across the citadel that is the engineering and spiritual epitome of the Inca Empire. There's a small shelter on the summit, often, bizarrely, with an optimistic dog or two hoping for a handout. On clear days you can see neighboring Llactapata ruins (p186) and the glacier-capped peaks of Salkantay and Veronica Mountains.

MARK EVELEIGH

BETO SANTILLAN/SHUTTERSTOCK

Machu Picchu ruins and Putucusi Mountain

Tips for Your Visit

Book early-morning tickets to enjoy fewer crowds at the ruins and to face less waiting time at the bus stops and at the checkpoints.

Be sure to use the toilets before you enter the archaeological site. There are are toilets outside the entrance, but strict rules mean that if you exit – even to use the bathroom – you will not be allowed back in.

Large packs (bigger than about 25L) and hiking poles must be left at the **luggage kiosk** *(S5)* before entering Machu Picchu.

LOCATION, LOCATION, LOCATION

The Río Urubamba, which starts its life in the glacial run-off of mighty Ausangate Mountain, and Río Ahobamba, which flows down from Mt Salkanty, were the two sacred rivers of the Incas. The fact that Machu Picchu was built almost at their confluence, at a spot almost encircled by the Urubamba, is unlikely to have been a coincidence.

The city is overlooked by several important mountains, including Salkanty's snowy summit and the soaring spire of Putucusi, just a kilometer away and likewise embraced in the coils of the snaking Urubamba. Few people seem to notice that by a geological quirk the rock face near Putucusi's summit bears an uncanny resemblance to the head of a condor, gazing back, almost at eye-level with the citadel. The condor, a powerful protective omen for the Incas, was considered to be an earthly incarnation of the *apus* (mountain spirits).

The question is not why the Incas chose to build on this spot but how they could ever have considered locating their great secret citadel anywhere else.

HIRAM BINGHAM III, PUBLIC DOMAIN, VIA WIKIMEDIA COMMONS

Museo de Sitio Manuel Chávez Ballón

The excellent Museo de Sitio Manuel Chávez Ballón (named for a resident archaeologist of the 1970s) costs S22 but is free with a Machu Picchu ticket between midday and 4pm. Here you'll find thought-provoking insights on the local people, who were well aware of the existence of the city long before the first foreigners laid eyes on it, including Melquiades Richarte. On July 24, 1911, this small boy, usually described as 'Pablito,' became Machu Picchu's first guide. There are excellent photo displays and artifacts and many of the exhibits have helpful information boards.

Left: Photo on display at Museo de Sitio Manuel Chávez Ballón

Scale Wayna Picchu's 'Stairs of Death'

The climb to the summit of Wayna Picchu is a bucket-list attraction for many tourists, but the 'race to the top' can be a risky challenge.

HOW TO

How to go: Book in advance by asking for 'Circuit 3, Machupicchu Realeza, Route 3-A: Wayna Picchu Mountain Route' ticket.

Getting here: To get to the trailhead for Wayna Picchu follow signs for Route 3-A, which loops around Machu Picchu's lower section. It's about 850m to the checkpoint where you'll be asked to show your ticket and register.

When to go: There are two slots each day for access: 7am and 9am.

Choosing your route: The simple short trail is about 2km (allow two hours) while the long trail, which visits the Temple of the Moon and winds down through cloud forest, is less crowded and runs for closer to 5km (three hours).

Tip: Remember your number among the hundreds in the register so that you can easily find the place to sign out at the end.

Some reputable tour companies forbid their Inca Trail and Machu Picchu guides from advising guests on the climb up Wayna Picchu (also spelled Huayna Picchu). While substantially lower than Machu Picchu Mountain, the steps are steep and narrow and can be slippery in wet weather. The fact that some people consider it a race to be first to the top has led to reckless behavior and some experienced guides claim to be astounded that fatalities and serious injuries are not more common.

Nevertheless, the climb remains incredibly popular thanks largely to the perceived challenge and the spectacular views. Since only 400 people are allowed in each morning it sells out almost daily. Many sections of the steps – such as the infamous 'Stairs of Death' – need to be climbed using the hands as well as feet and it's incredible that the Incas were able to build guardhouses, temples and terraces on these near vertical slopes.

ANDY WILCOCK/SHUTTERSTOCK

Path to Wayna Picchu summit

Train to Machu Picchu Pueblo
BETO SANTILLAN/SHUTTERSTOCK

INSIGHT

Machu Picchu by Rail

Whatever your intentions for visiting Machu Picchu, the mind-boggling rail options will likely play a big part in your planning. After all, Machu Picchu Pueblo is probably the only large town in the world accessible only by rail or on foot.

WORDS BY **MARK EVELEIGH**

Mark has traveled to and from Machu Picchu by various classes of train and has hiked the railway line to Hidroeléctrica.

Machu Picchu Before Trains

When American explorer Hiram Bingham III traveled along the Urubamba Valley in 1911 the last word in local transportation innovation was the mule trail dynamited out of the rock face 13 years before. There was a small settlement – barely a 'wide spot' on the mule trail – known as La Maquina, where a German lumberjack of dubious character (he might or might not have been Machu Picchu's first tomb raider) had a contract to cut ties for a railroad that, it was rumored, might pass this way one day.

There were also two wealthy hacienda owners, dedicated more or less to exploiting the local workforce, about 15km farther along the mule track. Machu Picchu Pueblo itself was yet to be born and the hot springs that would give the town its early name – Aguas Calientes – were yet to be discovered.

Then, it would have been impossible to imagine a time when up to 20 trains would clatter down the valley each day carrying 4000 visitors in six different budget categories. In 1928, 17 years after Bingham brought his momentous news home to the USA, the first train rattled into the little hamlet of Aguas Calientes. Now officially known as Machu Picchu Pueblo, the town's 6000 inhabitants rely on the railway line for their survival.

> Back then, it would have been impossible to imagine a time when up to 20 trains would clatter down the valley each day carrying 4000 visitors in six different budget categories.

Even today, there are only two ways to reach Machu Picchu Pueblo: you either take the train or you walk. Cargo transport through the narrow lanes takes the form of hand-carts or a fleet of eclectic ride-on carts that ply the streets at often surprising speeds. Even the large fleet of buses dedicated to carrying tourists and staff up the ostentatiously named Hiram Bingham Hwy to the ruins were transported into town on special rolling stock hauled by locomotives.

It's thought-provoking as you wander around the booming little tourist town to consider that almost everything you see was transported by rail. Travelers who complain about how expensive Machu Picchu Pueblo is should spare a thought for the fact that it's also so prohibitively expensive for the local workforce that few elderly people can afford to retire here and most leave for more affordable towns farther up the Sacred Valley.

Two Rail Routes to Machu Picchu Pueblo

Most people approach Machu Picchu Pueblo by rail from the southern direction, either from Cusco's Poroy Station (3½ hours) or from Ollantaytambo (two hours). There are several different levels of service plying this route.

A cheaper option is to travel by road to the village of Santa Teresa, north of Machu Picchu Pueblo. From there you can get a *colectivo* (shared taxi) to the railhead at Hidroeléctrica and then take a train to Machu Picchu Pueblo. There are direct buses each morning (S70, 8:45am) from Ollantaytambo to Hidroeléctrica station. Alternatively, Juan Javier Quispe Villalba *(WhatsApp: +51 902 888 881)*, a recommended English-speaking driver, often travels that route.

It's tempting to say that there are options 'to suit all budgets' for rail travel to Machu Picchu Pueblo. The harsh reality though is that calculated by Sol-per-minute, the Peru Rail and Inca Rail trains that service this route might be the most expensive trains on the planet.

Many people assume that the train fare is sufficient to deliver them directly to the UNESCO site, but unless you plan to make the steep three-hour return hike from town, you will need to pay a further US$12 for a return bus ticket along the Hiram Bingham Hwy, a series of gravel switchbacks that snakes up the mountain to Machu Picchu archaeological site.

If you're walking the four-day Inca Trail, your tour operator will take care of the booking for your return rail journey from/to Ollantaytambo. Costs for the two-day Inca Trail (p148) will include a ticket from Ollantaytambo to the stop known as 'Kilometre 104' and the return journey from Machu Picchu Pueblo.

Rail Services Explained

Voyager/Expedition Class

Fortunately for local people who live and work at Machu Picchu, there are some affordable trains (S12 each way) but international visitors are not allowed to travel in these carriages.

The cheapest 'international class' journey will set you back around US$66 for the two-hour journey between Ollantaytambo and Machu Picchu Pueblo. The 'Voyager' train is operated by **Inca Rail** *(incarail.com)* and the 'Expedition' by **PeruRail** *(perurail.com)*. Both PeruRail and Inca Rail run what they call a 'bimodal' transport option where they connect central Cusco with Ollantaytambo by bus for no extra cost.

The 20-minute PeruRail connection from Hidroeléctrica is cheaper than the connection from Ollantaytambo, but it's interesting to think that at US$39 each way, this 40-minute 'budget' train option is still eye-wateringly expensive.

There's no doubting it's a once-in-a-lifetime experience and few who make the trip end up resenting the outlay.

Prime Class

Inca Rail's premium service offers one-way tickets starting at US$103, including the bimodal bus connection from central Cusco. This train features a dining carriage specializing in Andean meals and live music.

Inca Rail 360°

Aimed especially at photographers and bookable through incarail.com, you get those all-important panoramic windows plus access to an open-air observation carriage for US$113 each way. This service also includes complimentary snacks and live music. You'll find a little more space than the Voyager class, but do note the new Voyager and Expedition carriages also have 'skylights,' albeit smaller than the 360° and Vistadome, that allow you to enjoy the overhead views.

PeruRail Vistadome

The Vistadome is a midrange rail service costing US$120 each way (book through perurail.com). The Vistadome is so-called because the carriages have large skylight windows in the ceiling that allow visitors to enjoy the spectacular scenery of the high peaks that loom over the Urubamba canyon. The service also features a partially open-air 'observatory' carriage.

Inca Rail 1st Class

Inca Rail's normal bimodal bus transfer is replaced for 1st-class passengers with a transfer in a premium private vehicle from Cusco to Ollantaytambo Station. A US$344 one-way ticket (see incarail.com) buys you a gourmet meal with live music in the dining carriage, plus access to a lounge/bar carriage and an open-air 'balcony'. Passengers also enjoy a unique *kero* ceremony – an Andean blessing to begin your visit to Machu Picchu in the most positive way.

PeruRail Hiram Bingham Luxury Train

South America's answer to the *Orient Express* comes at a hefty US$570 price tag. The *Hiram Bingham,* operated by Belmond Hotel Group, is the last word, taking Peruvian railway luxury to a whole new level. Guests are transferred by private car to Poroy Railway Station, about 25 minutes from Cusco center, and there the pampering begins with complimentary bucks fizz, fortified with a jolt of pisco. Traditional Andean dancers perform a blessing dance for the embarking guests before orders are taken for the a la carte three-course meal. Before eating, guests are free to move into the bar car, decorated in chic 1920s style, where complimentary drinks – champagne anyone? – are served and a three-piece band tunes up.

On the 9:05am outbound service from Poroy, Cusco, the bar-car is a place of civilized small talk over coffees and bubbly. On the service leaving Machu Picchu Pueblo at 5:50pm, the three-piece band frequently turns the journey into a rocking, rollicking party with a repertoire of tunes in Spanish, English, French, Russian and Hindi catering for the mixed nationalities of the passengers. At more than US$150 per hour, the 3¼-hour ride on the *Hiram Bingham* is certainly one of the world's most expensive railway journeys, but there's no doubting it's a once-in-a-lifetime experience and few who make the trip end up resenting the outlay.

Whatever Class You Travel in...

On the outbound service to Machu Picchu Pueblo, do your best to get seats on the left-hand side of the train to make the most of the dramatic views of the cascading river and snow-capped mountains. On the return journey to Ollantaytambo/Cusco, try to sit on the right.

About 20 minutes after you leave Ollantaytambo, look for the bridge that marks the beginning of the Inca Trail.

Price is not the only limitation to bear in mind: luggage is limited to 8kg for Inca Rail and 12kg for PeruRail, although it doesn't seem these restrictions are enforced often. Bear in mind, though, that you'll probably only need an overnight bag and most hostels and hotels in Cusco and Ollantaytambo have facilities to store luggage for guests.

Despite the high charges, Machu Picchu is such a bucket-list destination that all classes of these trains book up long in advance. During high-season especially, you should book all train tickets several months in advance. You'll need the two train tickets – most people 'mix and match' rather than go by the same mode twice.

Be aware that due to the spectacular geology, landslides are not uncommon and from time to time the line is cut, effectively isolating Machu Picchu Pueblo entirely from the outside world. It can pay to book through a reliable tour operator who will be able to advise on options should this – or another disaster* – occur.

---

* On December 30, 2025, two passenger trains collided on the line between Ollantaytambo and Machu Picchu Pueblo. The head-on collision between Inca Rail and PeruRail locomotives resulted in the death of one driver and injuries to around 40 people.

Food onboard the train to Machu Picchu Pueblo

MARK EVELEIGH

CITY GUIDE:

Machu Picchu Pueblo

BELOW: MARK EVELEIGH, RIGHT: MARK EVELEIGH

Machu Picchu Pueblo (often known as Aguas Calientes) is the end-point for the Inca Trail. Though much maligned as an expensive tourist trap, what might be the largest town in the world accessible only by rail has a unique and quirky appeal.

WORDS BY **MARK EVELEIGH**

Mark spent a happy week researching in isolated Machu Picchu village.

Arriving

There are only two ways to arrive in Machu Picchu Pueblo: by train (p176) or by walking the Inca Trail.

Train Amazingly, this town of around 8000 people is completely cut off from the outside world except by rail. While most visitors arrive by train from Cusco or Ollantaytambo, there's also cheaper train access via the 'Hidroeléctrica' (hydroelectric station) near Santa Teresa village (S120; five to six hours by road from Cusco).

HOW MUCH FOR A

Coffee S15

Pizza S45

One-way bus ticket to Machu Picchu S40

Getting Around

Shuttle buses Run from 5:30am until 7pm from Av Hermanos Ayar up to Machu Picchu archaeological site. Apart from these – and the aforementioned train – there is no public transport in Machu Picchu Pueblo.

Walking It takes less than 15 minutes to walk from one end of the village to the other. Free from traffic (apart from the electric delivery carts that ply the streets), Machu Picchu Pueblo is a pleasant place to wander.

Finding Your Way Around

The first thing you see after arriving at Machu Picchu Pueblo train station is a sprawling souvenir market, but once you meander through this you can get your bearings anywhere on the bank of Río Aguas Calientes. On the northern bank you'll find Av Hermanos Ayar and, parallel with it, Av Pachacutec with a seemingly endless selection of lively bars and restaurants. Plaza Manco Capac (named after the legendary founder of the Inca civilization) is officially the town center. The southern side of the river is appealing for being very local. Few tourists come here and you'll find some good, affordable eateries near Parque Amauta in this quarter, which is known as Barrio las Orquidias (Quarter of the Orchids).

Left: Inca statue with quipu, Machu Picchu Pueblo
Right: Río Aguas Calientes, Machu Picchu Pueblo

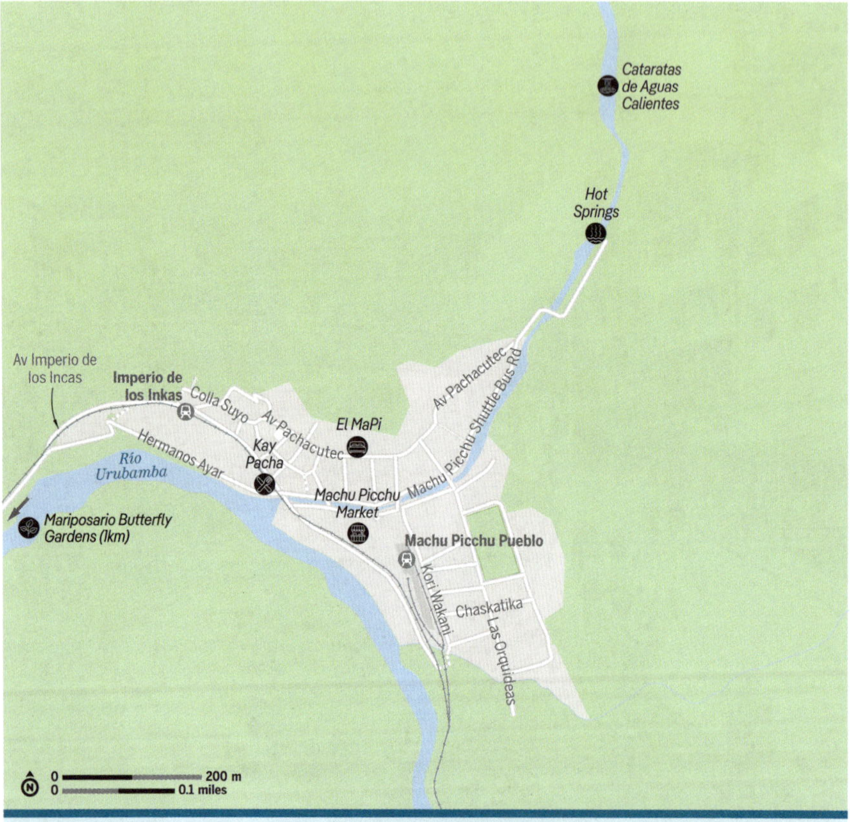

A DAY IN MACHU PICCHU PUEBLO

Start your day in leisurely style with coffee, croissants and people-watching on one of the sidewalk cafes along **Av Pachacutec**. Next wander past the slightly grimy-looking **hot springs** and continue up the valley to **Cataratas de Aguas Calientes** waterfall.

Grab lunch at **Kay Pacha** (p183), overlooking the railway line, before walking 20 minutes down the valley to the excellent **Mariposario Butterfly Gardens** (p185) for face-to-face contact with some of the fluttering gems of the jungle. Be sure to stop for a coffee at the park's cafe where bird feeders attract colorful avian species.

Avoid the tourist crowds and enjoy a traditional meal in the friendly local neighborhood known as **Barrio las Orquidias** (Quarter of the Orchids). End a perfect day with a pisco sour nightcap in the stylish bar at **El MaPi** (p183).

Where to Stay

Machu Picchu Pueblo is renowned for being expensive, which is understandable – the town is resupplied by rail and space is at a premium. The tourist area is on the northern bank of the Río Aguas Calientes, while the friendly and more cost-effective local quarters around Barrio las Orquidias is beyond the southern bank. There's something to match most budgets, from the luxurious Sanctuary Lodge (p159) to boutique backpacker hostels with US$12 bunks.

BEST PLACES TO STAY

Nativus Hostel $
Close to buses and with dorms, private rooms and a rooftop bar. *nativushostel.com*

Mandor Pampa Lodge $
Hike one hour downriver for a taste of homegrown vintage relaxation. *mandor.pe*

El MaPi $$
Machu Picchu Pueblo's first hotel, stylishly refurbished with sumptuous rooms. *inkaterra.com*

Inkaterra Machu Picchu Pueblo Hotel $$$
A gorgeous eco-resort, a lost world set in its own private reserve. *inkaterra.com*

Where to Eat

Make your way to the tourist center – the string of bars and restaurants along Av Pachacutec – for eclectic Peruvian and international menus...plus excellent two-for-one pisco sours (pictured below). 'Imported' regional specialties such as guinea pig and alpaca come at a premium here. South of the river are good-value local eateries where you can find three-course menus from around S20.

MACHU PICCHU MARKET

If it weren't for the fact that this mind-boggling collection of 300 or so market stalls was laid out in a grid formation it would be easy to get lost in Machu Picchu Market for quite some time.

Like most other things in Machu Picchu Pueblo, prices are a notch or two higher than other markets in the area but few tourists are able to resist the urge to pick up something unique on their way through the market to the train station. There's a colorful array of blankets, ponchos, bags and hats, as well as Andean instruments of every size and shape imaginable. If you're looking for something locally made and easy to transport, consider traditional Inca-style jewelry (such as pictured below) or locally grown organic coffee from valleys just downriver – they were producing beans long before the world had even heard of Machu Picchu.

FROM LEFT: BRENT HOFACKER/SHUTTERSTOCK, NICOLA MESSANA PHOTOS/SHUTTERSTOCK

BEST PLACES TO EAT & DRINK

Restaurante Amazonas $
Peruvian clientele come for great-value local, Chinese and international dishes. *9am-9pm Mon-Sat*

Cevicheria Fresco Mar $
Machupiccheños know that the freshest ceviche can be found here at local prices. *9am-5pm*

Kay Pacha $$
A great place for sunset cocktails while you watch the bustle from this 3rd floor terrace. *9am-10pm*

Minkay Wasi $$
Snack on empanadas while you sample fiery infused pisco (coca, *muña* – Andean mint, fruits). *7am-9pm*

Hike to Machu Picchu Ruins

For a more adventurous alternative to the typical bus ride, hike up (or down) the stepped Inca Trail between Machu Picchu Pueblo and the world-famous archaeological site.

HOW TO

Getting here: Simply set off downriver from Machu Picchu Pueblo, cross the bridge and follow the steps.

Difficulty: The hike is steep so take your time and allow two to three hours to get to the top and one hour to return. The route is well sign-posted and well maintained so you can't get lost.

Cost: The hike is free, but if you choose to bus up and walk down, buy a one-way ticket at the Consettur office on Av Hermanos Ayar. You'll need your passport and S40.

For some the return 7km hike from Machu Picchu Pueblo to the Machu Picchu archaeological site is a good way to test the strength of those thigh muscles after the Inca Trail. For others it's a little too much of a good thing and a bus ride up followed by the 3.5km descent on foot is more appealing. There are several shady picnic spots with good views along the way so consider getting provisions in town or, better still, buy a ham and cheese roll (a *classico*) from the vendors on the little terrace at the top of the steps.

The descent is unsurprisingly far easier than the climb up and can be done in around an hour. Take time, however, because the tangled jungle offers a wonderful chance to spot colorful birds and butterflies (and even, on occasion, bears). After about 10 minutes you'll see a section of stepped Inca terraces that are missed by visitors who journey on the buses.

Break your journey with a visit to Museo de Sitio Manuel Chávez Ballón (p174) or stop by the Mariposario Butterfly Gardens (right).

Above: Caracara; Right: Hikers en route to Machu Picchu

AGUAS CALIENTES' HISTORY

Machu Picchu Pueblo (sometimes known to locals as MaPi Pueblo or, more often, Aguas Calientes) has a fascinating history that might surprise visitors. When the American explorer Hiram Bingham passed this way in 1911, the little collection of timber shacks at the spot where the Ríos Aguas Calientes and Alcamayo flowed into the Urubamba was known only as La Maquina (the Machine). Historians believe that around 1867 a German adventurer called Augusto Berns had a timber yard here and, according to some sources, might even have looted Machu Picchu almost 50 years before Bingham supposedly 'discovered' the site.

Just an hour's walk down the Urubamba Valley, the small rural settlement of Mandor Pampa – an idyllic and unspoiled escape today – was the more important settlement back then. It was only after the railway was constructed in 1928 that La Maquina became famous for something more than hunks of rusting metal and Machu Picchu Pueblo came into existence.

MARK EVELEIGH

Butterfly, Mariposario

Visit a Butterfly Sanctuary

Home to stunning local butterfly species, **Mariposario** *(facebook.com/mariposasdemachupicchu; S20)* was established in 2006 by residents of Machu Picchu Pueblo as a sanctuary and research center committed to studying and preserving some of the region's most fascinating lepidoptera. An interpretation center, breeding laboratory and flight area allow visitors to get close to colorful species such as blue morphs, swallowtails and monarchs. Leave enough time to visit the cafe: perfectly positioned to look out over the river and forest, it is an exceptional spot for a bit of bird-watching.

Along the Way We Met...

ROSA SOLIS SALDIVAR People say Machu Picchu Pueblo is a rip-off and a tourist trap. They don't realize that this town is unavoidably expensive for locals too. I specialize in giving tourists a deeper insight into the uniquely cosmopolitan community that lives among the overcrowded high-rises and steep-staired favelas.

Rosa Solis Saldivar, born in Machu Picchu Pueblo, runs tours of her hometown. (WhatsApp: +51 990 725 647)

ROSA'S TIP: *Get to know the backstreet communities that keep the World Heritage Site functioning.*

Venture Out to Llactapata Ruins

Most activities in this area tend to come with a hefty price tag but here's a real adventure that will cost you very little. If Machu Picchu was the famous 'Lost City of the Incas' then Llactapata ruins has been described as the 'Lost Suburb.'

HOW TO

Getting here: Simply walk along the track beside the railway line from Machu Picchu Pueblo to Hidroeléctrica then turn up the Ahobamba Valley and follow signs.

Distance: The Llactapata ruins site is 16km from Machu Picchu Pueblo. Allow a leisurely six hours.

Cost: The site is free to access.

Where to stay: Llactapata Lodge is just a 20-minute walk from the ruins. Mandor Pampa Lodge is a delightful place to break the return journey.

Tip: Refrain from giving tidbits to the very friendly village dogs as it entices them to hang out on the railway tracks.

Despite being visible from Machu Picchu ruins, Llactapata ruins are so isolated that after Hiram Bingham first brought it to the attention of the broader world, it again effectively disappeared from wider public knowledge for several decades. Getting here is a big part of the adventure.

You can take the train from Machu Picchu Pueblo to the end of the line at Hidroeléctrica (one way S130) and begin the hike there. Better still, enjoy a gorgeous hike from Machu Picchu Pueblo with spellbinding views along the Urubamba and Ahobamba canyons. Allow one or two nights for a peaceful escape.

The Hiking Route

There are less than 5km between Machu Picchu ruins and Llactapata as the condor flies and yet the steep valleys meander so wildly that the 16km hike will take five to six hours. Most guides will tell you to set out walking through the railway tunnel next to town, but avoid the tunnel entirely by walking downhill toward the Machu Picchu Bridge and rejoin the track by the railway there. The 11km walk to Hidroeléctrica will take around two to three hours, with stops at eating places. From 'Hidro' a track leads up the Ahobamba Valley. A suspension bridge will take you across the river, but the steep climb to Llactapata is likely to take another three hours.

Llactapata Ruins

Llactapata archaeological site (2733m) appears deceptively small but most of the complex

FROM FAR LEFT: MARK EVELEIGH, HANA SCHUSTEROVA/SHUTTERSTOCK

WHERE TO STAY

Break your journey at family-run **Mandor Pampa Lodge** *(mandor.pe; $)*. Near the spot where Bingham camped, it's a private nature sanctuary that makes a restful alternative to accommodations in town.

With breathtaking views across the valley to Machu Picchu, **Llactapata Lodge** *(WhatsApp: +51 952 712 467; $)* is unforgettable for its easy access (just a 20-minute walk) to Llactapata ruins and the hearty home-cooked meals that Gisela and Felix serve up, which are included in the room price! Despite being supplied entirely by mules, the lodge has excellent facilities including solar hot water and wifi.

Left: Llactapata; Below: Río Ahobamba

is still covered by jungle. One theory is that the main temple's central corridor once supported a golden sheet that was used to reflect the sun during the June winter solstice. The ray of gilded sunlight would be re-directed at Machu Picchu, which, at 300m lower, would still have been shrouded in shadow. The effect would have been spectacular for a people who worshiped the sun.

Wild and isolated, Llactapata is a wonderful contrast to the regimented walking trails and crowds at Machu Picchu. It's a privilege to explore the jungle, amid ancient masonry, haunted by colorful birds and even bears.

MARK EVELEIGH

Train travels along Río Urubamba
MATTHEW WILLIAMS-ELLIS/GETTY IMAGES

INSIGHT

Riding Back to the Beginning

After the final steps into Machu Picchu, it's time to revisit your journey in reverse. Memories of your experience on the ancient pilgrimage flood to mind - and some come to vision - as you come full circle, arriving back where you started.

WORDS BY **AGNES RIVERA**
Agnes wrote this after her fourth train ride from Aguas Calientes to Ollantaytambo in three years.

A Sacred River

Not long after touring the terraced citadel of Machu Picchu, you'll likely find yourself in another queue, this time to board a return train at the Machu Picchu Pueblo (Aguas Calientes) station. The scenic departure to the Sacred Valley and then onward to Cusco is a journey that unwinds the Inca Trail in reverse. If walking the trail was an adventurous pilgrimage through the past, then it's only fitting that the ride back is a meditative return to the present. And there to constantly guide you is the Río Urubamba.

Hushed by the huffs and puffs of the locomotive warming up to its 40kph pace and the excited, multilingual chatter of other passengers, the Río Urubamba rushes into view as the trail pulls past a group of white stucco buildings, the final signs of the tourist town. It's a near two-hour, 43km ride to the Ollantaytambo station, then another hour and a half to complete the 92km journey to Cusco.

Fed by high Andean glaciers near La Raya Pass (4335m), between the regions of Cusco and Puno the snaking river is referred to as Vilcanota. Flowing through the Sacred Valley, it connects the major Inca towns of Pisac and Ollantaytambo, then undergoes a name change to Urubamba. After wrapping around three sides of Machu Picchu, flanked by tropical foliage and the massive boulders it has polished with time, the river merges with the Ríos Ucayali and Marañón, before eventually connecting to the Amazon.

> The rhythm of the train, a gentle rocking side to side, is reminiscent of hiking boots hitting the ancient trail, landing upon uneven stones

Heading against the northbound current of the watercourse, the train curls through tight canyons, bends around sheer rock faces and – when it's not possible to navigate around them – dips beneath the mountainsides via tunnels. It's like a low-slung Inca Trail. And just as the multiday trek traverses high-altitude microclimates, the change in vegetation witnessed through the train windows is as though you've pressed rewind on the memories of your unforgettable hiking journey: ascending from the humid subtropics back into the Andean highlands.

The large windows are curtained by just-beyond-reach verdant broad-leafed trees. Flashes of color appear and vanish: the fiery talon-shaped flowers in the branches of pisonays (a favorite nectar-rich food for beaked creatures), red and yellow bracts of heliconias perched below, and the purple of wild morning glories wrapping around the bases of tree trunks.

Referred to as Willkamayu (sacred river) in Quechua and later Hispanicized to Vilcanota, the rushing river dictates the train journey, just as it did the agricultural and spiritual beliefs of the Incas. It was believed to be a mirror of the Milky Way – two rivers: one terrestrial, another celestial. The sacred river was the threshold between the earthly *(kay pacha)* and the ancestral worlds above *(hanan pacha)* and below *(ukhu pacha)*.

The rhythm of the train, a gentle rocking side to side, is reminiscent of hiking boots hitting the ancient trail, landing upon uneven stones, or the rapids of the river passing by. At times it veers away from the body of water, only to round a curve and be pulled back toward this guiding and magnetizing force. The Incas were drawn to build some of their most important constructions near these banks precisely because of the river's bounty and significance.

Memories of Recent Archaeological Sightings

Landscapes of various palettes and densities open further as the altitude rises; from Machu Picchu Pueblo to Ollantayambo the gain is 700m, which will be matched by the time the train pulls into its final destination, Cusco. Opaque rainforest gives way to bamboo, and bamboo to open grassland, and eventually agricultural fields as you near Ollantaytambo.

At Km 104, where trekkers opting for the two-day Inca Trail begin their hike, a wooden footbridge coolly straddles the rushing river. For those who've completed either the Classic or the shorter version, the modern construction triggers visions of the Wiñay Wayna archaeological site, a short hike away.

Occasionally the train pauses, as if to catch its breath. At one resting period, well beyond the limits of the cloud forest, still frames of eucalyptus trees appear. An introduced evergreen, the stiff branches lean eternally west from decades of harsh winds funneled through the valley. An oncoming parade of train cars brushes past and, once again, the east-bound locomotive continues forth, past the hamlet of Pampacahua, where bursts of orange and pink lantana bloom and tuna fruit ripen in the dry air.

Near Km 88 and on the opposite side of the river, the terraces of Qorihuayrachina (Quechua for 'where the wind refines gold') run down toward the water's edge and scale the base of mountains like rows of empty seats in an amphitheater. Covering over 5 sq km, the hilltop complex of dwellings and towers was brought to global attention at the turn of the 21st century, with research pointing to it having been an administrative center and former checkpoint. Victim to heavy rains in 2010, what remains is visited by those who start their Inca Trail journey at Km 88.

SIMONMAYER/GETTY IMAGES

Trackside scenery

As the train rolls through a tunnel, a roughly 10m passage through a massive boulder, the flash of darkness is an opportunity to imagine how these sturdy terraces must have appeared in the centuries prior to the Spanish conquest, brimming with medicinal plants, maize and quinoa.

> Your time traversing the mountains suddenly feels worlds away as the train slows to 35kph, giving you one last chance to imprint the sensory memories collected over the past four days

As the river leads the train around another bend, Apu Wakay Willka reveals herself – a glacial guardian rising to 5860m. Meaning 'sacred tears,' her Quechua name is rarely used; instead, she is commonly referred to by her Spanish name, Veronica. During the trek, she played peekaboo behind closer mountains and often wore a veil of clouds. Now unobscured, cellphones rise in unison to snap her photo as if she wore the sly smile of *Mona Lisa*. In brutal reality, the Wakay Willka snowcap melts into tears, her original name more fitting than ever.

Back at eye-level, the curved terraces of Salapunku, a *tambo* (rest house) with pre-Inca origins, appear startlingly close to the north-facing windows of the train car. Located at Km 84, at the intersection of Ollantaytambo with the Machu Picchu region, the site was likely a guardpost. It is believed that ceremonies, as well as a shrine dedicated to the *apu* (mountain spirits), were held onsite as Salapunku faces Wakay Willka. A trapezoidal doorway to the lower left of the site would have been difficult to see from the viewpoint across the river at the beginning of the trek – but if you look quick enough while on board the train, its gaping black insides appear like an alluring portal to this low-sitting ruin.

Familiar Markers

Two kilometers later, seen through the south-side-facing windows is the footbridge at Km 82, the swaying starting line of the Classic Inca Trail. Seeing it from this angle sparks simultaneous disbelief and self-congratulatory been-there, done-that pride. But it also feels like the perfect closing of an imperfect circle: rather than back-tracking through the same mountain-defined paths, your near arrival to the beginning has been shaped by water, a symbol of continuity as well as transformation.

Though you can't yet feel it on your shower-deprived skin, the increasingly dry air is visibly apparent in the change in vegetation upon the countryside. Resilient yellow *retama* shrubs, skirted by the native Andean *chilca (Baccharis latifolia),* soon give way to fava beans and corn on mono-level agricultural plots. Occasional *mototaxis* (three-wheeled motorcycle rickshaw taxis) and motorbikes flash by on dusty roads running parallel to the rails and in front of small adobe homes with rectangular doors.

Your time traversing the mountains suddenly feels worlds away as the train slows to 35kph, giving you one last chance to imprint the sensory memories collected over the past few days: the singsong of endemic Andean birds, gusts of high-rising wind kissing your cheeks and breezing through dry grass, the tingle of coca leaves easing the climb up slick stone – and the bittersweet ache in your chest at catching your first glimpse of Machu Picchu through Inti-punku, relinquishing your peregrination days.

Just before sunset the train glides into Ollantaytambo and comes to a halt. Even the clouds are motionless in the late afternoon sky. Travelers, coming and going, spill onto the platform, some beginning their journey, others returning to where they started. And just like that, without a show of goodbye or prolonged farewell, our guide, the sacred Willkamayu, has disappeared from view, trusting we will find our way home.

Río Urubamba

IRYNA SAVINA/SHUTTERSTOCK

OTHER ROUTES AROUND THE INCA TRAIL

If you wish to hike your way to Machu Picchu but want to skip the advance planning and large expense of walking the Inca Trail, you will be glad to know there are other incredible routes to choose from. The Salkantay Trek is considered the best alternative to the Inca Trail, and is as popular as it is challenging. The Lares Trek is an off-the-beaten-track gem. Both take you to Machu Picchu. The Choquequirao Trek explores a spectacular Inca ruin that is three times the size of Machu Picchu and nowhere near as crowded. Add in some day hikes from Cusco and you'll find there are many paths to adventure beyond the Inca Trail.

Hiker, Lares Trek (p220)

AJWOMER/SHUTTERSTOCK

Challacancha

Voted one of the 25 best hikes in the world by National Geographic's *Adventure Travel Magazine* and Peru's second most popular trek after the legendary Inca Trail (but without the need for all the permits), the Salkantay Trek is great for anyone wanting to experience a challenging, yet rewarding, hike that ends in Machu Picchu. The emphasis here is on dramatic and varied natural landscapes. While the majority of people join a tour group, many hikers go solo. Whichever way you choose, note that this hike is best undertaken by experienced hikers.

Vesna Maric

Mt Salkantay (p199)

SAHARSH AGGARWAL/SHUTTERSTOCK

Machu Picchu

SALKANTAY TREK

74.5KM
4 DAYS' WALK

THIS LEG:

- Challacancha
- Soraypampa
- Humantay Lake
- Salkantay Pass
- Huayracmachay
- Chaullay
- Santa Teresa Valley
- La Playa Sahuayaco
- Lucmabamba
- Llactapata
- Hidroeléctrica
- Machu Picchu Pueblo
- Machu Picchu Archaeological Site

Walking Notes

The Salkantay Trek is a challenging hike, with long and demanding days. The first two days require hiking at a very high altitude, and the second two are a descent through the rainforest. Most complete the walk in four days, with days two and four covering some 24km each. The weather and terrain are changeable, but the views are always spectacular.

Breaking Your Journey

Distances between accommodation and food stops are long, but overnight stops generally include Soraypampa (day one), Collpapampa (day two), Lucmabamba (day three) and Machu Picchu Pueblo (day four), with some adding an extra overnight in Llactapata (day four) to break up the longest leg.

Vesna's Tips

BEST MEAL Dinner or breakfast at Lia B&B by Fredy & Esther (p205) in Lucmabamba.

TOP VIEW Getting a glimpse of Machu Picchu from Llactapata (p204).

FAVORITE STOP Tasting fresh local coffee at a coffee farm (p203) in Lucmabamba.

TIP Keep pack weight to a minimum and take lots of layers. You'll have all weathers in a day.

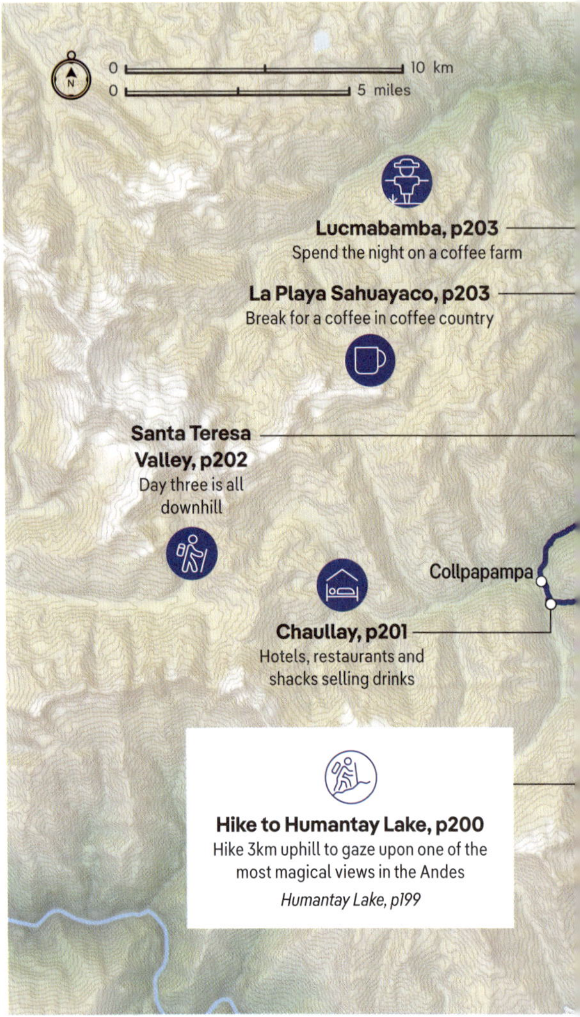

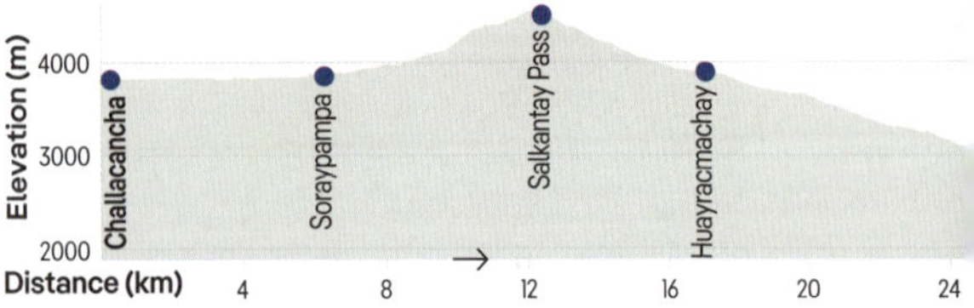

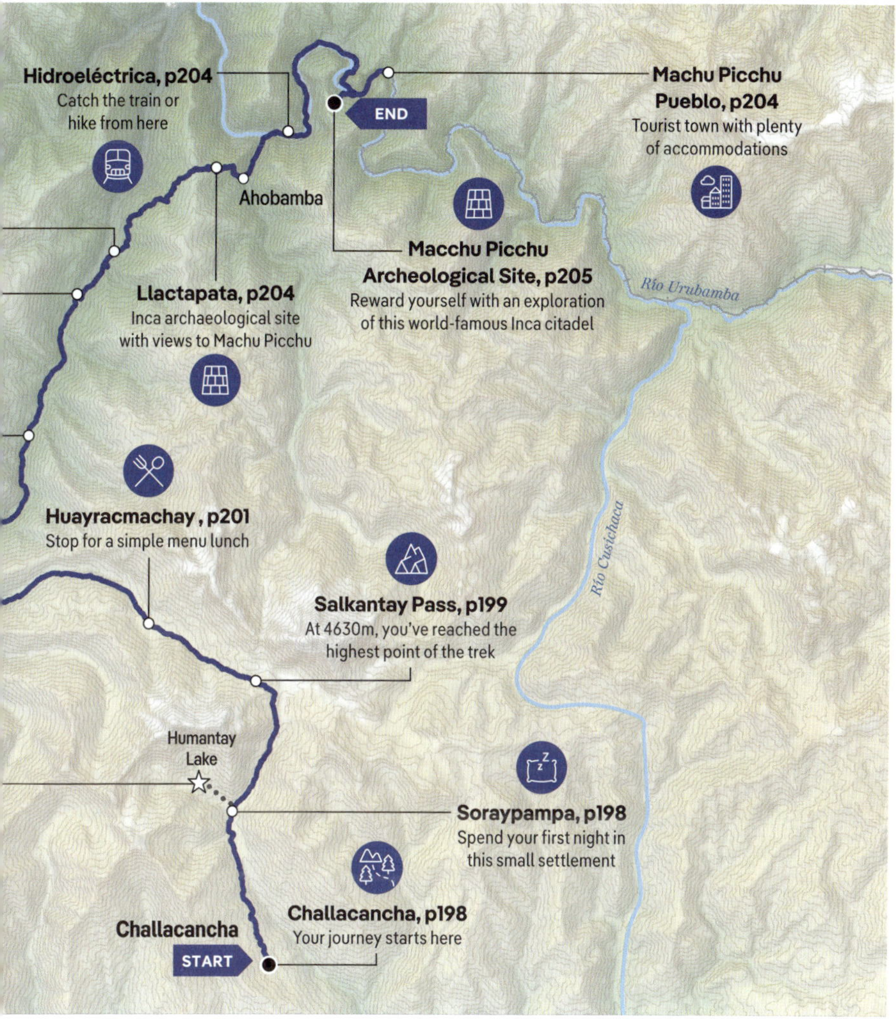
Hidroeléctrica, p204
Catch the train or hike from here
Ahobamba
END
Machu Picchu Pueblo, p204
Tourist town with plenty of accommodations
Macchu Picchu Archeological Site, p205
Reward yourself with an exploration of this world-famous Inca citadel
Río Urubamba
Llactapata, p204
Inca archaeological site with views to Machu Picchu
Huayracmachay , p201
Stop for a simple menu lunch
Río Cusichaca
Salkantay Pass, p199
At 4630m, you've reached the highest point of the trek
Humantay Lake
Soraypampa, p198
Spend your first night in this small settlement
Challacancha, p198
Your journey starts here
Challacancha
START

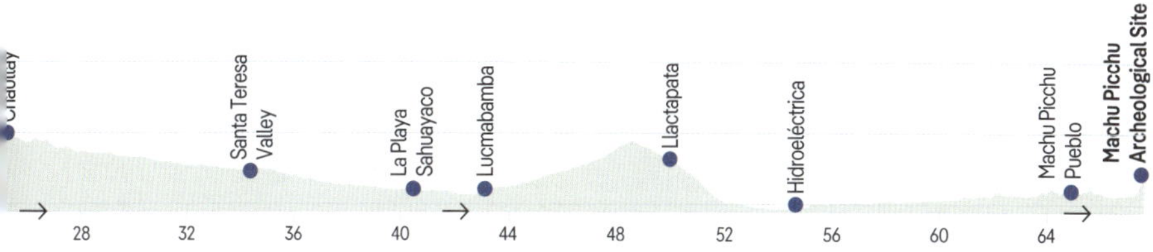
Santa Teresa Valley
La Playa Sahuayaco
Lucmabamba
Llactapata
Hidroeléctrica
Machu Picchu Pueblo
Machu Picchu Archeological Site
28
32
36
40
44
48
52
56
60
64

GETTING THERE You'll start all your hiking days early, but day one of the Salkantay Trek is super early, when the streets of Cusco are full of sleepy hikers mostly setting off in guided groups. If you've opted for a guided trek, your tour operator will pick you up in Cusco. If you've decided to hike independently, set off as early as 3:30am or 4am, either by bus (S15) or taxi (S110). Buses depart from Cusco's Arcopata Terminal, while a private taxi can usually be arranged by your hotel or hostel. It's a 2¼-hour drive to the tiny town of Mollepata, where you must get your municipal access permit (S20). Grab a quick breakfast and good coffee at **Tilcafe**, then catch a taxi to Challacancha (S50), the trail head, which takes another hour on a serpentine mountain road.

Challacancha

Leave all the transportation behind and get your limbs moving with a moderate 7km (three-hour) hike from Challacancha to Soraypampa, where you'll be spending your first night. En route there are incredibly beautiful views of the high mountains with their low shrubbery and brown colors, and snowy peaks all around. As you hike this part of the trail, you will gain around 100m in elevation, rising from 3800m at Challacancha to 3900m in Soraypampa. Although the gain is low here, the altitude may make it feel more demanding. This is a good stretch to work out how affected you might be by the altitude, before hitting the relatively short, but demanding, hike to Humantay Lake in the early afternoon. Drink plenty of water to manage altitude sickness.

Once you've left Challacancha, there are no snack shacks or facilities until you reach Soraypampa. It often rains up here, so make sure you've got your rain poncho handy.

Soraypampa

FROM LEFT: JOAO D'ANDRETTA/SHUTTERSTOCK, MILTON RODRIGUEZ/SHUTTERSTOCK

Soraypampa

If you set out early, you should be in Soraypampa (3900m) by noon. This very basic settlement is based mostly around accommodations for group and solo hikers, run by a few local families. Either find your accommodations on the go or locate your pre-booked place, and get some lunch at your hostel. There are no 'restaurants' as such as all hostels here serve food, and meals are included in the price of a room.

Challacancha

7km

Your day begins with an early start in Cusco

Hikers en route to Humantay Lake

DETOUR: Humantay Lake

After lunch and some rest start the hike up to the stunning Humantay Lake (p200). Allow around three hours for the 3km up-and-down trek, as the consistent ascent at high altitude means most hikers need to pace themselves carefully. Return to Soraypampa for dinner and your first night on the trail.

Salkantay Pass

Wake up at the crack of dawn for a good breakfast before beginning the hardest day of your hike. Try to get going by around 6am, when the sun has just risen, so that you can

Continues on p201

SACRED APUS

As you hike the Salkantay Trek, especially on days one and two, you'll not find it hard to understand why the Incas worshiped these powerful mountains. Protective deities that watch over human and animal communities, they are known locally as *apus*.

The Cusco region has three *apus*: the majestic peaks of Apu Salkantay (6271m), Apu Ausangate (6372m) – the region's highest mountain and the fifth-highest peak in Peru – and Apu Veronica (5860m), located in the Sacred Valley. Apu Veronica's original Quechua name is Wakay Willca, meaning 'sacred tear' or 'sacred weeping mountain.'

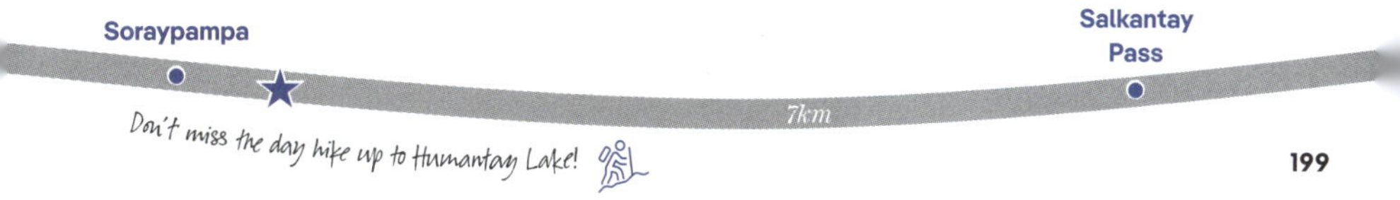

Hike to Humantay Lake

The hike to Humantay Lake from Soraypampa can be undertaken as a detour on the Salkantay Trek or as a standalone day hike for those who want to see Andean beauty without a multiday commitment.

HOW TO

Nearest stop: Soraypampa

Altitude: 4200m

Distance: 3km

Time: Allow three hours for walking, plus 30 minutes at the lake

Getting here: From Cusco, get a bus, van or private taxi to Mollepata, where you'll pick up your municipality pass. From there, get a taxi to Soraypampa, and return to Cusco by evening. The trailhead is clearly marked from the main path in the settlement.

Horse rentals: Soraypampa locals rent horses (S90) for the uphill climb at the start of the hike to the lake.

One of the loveliest day hikes in the area, the trek up to Humantay Lake is quite demanding due to the lake's altitude. The up-and-down trail is well marked, but the terrain is rocky and has slippery sections. Although it's only a day hike, you should prepare well, ensuring you are equipped with a good rain poncho, proper hiking boots and so on. As you huff and puff up the hill, take regular breaks and drink lots of water.

As you emerge at the lake, gasping for breath, you'll find yourself in one of the dreamiest spots in the Andes. The lake's turquoise waters are a mirror reflecting the glacier behind, and the reflection of the layers of mountain rocks in the water forms a beautiful geometry. Wait for the hiking groups to disperse and spend a moment or two of peace and quiet in this magical scenery. Gazing upon it, you will surely feel in awe of nature and gratitude for life and its beauty.

At the end of the day, you'll have had a taste of the start of the Salkantay Trek and the incredible natural landscapes of the Cusco region.

Humantay Lake

ETZON QR/SHUTTERSTOCK

Continued from p199

stay ahead of most tour groups – the path can get quite crowded! The trail up to the pass is easy to follow, as there's just one path.

The day begins with the 7km (three-hour) ascent to the highest point of thc hike, Salkantay Pass (4630m). Salkantay (6271m) is Cusco region's second-highest mountain and is one of the sacred peaks, known as *apus* (p110), of the Peruvian Andes. Apu Salkantay's incredible power is very much in evidence as you climb the difficult ascent known as the Path of the Seven Snakes – a tight, serpentine path that winds relentlessly up. Once at the top, you will have a magnificent view over the surrounding valleys: Salkantay will be the one directly facing you.

Note that the pass is often covered in low cloud, and can be quite windy and cold. If you're lucky and it's clear, you'll be able to get some great photos and see Humantay, Tucarhuay, and Pumasillo mountains. Weather permitting, stop for a snack here – there are no facilities on the pass itself, so bring your own – or if the weather is bad, carry on down toward the village of Huayracmachay for a break.

Huayracmachay

You will descend 7km (allow an hour and a half) from Salkantay Pass toward the village of Huayracmachay (3850m). This is a rocky, steep section and you will need to pay attention to where you step. If you have any knee problems, you'll feel them on this stretch. Pause and take in the impressive views of the surrounding valley. If you're carrying a filter water bottle, the glacial streams that flow off the mountain to the left of the trail are a great spot to refill. When you reach the rural settlement of Huayracmachay,

NELL REID/SHUTTERSTOCK

Salkantay Pass

you'll find a few small restaurants that serve a menu lunch (S15).

Chaullay

After leaving Huayracmachay you'll enter the Andean cloud forest – the lush edge of the rainforest. Hiking this 9.5km stretch (allow 3½ hours), the landscapes traveled through this morning will seem like a bizarre memory. It's a rare experience to begin a day of walking in the barren, mossy Andes and end it in the lush Amazon! As you walk you'll be surrounded by tropical forest and you'll notice the temperature increase significantly.

The easy-to-follow path guides you down a fairly gentle descent on a dirt track all the way to Chaullay. Note that there are biting insects galore, so apply your repellent! In Chaullay (2860m) you'll find hostels with restaurants and shacks selling snacks and drinks.

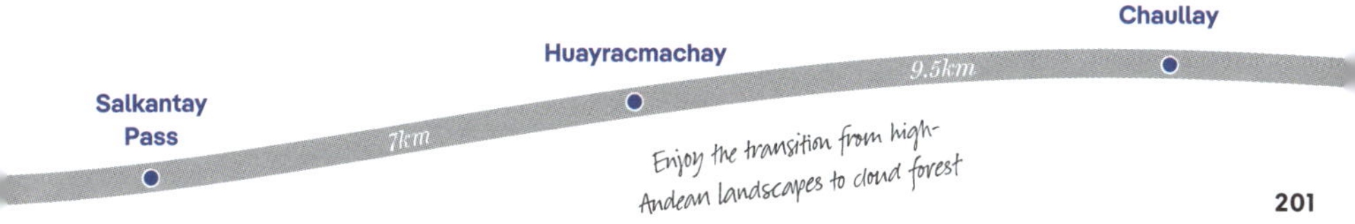

Horse, Salkantay Trek
ORORU/SHUTTERSTOCK

TREKKING WITH A TOUR COMPANY

Most people join a tour company from Cusco to tackle the Salkantay Trek – it's in fact the ultimate group experience for many hikers. Expect groups of around 10 to 15 people and prices starting from US$650 per person for a four-day hike.

Sleeping is in tents or domes, depending on the company. All tours include local guides. Cooks and horses take your luggage (5kg maximum), and the rest of your luggage can be stored by the company for the duration of the trek. You will be picked up and dropped off in Cusco. All your meals are cooked for you at the company accommodations site, and your accommodations and meal(s) in Machu Picchu Pueblo (also known as Aguas Calientes) are also organized, together with transportation, admission and a guide to the Machu Picchu archaeological site.

If you choose to go with an agency, remember that you have to tip your guides, cooks and horse handlers at the end of your trip. Apart from that all you need to do is – walk!

Santa Teresa Valley

Getting up bright and early in Chaullay, have yourself a good breakfast and walk a short distance along the main road through the settlement of **Collpapampa.** Coming out of town, there are several smaller paths that lead off the main road and many hikers get confused here. Generally, these are shortcuts that all lead down to the Santa Teresa Valley. Look for the path with a green safety rail that veers off to the left river bank, just before the road crosses the river – if you're feeling lost, this single-track trail is a safe bet. You can also stick to the main road or follow a tour group. You'll be walking 17km today (allow five to six hours) and it's all downhill.

Along the Way We Saw...

ANDEAN COCK-OF-THE-ROCK 'What is this strange pig-like noise,' we wondered as we descended through the cloud forest. Then we spotted a bright orange/scarlet bird with an oddly shaped head and black-and-white wings – a thing of strange beauty because it was hard to locate its beak! It was not until later, when we could search for it online, that we realized we had seen Peru's national bird known locally as *tunqui,* the so-called Andean cock-of-the-rock *(Rupicola peruvianus),* named for its vague resemblance to a rooster. This gorgeous bird lives in the cloud forests of the Andes, so take your binoculars with you and keep your eyes peeled!

Vesna Maric

Following the single path through the forest, you will soon reach a steep section that forks at the top – keep right and you will gradually emerge at the river course. Descending through the Santa Teresa Valley you'll see waterfalls, birds, hot springs and fruit trees. If you're lucky, you may spot the national bird of Peru, the Andean cock-of-the-rock *(Rupicola peruvianus),* with its bright red head and black-and-white wings. Listen out for its spectacular snorting sound. About an hour into the walk, you will walk past passion-fruit plantations and **fresh fruit shacks** selling freshly squeezed juice – a great opportunity for a short break before continuing on your way.

La Playa Sahuayaco

As you approach the settlement of La Playa Sahuayaco, the trail splits again. Stay on the left bank of the river and cross the bridge if you want to stay in La Playa, but consider continuing on to Lucmabamba (elevation 2000m), another hour away, as it's a much better option.

If you are tired and want to catch a van into Lucmabamba from La Playa Sahuayaco, you'll need to reach the main road. In this case, cross to the right along the riverbank and walk across a small suspension bridge then hike up the trail to the road. As you enter La Playa, there's a **cafe** where you can stop for a coffee break if you wish – this is coffee land, after all! Look for a double-story, wooden restaurant with 'Coffee' signs.

Lucmabamba

Plan to spend your third night on the trail at one of the **coffee farms** in Lucmabamba, where breakfast, hot showers, dinner, coffee and a tour of the plantation are all included in the price of a bed for the night. On the coffee plantation tour, you'll learn all about coffee plants and the process of picking and fermenting coffee. You will even get to roast and grind your own beans for a fresh cup. Peru's excellent-quality coffee is exported worldwide – it is a primary agricultural industry in the jungle.

Llactapata

Day four – the final day of the Salkantay Trek for most people – involves an intense day of walking to Machu Picchu Pueblo (Aguas Calientes), but you can break this day up by hiking to Llactapata and spending the night there. The trail is signposted off the main road, but ask a local to make sure you're heading in the right direction – many solo hikers have taken the wrong path and added extra kilometres to an already long day.

Ascend the mountainside through coffee plantations on a steep, winding trail. It takes two to three hours to reach the top point of the path from where you'll enjoy expansive views of the Santa Teresa Valley all the way. Mind that the path is very rocky, muddy and slippery here, especially if it has been raining. Entering a bamboo forest, the trail flattens out and the path forks: if you take the left branch (signposted as a shortcut to Hidroeléctrica) for a few minutes, you'll come to a **viewpoint** where you might get your first glance of Machu Picchu citadel in the distance. There is also a **snack shack** that sells sandwiches, juice and coffee.

The bonus part of this bit of the trek is that it joins the original Inca Trail – retrace your steps and return to the main path, then take the right fork to the **Llactapata ruins** (p186), an Inca archaeological site with views of Machu Picchu in the distance. From the ruins, it's a steep 1½- to two-hour downhill walk to **Ahobamba** and the river valley.

Hidroeléctrica

At the river valley, cross the bridge and follow the road to Hidroeléctrica (1800m), home to an impressive 250m-tall artificial **waterfall**, which generates electricity for the entire city of Cusco. Just before Hidroeléctrica is a checkpoint where you will need to show your passport. Have lunch in Hidroeléctrica at one of the several generic roadside restaurants that serve soup and rice dishes for around S15.

Machu Picchu viewed from Salkantay Trek

DANIELPRUDEK/GETTY IMAGES

From here, you can get a train to Machu Picchu Pueblo (Aguas Calientes): tickets are available online via the Peru Rail website *(perurail.com)* or you can purchase them at the Hidroeléctrica train station.

Otherwise, it's another 10km (around three hours) to Machu Picchu Pueblo, walking along the railway for a final flat and scenic stretch.

Machu Picchu Pueblo

Most hikers are very sore and tired by the time they arrive in Machu Picchu Pueblo (p180), so it's highly recommended that you book your accommodations in advance. There

is a whole range of options – from fancy hotels to backpacker hostels – and you'll be glad to be able to go straight to your bed rather than have to look for accommodations on the spot.

Machu Picchu Archaeological Site

If you still have energy to spare, climb the 1700 stairs from Machu Picchu Pueblo to the citadel (p184). It's a beautiful climb through lush forest, but it's hard going, especially after several days of hiking. Many feel it's the best way to reach Machu Picchu archaeological site (p166), and the very thought of seeing this impressive sight is enough to spur hikers on.

Otherwise, you can catch a **bus** *(comprar .caminoalamaravilla.com; one way S82; 25 minutes)* to the site, which must be booked in advance. Registered guides flaunt their services outside the entry gate and charge around S50 per person – hiring one will definitely enhance your experience.

BEST PLACES TO SLEEP

Refugio Nacho $
Wooden huts with glass roofs come with wi-fi, but no heating or hot water. Basic dinner and breakfast included. *(refugionachosoraypampa.com; Soraypampa)*

Soraypampa Hostel $
Wooden huts with wi-fi, outdoor toilets and cold showers. Basic but filling dinner and breakfast included. *(soraypampahostel.org; Soraypampa)*

Salkantay Hostel Chaullay $
Good rooms with private bathrooms and hot showers. Delicious dinners of rice, avocado and chicken, and a generous breakfast, are included. *(salkantayhostelperu.com; Chaullay)*

Lia B&B by Fredy & Esther $
Wonderful coffee farm stay. Includes dinner, breakfast, coffee, a tour of the plantation and comfortable rooms with hot showers. *(fredy-bb-lucmabamba.cuzco-hotels.com; Lucmabamba)*

Llactapata Lodge $
Stunning spot with endless views, encompassing Machu Picchu in the distance. Dinner and breakfast included. *(llactapatalodge.com; Llactapata)*

Soraypampa Hostel

JON CHICA/SHUTTERSTOCK

Cachora

Of all the Inca Trails near Cusco, none are as challenging as the Choquequirao Trek, whose path plunges steeply into the Cañón del Apurímac before clawing its way up the other side in endless switchbacks. Of course, big challenges come with big rewards, including Inca ruins far larger – though less excavated – than Machu Picchu. Channel your inner Lara Croft or Indiana Jones and become one of the few tourists to explore Choquequirao.

Mark Johanson

Choquequirao ruins (p216)
YURI ZVEZDNY/SHUTTERSTOCK ©

Choquequirao

CHOQUEQUIRAO TREK

60KMS
4 DAYS' WALK

THIS LEG:

- Cachora
- Saywite
- Capuliyoc
- Cocamasana
- Chiquisca
- Playa Rosalinas
- Santa Rosa
- Marampata
- Choquequirao Base Camp
- On to Machu Picchu

Walking Notes

Choquequirao is not for first-time hikers, nor those out of practice. This is a tough trail full of demanding hairpin turns – though you can tackle it over as many days as you'd like. Be sure to visit during the dry season (May to October) or in the shoulder months (April and November); at other times it can be dangerously slippery and infuriatingly buggy.

Breaking Your Journey

Unless you're making the arduous journey onward to Machu Picchu (eight days in total), the Choquequirao Trek will be round-trip from Capuliyoc. Most hike it in four days, three nights. Those carrying their own camping gear might factor in five days. Extremely fit hikers sleeping and eating in guesthouses could do it in three, but it's a grueling feat.

Mark's Tips

BEST MEAL A pre-hike feast of *lomo saltado* (stir-fried beef with onions, tomatoes, potatoes and chili) at Cachora Bar Restaurant (p211)

FAVOURITE VIEW Choquequirao and the Cañón del Apurímac from the ceremonial platform of Ushnu (p216).

ESSENTIAL STOP I love the villagers in Marampata (p213), who are always eager for trail gossip.

TIP Hire a horse in Capuliyoc (p210), or a mule to carry your gear.

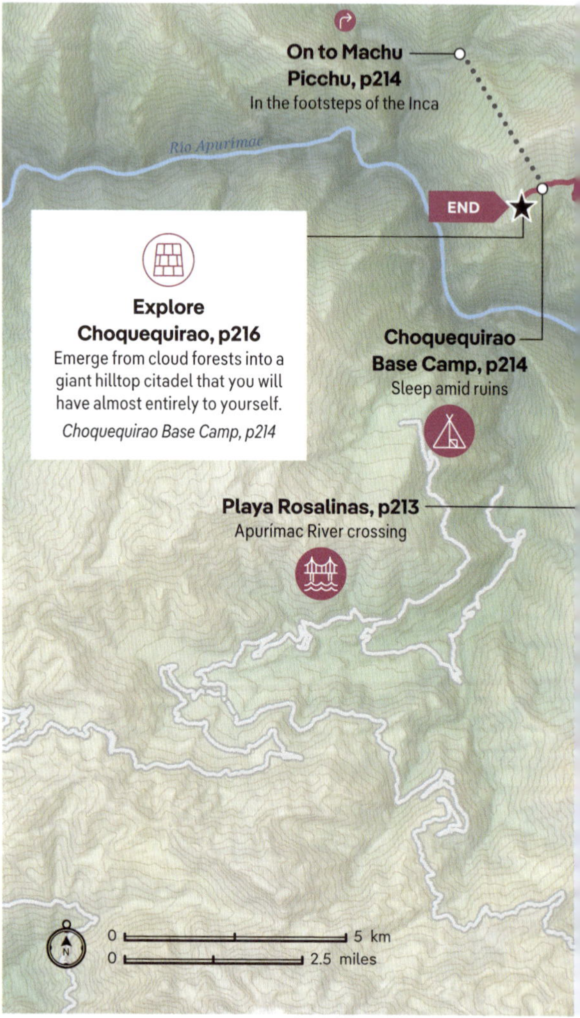

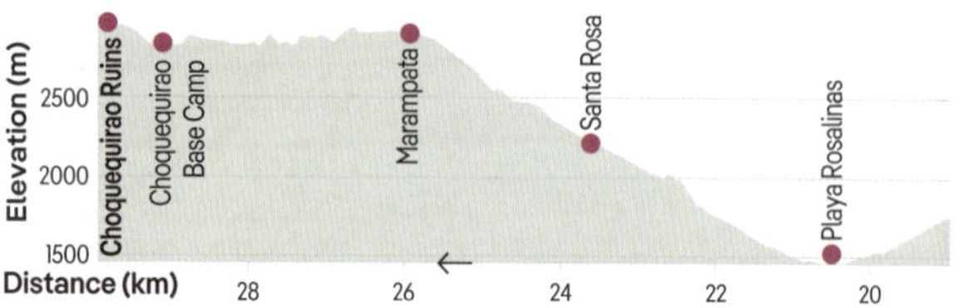

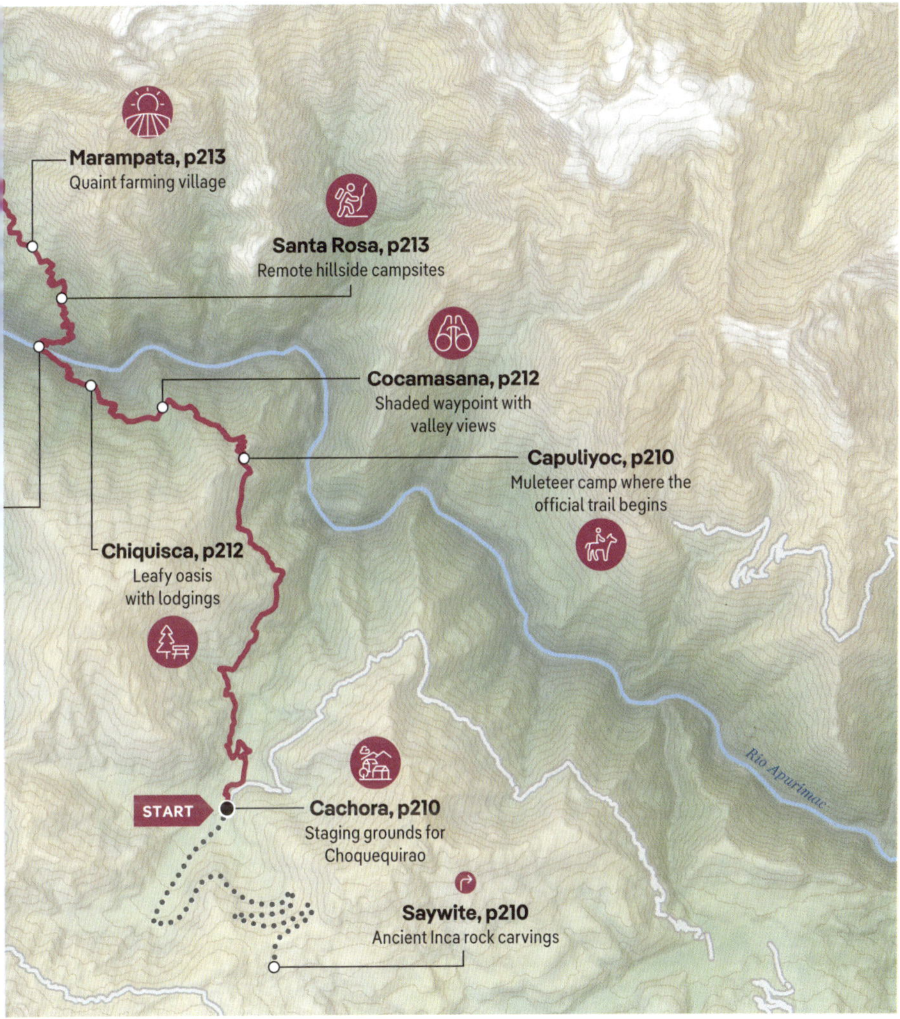
Marampata, p213
Quaint farming village
Santa Rosa, p213
Remote hillside campsites
Cocamasana, p212
Shaded waypoint with valley views
Capuliyoc, p210
Muleteer camp where the official trail begins
Chiquisca, p212
Leafy oasis with lodgings
START
Cachora, p210
Staging grounds for Choquequirao
Saywite, p210
Ancient Inca rock carvings
Río Apurímac

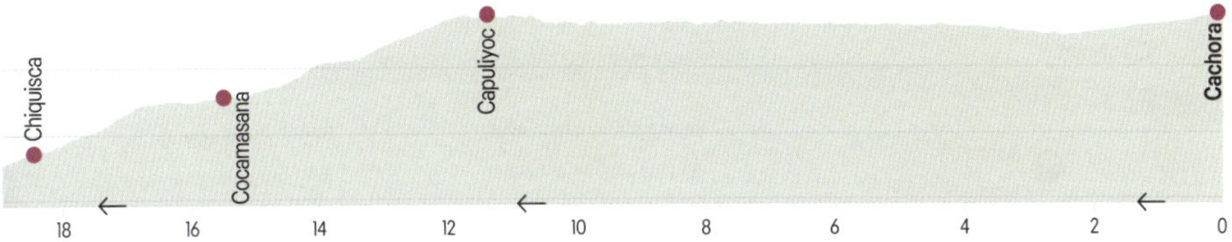
Chiquisca
Cocamasana
Capuliyoc
Cachora
18
16
14
12
10
8
6
4
2
0

GETTING THERE There are two ways to Cachora from Cusco. The fastest (a little under four hours) is to catch a *colectivo* (share taxi) to Curahuasi from Cusco's Paradero a Curahuasi on Av Arcopata, then a second *colectivo* from Curahuasi to Cachora. Alternatively, from Cusco's Terminal Terrestre, take any bus headed to Abancay and ask the driver to let you off at Ramal de Cachora, near Saywite. Then, take a *colectivo* the final 15km to Cachora. Plan to depart around 7am, as there are less options later in the day.

Cachora

Cachora is the charming, flower-filled mountain town from which most trekkers stage their journeys to Choquequirao. Settle into one of the lovely valley-facing guesthouses such as **Casa de Salcantay** (p215) or **CasaNostra Choquequirao** (p215), both of which will store any excess baggage while you're gone. Take some time to wander around Cachora's shaded plaza, with its adobe **Iglesia San Pedro** and small tourist information panels. You've got a big day ahead, so grab a calorie-heavy dinner at **Cachora Bar Restaurant** (right) or **Inca Dream** (right), the two most established restaurants in town.

NOMADKATE/SHUTTERSTOCK

Cachora

DETOUR: Saywite

The **Inca ruins of Saywite** *(S15)* lie just off the main highway from Cusco, near the turnoff for Cachora, making them a great detour for amateur archaeologists. Quiet and lightly visited, this ceremonial complex was likely dedicated to the cult of fertility and water, as evidenced by the stone canals, fountains and pools. The site is perhaps best known for its remarkable **Saywite Monolith**, an intricately carved boulder that depicts a miniature world of terraces, animals, waterways and ritual spaces. Two meters long by 4m wide, it's believed to represent an Inca hydraulic model. The complex surrounding the monolith includes ceremonial platforms, a solar clock and lookout points with sweeping views of nearby peaks. Saywite takes less than an hour to explore, but lets you engage closely with Inca craftsmanship and symbolism.

Capuliyoc

Capuliyoc gets its name from the capuli, or wild cherry trees, which grow here in abundance. The 11km stretch of farmland linking

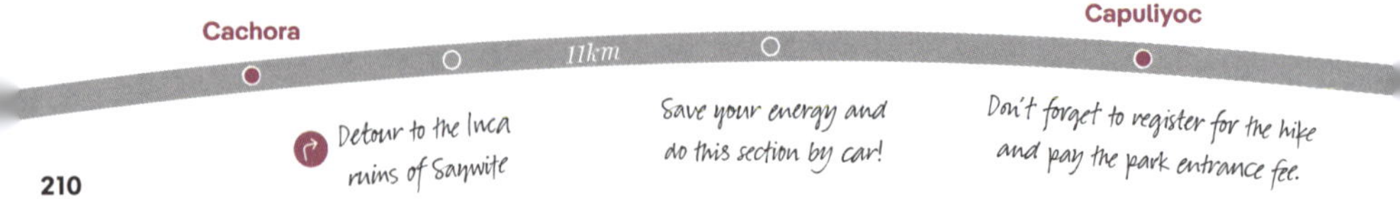

it with Cachora was once considered the start of the Choquequirao Trek. Yet, over the past decade, the former trail has morphed into a well-maintained road, and most hikers now zoom past in a 30-minute *colectivo* ride. Ask your driver to go slow as it's a thin road on the side of a cliff with no railings! Plus, the scenery here is lovely and pastoral, with fields of potatoes and corn leading down to farms of lima beans. Look out for condors in the sky above, which locals view as a good sign of a healthy harvest.

Unlike Cachora, Capuliyoc is more of a muleteer station than a proper town. Trekkers on guided trips typically load their gear onto mules here and hire 'emergency horses' – which tired hikers can use on the uphill legs. There are a few stalls where you can buy last-minute snacks or clothes, and have a final meal. Then, before departing along the cliff's edge, you'll need to pay an entrance fee for **Parque Arqueologico de Choquequirao** *(S60; entry 7am-4pm)* and register your name in the guest log.

BEST PLACES TO EAT

Cachora Bar Restaurant, Cachora $$
Busy spot on the plaza with the largest menu – and dishes! – around, including hearty Peruvian staples. *(instagram.com/cachora_bar_restaurant; 7am-8:30pm Mon-Sat)*

Inca Dream, Cachora $
Quiet restaurant for morning coffees and evening sours. Dine with fellow travelers on chicken dishes or fried trout. *(inkadreamruins.wixsite.com/misitio; breakfast-dinner)*

La Cabañita, Chiquisca $
Also a great guesthouse, the enclosed restaurant has sweeping Apurímac vistas and lovely owners who enjoy chatting. *(98-497-4775; breakfast-dinner)*

Refugio Choquequirao Restaurante, Marampata $
Adobe restaurant covered in Andean murals with wide canyon views and rare vegan food. *(instagram.com/campingrefugiochoquequirao; breakfast-dinner)*.

Saywite Monolith

LINA CHERO PHOTOGRAPHY/SHUTTERSTOCK

Cocamasana

Now, the real adventure begins as you descend from 2920m into the Cañón del Apurímac on long, serpentine switchbacks. This is the same trail that American explorer Hiram Bingham hiked in 1909 when he surveyed Choquequirao (two years before documenting Machu Picchu) with the help of local farmers.

The first leg of the trek is almost entirely downhill through arid, vertical grasslands – the result of an historic wildfire. As a consequence, you get strong sun, but also wide-open views of almost the entire trail to come on the far side of the canyon. Look, too, for the **Padreyoc Glacier** glistening in the sky on the northeastern horizon.

Continue downhill, searching for mountain herbs like *huacatay* (Peru's 'black basil') and *muña* (an Andean mint), both of which feature in dishes you'll find at restaurants on the trail. At around 5km, you'll come across the **Mirador de Cocamasana** (a great lookout for spotting more condors). One kilometer later is the two-house 'village' of **Cocamasana**, which has a campground, huts and a small restaurant.

Chiquisca

From Cocamasana, continue downhill past rows of prickly pears and agaves, whose stalks look like giant asparagus blowing in the wind. Thankfully, the path here isn't quite as steep as the previous leg. Yet, your knees may still be wobbly by the time you stroll into Chiquisca 4km later. This lovely oasis shaded in avocado trees has two options for dining or sleeping, **La Cabañita** (p211) and **Camping Hospedaje Llamayoq Wasi** (p215), which have small pools

Along the Way We Met...

MAMÁ PANCHITA I'm originally from Cachora, but my husband Julio was born in Marampata, so we came to live here in 1977. I love how pretty it is. There is a tranquility here, living in the pure air, eating what we grow. Each year, we harvest potatoes, onions, carrots, broccoli, cabbage and cauliflower. It's all organic, grown with compost. We also have a mule caravan bring us supplies once a month, and that's how we're able to attend to the visitors.

Panchita hosts visitors in Marampata at Hospedaje Mamá Panchita, which has a campground, A-frame cabins and a restaurant.

PANCHITA'S TIP: *You don't have to bring your own food and tents anymore because families are now working in tourism.*

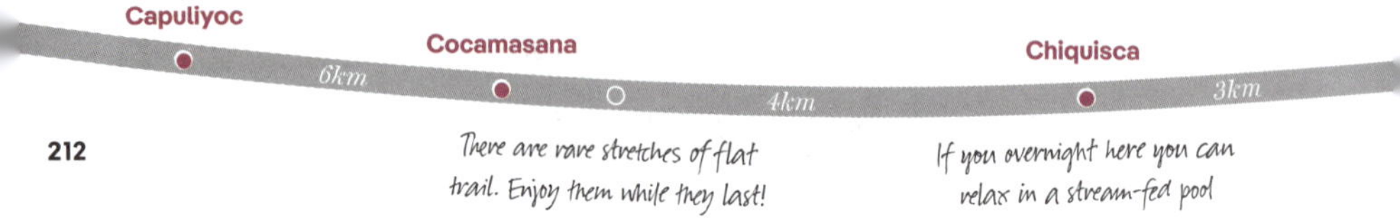

fed by streams. There are also sheltered benches and public restrooms off the central (dirt) plaza. Many travelers enjoy stopping here either on their first night or when returning to Capuliyoc.

Playa Rosalinas

The final 3km push downhill flattens out near the riverbed and tracks along a gorgeous red-rock promenade. Your ears may pop by the time you reach 1500m, near the old **Playa Rosalinas campground**, which was abandoned years ago. Some trekkers still squat here, but it can be hot, buggy and prone to flash floods. Swimming is also not recommended due to the fast-flowing waters. Instead, push onward over the Río Apurímac on the hanging bridge, **Puente Rosalinas**, where you'll get a nice blast of wind blowing through the canyon (hold on to your hat!). 'Apurímac' means 'where the gods' speak' in Quechua and if you listen closely, you can almost hear voices roaring in the river while you cross.

Santa Rosa

There's no way of sugar-coating what comes next: the relentless uphill slog to Santa Rosa is sure to be your least-favorite part of the journey. Most people have never hiked this many switchbacks without any flat stretches for respite. If you haven't seen many other hikers on the trail, you will here, resting on rocks, panting and sweating, fumbling with their water bottles.

We're talking about 500m of altitude change just to get to **Santa Rosa Baja**, which has a buggy campground and shaded snack stand. Then, there's another 100m gain to reach **Santa Rosa Alta**, which has a much cleaner guesthouse and campground, but is more exposed to the sun. Plan to do this leg in the early morning or late afternoon if you can; there is little shade and, since you're still deep in the canyon, it can be very hot.

NOMADKATE/SHUTTERSTOCK

Marampata

Marampata

The trail onward involves an even greater altitude gain than the previous leg from Playa Rosalinas to Santa Rosa, yet it somehow feels more enjoyable. That's because, as you rise, the temperatures drop and you ascend into the Peruvian cloud forest, which is full of bushy trees and colorful orchids. Some lucky trekkers even spot spectacled bears roaming the hillsides.

At **Uchuhuerta**, cross the small stream and zigzag up your final switchbacks to **Marampata**, the largest village on the trail. Marampata lies amid terraced fields of potatoes and corn in a serene mountaintop setting. Miraculously, there are solar-powered streetlights, hot showers and

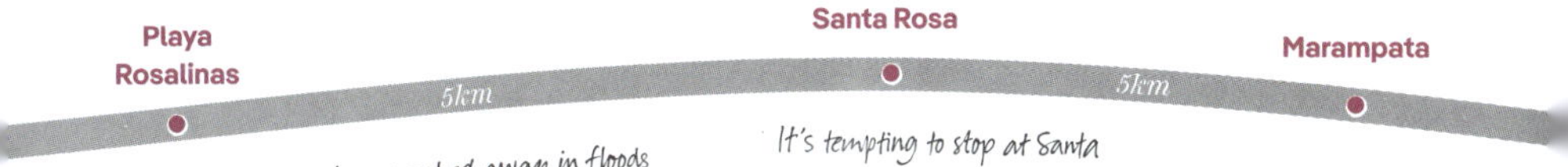

The bridge has been washed away in floods (and rebuilt) countless times. Look for old bridges rusting near the riverbed below.

It's tempting to stop at Santa Rosa Baja, but the toilets at Santa Rosa Alta are far superior.

even restaurants with satellite wi-fi, such as **Refugio Choquequirao Restaurante** (p211). Almost all travelers who aren't continuing onward to Machu Picchu sleep here, either in campgrounds or in A-frame cabins like those at **Hospedaje Mamá Panchita** (right).

Choquequirao Base Camp

You'll likely pass grazing llamas as you trek in and out of puffy clouds on the final 7km stretch to the **Choquequirao Base Camp**. About 20 minutes into the hike, expect your first proper glimpse of the **ruins** (p216) – particularly the immense agricultural terraces, which plunge down broccoli-green hills. Continue onward along the edge of a steep cliff until you reach a large wooden gate with a sign welcoming you to Choquequirao. Sadly, this greeting is a bit premature – you've got another 3km to go!

The final push sends you into a lush forest of moss-covered trees, fluffy ferns and vibrant bromeliads. Follow the trail as it veers up and then down again, occasionally flattening out – at least, for a few precious steps. Just before you reach Choquequirao's official gate – and pass 3000m in altitude! – you'll find a sign leading off to the left toward the **Pikiwasi Sector** and its campground. Note that only backpackers continuing onward toward Machu Picchu are allowed to camp here; all others must visit for the day from Marampata.

NOMADKATE/SHUTTERSTOCK

DETOUR: On to Machu Picchu

Most hikers will turn around at Choquequirao and trace their footsteps back down the Cañón del Apurímac and up the far side to Capuliyoc and Cachora over the course of two more days. However, some intrepid backpackers continue onward toward Machu Picchu (p166) via the

Along the Way We Met...

EVERT QUISPE The first time I hiked this trail was 15 years ago when I was studying to be an electrical mechanic. Choquequirao changed everything. I overcame my fears, and accomplished a big challenge. I was feeling the energy of these apus, the mountain gods. They encouraged me and helped me decide to change my career and study tourism at the university. Every time I come back here, I ask the apus for more advice.

Evert is a hiking guide working for QN Travel Peru.

EVERT'S TIP: *Do some training at home before you attempt Choquequirao. Also, make sure to break in your hiking boots.*

View from Choquequirao Trek

trail to **Yanama**, which is signposted just before the official Choquequirao gate. Beyond here there are fewer facilities and higher altitudes. You'll need to carry water and camping gear, planning for another six days of backpacking.

The trail beyond Choquequirao plunges down canyon into the **Río Blanco**, rises precipitously up the far side to **Maizal**, and winds over to more campgrounds in Yanama, **Totora** and **Playa Sahuayaco** before ending at **Hidroeléctrica** near **Machu Picchu Pueblo** (also known as Aguas Calientes), the village at the base of Machu Picchu archaeological site. Guided trips often skip some of the final legs as you can arrange a car transfer as early as Yanama, where there is now a road.

BEST PLACES TO SLEEP

Casa de Salcantay, Cachora $
Manicured gardens, strong wifi, and young, friendly hosts make private rooms here an excellent value. (*salcantay.com*)

CasaNostra Choquequirao, Cachora $
Found down a winding road on the outskirts of town with an oasis-like vibe and solid bar-restaurant. (*choque quiraotrekk.com*)

Camping Hospedaje Llamayoq Wasi, Chiquisca $
You can camp or bunk up in the long block of garden-facing rooms with shared baths, hot showers and rare wi-fi. Oh, and there's a pool, too! (*92-828-7323*)

Hospedaje Mamá Panchita, Marampata $
The namesake *mama* is a real joy, and some of her A-frame huts even have balconies. You can camp in the flower-lined fields. (*instagram.com/choquequirao_mama_panchita*)

Choquequirao Ruins

Explore this massive complex without the crowds

Turn back the way you came or continue on to Machu Picchu

EXPERIENCE ★

Explore Choquequirao

Ever wondered what it was like to visit Angkor Wat, Chichén Itzá or Machu Picchu before the roads and tour buses arrived? This is the appeal of Choquequirao, a citadel so far up in the Andes that the only way here is on your own two feet.

HOW TO

When to go: The dry season, between April and October, offers ideal conditions.

Cost: Entry to Parque Arqueológico de Choquequirao is S60. You pay at the trailhead in Capuliyoc (p210), but need to show the ticket at the Choquequirao entry gate.

Restrooms: The only toilet facilities are at the campground; there is no potable water.

Guides: There are no information panels anywhere at Choquequirao, making a guide essential for a greater understanding of the site.

More info: peru.travel/en/attractions/choquequirao

Enter via the Plaza Principal

Choquequirao is a vast archaeological complex that sprawls across three hilltops, 12 sectors and 6 sq km. To see it all would take more than a day, yet most visitors explore the highlights in just a few hours. Enter through the main gate and walk along the stone path through terraced agricultural fields. Follow the trail as it winds above the terraces to the **Plaza Principal**, which houses several prominent structures, including temples, fountains, baths and the multilevel residences of the elite.

Climb to the Hilltops

On the south side of the plaza is the **Templo del Muro Triunfal**. The niches in the temple walls here would have held the mummified remains of important leaders. Follow the path up to the ceremonial shrine on the hilltop, **Ushnu**, a place of offerings that has sweeping views of the Cañón del Apurímac.

You can also climb above the Plaza Principal on the north side, following an old aqueduct to a string of storage houses, which line the uppermost **Qullqa Sector**. Clouds frequently swirl in and out of these ruins, obstructing views before revealing them again.

Descend to the Lower Levels

Choquequirao's famous **Llamas Sector** requires a precipitous 30-minute descent from the Plaza Principal into terraced fields. Your reward is a set of stone

ERICK MANGA/SHUTTERSTOCK

WHAT DO WE REALLY KNOW ABOUT CHOQUEQUIRAO?

Built in the 15th century, Choquequirao was a ceremonial center, administrative hub and checkpoint controlling access to the Vilcabamba region. Archaeologists believe it may have been one of the last refuges of the Inca when Spaniards arrived a century later. Its name in Quechua loosely translates to 'cradle of gold,' though most of its treasures have vanished over the years. While it may be three-times the size of Machu Picchu, only about a third of it has been rescued from the jungle.

Left: Choquequirao ruins
Below: Stonework llama

terraces adorned with 24 llamas, which were designed using white stones. Continue walking for another 15 minutes to reach a lookout point on the far side of the hill, which offers the best perspective for photography.

From Templo del Muro Triunfal, you can drop down into the **Pikiwasi Sector**, which has a few excavated homes that likely belonged to middle-class workers. There are many more poking out of the dense forest, unexcavated, making it a fascinating area to comprehend just how much of this site remains a mystery. Keep walking past the campsite to exit Choquequirao.

ERIK LLONTOP MARTINEZ/SHUTTERSTOCK

INSIGHT

Choquequirao: the Next Machu Picchu?

Choquequirao receives about the same number of annual tourists as Machu Picchu gets in just two days. Yet, there are plans underway for roads and even a cable car that could forever alter the trajectory of this isolated Inca citadel – for better or worse.

WORDS BY **MARK JOHANSON**
Mark is a Chile-based journalist and author of the book Mars on Earth.

BETO SANTILLAN/SHUTTERSTOCK

Hikers, Choquequirao Trek (p206)

ACADEMIC-EXPLORER HIRAM BINGHAM conducted a series of expeditions in the early 1900s that produced the first modern maps of both Choquequirao and Machu Picchu. From that shared beginning, their histories diverged wildly. By 1913, Machu Picchu had been mistakenly celebrated as a rediscovered 'lost city,' a label that drew widespread attention and rapidly growing crowds. The ruins went on to became Peru's most recognizable symbol and, by the end of the 20th century, you could arrive by train and bus.

What happened to Choquequirao over that same time period? Not a whole lot.

Although it's actually a larger archaeological complex than Machu Picchu, Bingham didn't find the ruins nearly as intact. And due to the remote location, archaeologists have been slow to unearth additional treasures ever since true excavations began in the 1970s. This has meant less interest and fewer visitors. Yet, over the past decade, that's started to change...

A Cable Car to Choquequirao?

In 2013, Peru's then-president Ollanta Humala announced plans for a US$47 million cable car line that would cut the time to reach Choquequirao from two days on foot to just 20 minutes by air. This sparked global headlines and renewed interest in the site; travelers rushed to visit before the cable car changed Choquequirao forever.

More than a decade has passed and there is still no cable car. Yet, the project remains in development. Ex-president Dina Boluarte presented it to foreign investors at a ceremony in 2025, saying the 10.6km-long gondola (now valued at US$261 million) would allow more than one million annual visitors to reach Choquequirao; currently the site receives fewer than 10,000 annual visitors for an average of 27 people per day.

Choquequirao forms part of the greater Vilcabamba–Choquequirao–Machu Picchu biological and cultural corridor, a vast landscape that links multiple Inca sites through one of the most spectacular mountain ecosystems in South America. 'In this sense, the future of Choquequirao is inseparable from the long-term vision for Machu Picchu National Park and the wider goal of diversifying how travelers experience Peru's network of mountaintop citadels,' explains Nick Stanziano, founder and chief explorer at SA Expeditions, a trekking company based in Lima. 'Thoughtful development here can expand accessibility while distributing tourism more evenly across the region.'

> 'The future of Choquequirao is inseparable from the long-term vision for Machu Picchu National Park and the wider goal of diversifying how travelers experience Peru's network of mountaintop citadels.'

If the proposed cable car becomes a reality, Stanziano thinks it could open up new avenues for exploration. 'Travelers could soon connect to Machu Picchu through a series of different modes of transport – cable car, walking, train – creating a completely new and more accessible route through the Vilcabamba range.'

New Roads Winding into the Andes

Cable car or not, the Choquequirao region is already evolving. Before 2020, it was only possible to camp and purchase basic goods along the trail. Now, there are cabins, simple restaurants, hot-water showers, satellite wi-fi and other amenities scattered along the trail, which were unimaginable just a few years ago. Meanwhile, locals say private companies have begun buying up land in several villages, with plans to develop lodge-to-lodge trips similar to what's currently available on the Lares and Salkantay Treks.

Dirt roads are also snaking through the Andes closer to Choquequirao each year. One now descends into the Cañón del Apurímac from Huanipaca, with an end goal of one day reaching the river, from where you could hike up the far side to Choquequirao. On the back end of the ruins, the road from Machu Picchu Pueblo (also known as Aguas Calientes), gateway to Machu Picchu archaeological site, now goes all the way to Yanama, making it easier to connect the two Inca sites with a combination of hiking and driving. 'Alternative Choquequirao Treks' have been popping up every year.

'These are complementary routes that would boost tourism, but fundamentally, the construction of the cable car is generating the most excitement,' says Octavio Fernández Carrasco, an archaeologist with the Ministerio de Cultura Peru, who cautions that the project is still not backed up by a technical report. Carrasco also notes that increased tourism will require more investment.

'Given the contemporary context, signage needs to be much more dynamic, harmonious and in dialogue with the surroundings,' he says. 'Furthermore, the signage should be coded and classified to serve a more efficient function in orienting, informing and educating visitors.'

Once these issues are resolved, Carrasco believes the site could finally live up to its tourism potential, adding: 'I think there's going to be a significant tourism boom.'

Calca

The Lares Trek is a true off-the-beaten-track route that takes you into the majestic altitudes, vast stillness and epic landscapes of the Andes. Locals herd their alpaca flocks, a condor might glide overhead, a lake reflects the mossy greens of the surrounding hills as the ground crunches beneath your feet. It's a rare adventurer that heads out this way. While the altitude, rough terrain and climate make this route a challenge, the beauty and silence feel sacred.

Vesna Maric

Lares Valley
CHRISTIAN DECLERCQ/GETTY IMAGES

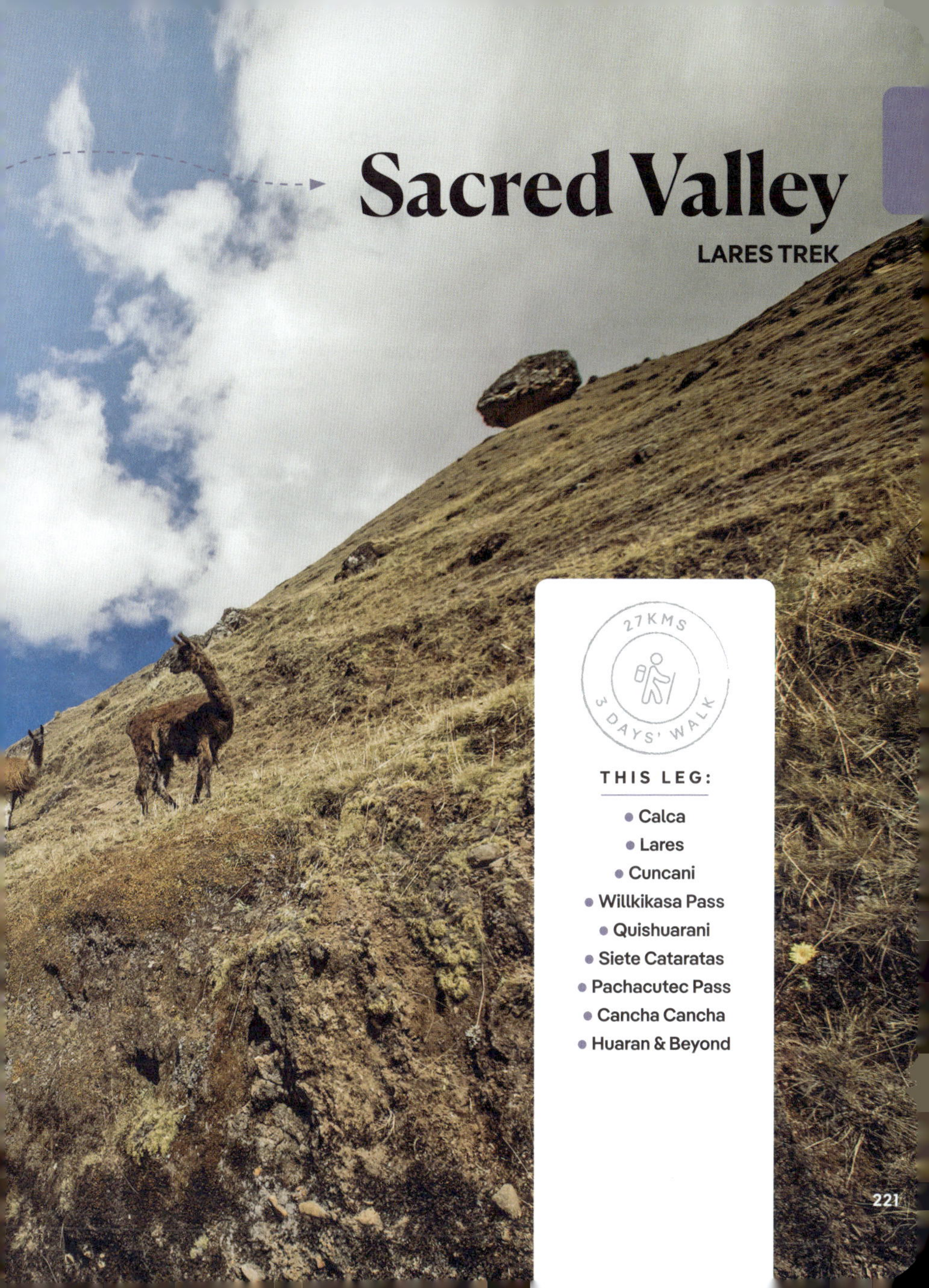

Sacred Valley

LARES TREK

27KMS
3 DAYS' WALK

THIS LEG:

- Calca
- Lares
- Cuncani
- Willkikasa Pass
- Quishuarani
- Siete Cataratas
- Pachacutec Pass
- Cancha Cancha
- Huaran & Beyond

Walking Notes

There are several different Lares Treks and the one we outline here is only one possible route. It is a challenging hike, with demanding routes made more difficult by the ever-changing weather and freezing night temperatures during the dry season. You will need to take a tent and cooking gear, as there are no services along the way. Make sure you also get a reliable map of the trek you want to undertake on your own or hire a professional guide.

Breaking Your Journey

If you start in Lares and finish in Ollantaytambo, you can do this trek in three days, with some eight to 10 hours of hiking on the first two days. Overnight stops might include Quishuarani, Cancha Cancha and Ollantaytambo.

Vesna's Tips

BEST MEAL A picnic lunch at the Willkikasa Pass (p225).

FAVOURITE VIEW The 360-degree views from Pachacutec Pass (p227) are unforgettable.

ESSENTIAL STOP Gazing at the flourishing flora as you descend into the Sacred Valley.

TIP Do fitness and cardio training, and work on your legs and back for strength before starting this hike.

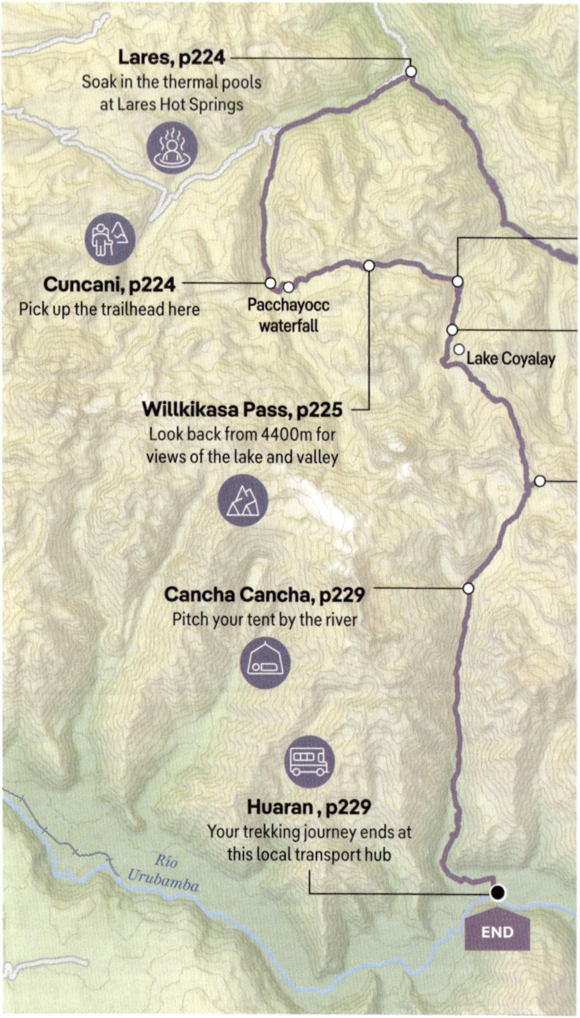

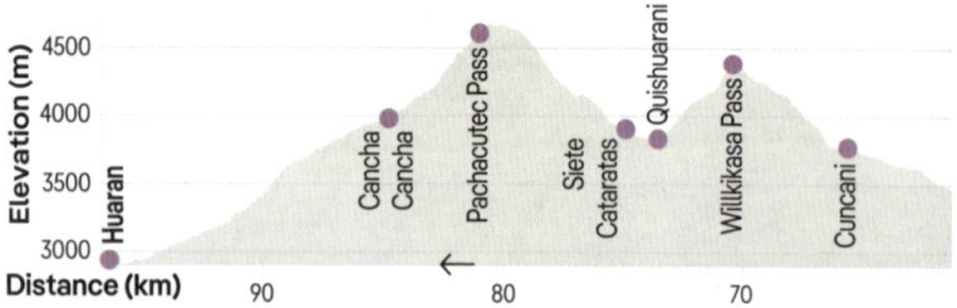

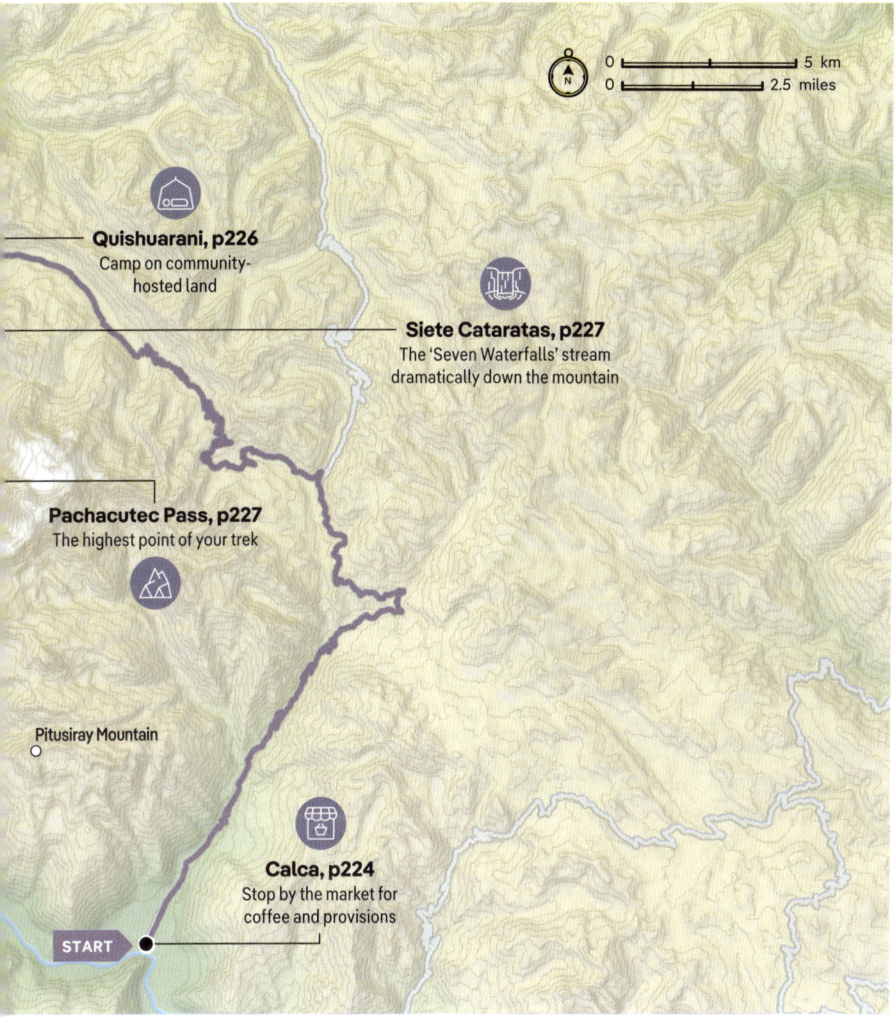
0 5 km
0 2.5 miles
N
Quishuarani, p226
Camp on community-hosted land
Siete Cataratas, p227
The 'Seven Waterfalls' stream dramatically down the mountain
Pachacutec Pass, p227
The highest point of your trek
Pitusiray Mountain
Calca, p224
Stop by the market for coffee and provisions
START

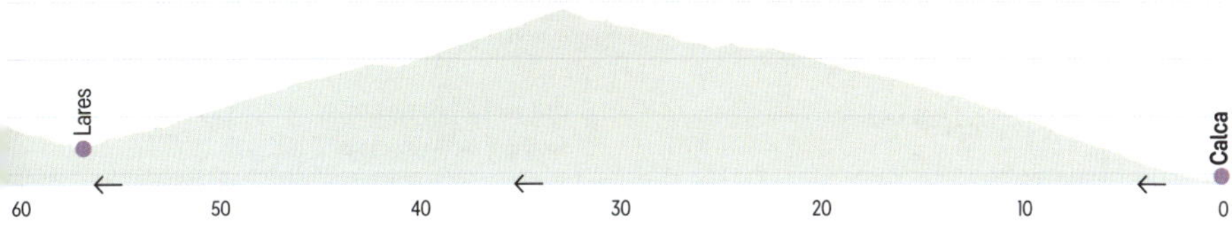
Lares
Calca
60
50
40
30
20
10
0

GETTING THERE From Cusco, your journey to Lares will start before dawn, in the dark early-morning hours. You'll first need to reach the town of Calca: buses and *colectivos* (1½ hours, S10) leave from the terminals on Calle Puputi and Av Tullumayo.

Calca

Once you reach Calca, head for the very cute **Calca market** where you can get some provisions. Don't miss spending a little time in this great local spot – enjoy breakfast and local coffee on the 1st floor while you watch life unfold on the market floor beneath. There are mountains of soft white cheeses, different fruit and vegetables, and, yes, piles of *cuy* (guinea pigs) ready to be roasted. All the produce from the rich fields of the Sacred Valley is on display here, and it's a spot few tourists see. After this, head to Calca's terminal to catch one of the regular *colectivos* to Lares (S10), which leave when full.

Lares Hot Springs

FROM LEFT: JAN SCHULER/ALAMY, RYAN MORRIS/GETTY IMAGES

Lares

The journey from Calca to Lares takes about three hours and is an event in itself: you'll travel along a winding mountain road that leads up to a spectacular pass at 4200m. You'll really feel as if you're driving into the heavens – the low cloud can literally cover everything around you. The road then winds down to Lares.

If you have time, spend a few hours dipping in the **Lares Hot Springs** *(S20; 4am-10pm)*, a series of thermal pools that are as soothing as they are therapeutic. A 20-minute hike uphill from the town center, locals have visited Lares to alleviate various ailments for centuries. There are three main pools ranging in temperature from 91°F to 111°F (33°C to 44°C), as well as a cold pool. Try to time your visit for a weekday, when it's less crowded and don't be put off by the slightly brownish color – it's the minerals in the water! These minerals are believed to help soothe muscle tension and improve circulation.

Some people choose to spend the night at the basic hotel by the springs, see local life then head out hiking early the next morning. However you decide to organize your time, a relaxing dip here is time well spent.

Cuncani

Begin your hike at the trailhead (3200m) just above the Lares Hot Springs or, if you are starting your hike later in the day and want to

Hiker rests, Lares Trek

save a bit of time before sunset, get a local taxi (S5, 20-minute ride) to the nearby trailhead at **Cuncani** (3600m). Starting at Cuncani, you'll hike 7km (allow four to five hours) on day one, spending your first night in Quishuarani.

Willkikasa Pass

From the Cuncani trailhead, walk up for about 1½ hours to the **Pacchayocc waterfall and lake** on an easily identified path – this is a beautiful, demanding walk with vast high-mountain views and incredible silence. You will pass local shepherds and their dogs, which are likely to bark at you. Stay calm and carry on. Look out for the Peruvian viscachas

PREPARING FOR THE LARES TREK

Day One
7km/four to five hours
Cuncani – Willkikasa – Quishuarani

Day Two
11km/seven to eight hours
Quishuarani – Qoyalay Lake – Pachacutec Pass – Cancha Cancha

Day Three
9km/four hours
Cancha Cancha – Huaran

Camping
You can set up your tent where you see fit, such as any flat spot near running water, although there are a couple of local-run 'campsites' in the settlements of Quishuarani and Cancha Cancha, both at around 3900m. At this height, in the dry season, the temperatures at night will reach below freezing, so keep this in mind.

Have a picnic at the peak, taking in the valley you just passed through, below

CHRISTIAN DECLERCQ/GETTY IMAGES

Hikers, Lares Trek

(similar to a chinchilla) perching on the rocks. As you walk for another 30 minutes toward the highest point of the day, the **Willkikasa Pass** (4400m), look behind you at the incredible views of the lake and the valley – as you pause to catch your breath, you'll have a great sense of achievement. Consider having a picnic lunch here.

Quishuarani

Descend for an hour and a half from Willkikasa Pass to the camp in the settlement of **Quishuarani** (3850m). It's a rocky path for the first part, so care must be taken as you descend, but it then evens out as you enter the valley, and wide meadows open up before you. After you set up your tent, you can gaze at the amazing views of the frozen Andean peaks and the Siete Cataratas. This is the direction your path will take on day two.

Along the Way We Saw...

ANDEAN VISCACHA The very cute Andean viscacha, the cousin of the chinchilla, lives in the the rocky heights of Peru and as far as northern Argentina. Don't be fooled by its cuddly exterior: these remarkably resilient rodents adapt to extreme environments – some live above 5000m! They are watchful animals subsisting on herbs, lichens and moss and living inside rock shelters. In Andean folklore, the viscacha is a symbol of patience and strength.

Vesna Maric

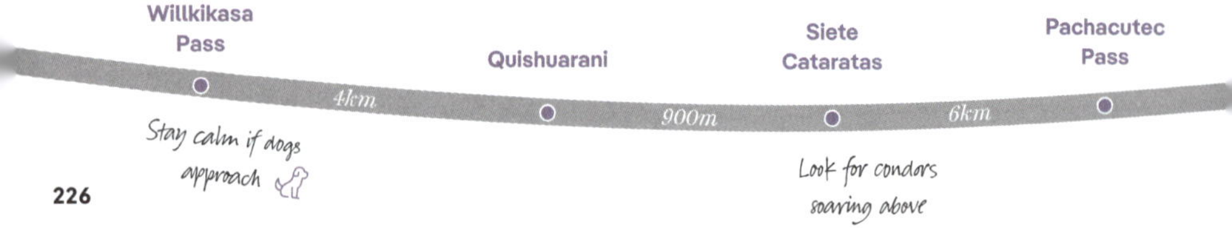

Unless you pitch your tent at an independent location in Quishuarani – ask for permission if it's near anyone's house – you can set up camp on a small bit of land where the local community hosts hikers and groups. Ask a local to show you the way. There is a very basic toilet here and running water, but no showers. Locals may even serve you some cooked food for a fee. These are very remote settlements of Quechua speakers, so it's best to have some basic Spanish-language skills – don't expect English to be spoken.

Siete Cataratas

Head out early after breakfast, because it's a long way up to the Pachacutec pass – allow four to five hours for the over 900m ascent. This is the highest and the toughest part of the trek. The terrain is reasonable but the altitude is very high and the ascent is relentlessly uphill, often through cloud, rain and/or snow.

As you start the morning, you will pass the spectacular **Siete Cataratas** – Seven Waterfalls or 'Qanchispaccha' in Quechua. The seven waterfalls stream down the mountain in separate streams, and the contrast between the dark mountain rock and frothing white waters is impressive. Climbing up, you'll spot **Lake Coyalay** in the valley bellow, a tranquil lake, whose colours change from blue to green to grey, depending on the skies above. Take your time to enjoy the views – on a clear day you should be able to spot the Andean ibis and Andean geese, and maybe even a condor overhead. You will cross 6km overall before reaching the Pachacutec Pass.

Pachacutec Pass

From the very top of **Pachacutec Pass** (4700m) you'll have views of the dramatic peaks of **Pitusiray** and **Qolque Cruz** mountains,

Siete Cataratas

ROY VEREIJKEN/SHUTTERSTOCK

VESNA MARIC

WHAT TO PACK FOR THE LARES TRAIL

- Tent, sleeping bag and mat.
- Gear for cold and freezing temperatures.
- Food, camping stove and cooking utensils.
- Snacks – there is no option to get any supplies along the way.
- Water filter so that you can refill in rivers along the way.
- Layered clothing – be prepared for every kind of weather and fast and extreme changes.
- Offline map.
- One or two power banks to charge your phone.

which provide a humbling backdrop with their immense beauty. The descent from here to camp takes five hours in total.

It's another 1.5 to 2km (allow an hour to an hour and a half, depending on conditions) across what is a sort of 'false plain,' meaning that the trail goes up and down, before you start your descent to Cancha Cancha in earnest. If the weather is clear, you will be able to see lakes and mountaintops all around you from the top of the pass. If the weather is bad, the visibility can be very poor, and you won't see much except clouds! This can make for a rough part of the hike. Once you start to really go downhill, it's another two hours to the community of Cancha Cancha where you can set up camp.

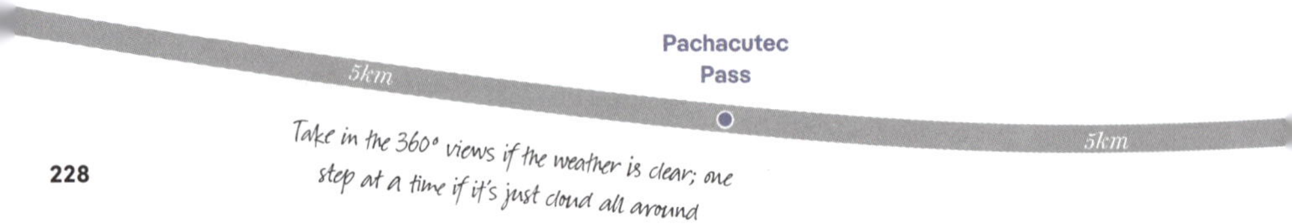

Take in the 360° views if the weather is clear; one step at a time if it's just cloud all around

Hikers ascend Pachacutec Pass

Cancha Cancha

Cancha Cancha is a small settlement where you can set up your tent by the river. You'll be surrounded by grazing horses, alpacas and llamas. This is an open landscape so it can be quite windy – look for a sheltered spot so that you can cook. The following morning you will start the last leg of the Lares Trek, a 9km four-hour descent into the Sacred Valley.

Huaran & Beyond

From Cancha Cancha, it is a beautiful, lightly downhill walk where the landscape shifts from the harsh Andean high-mountain scenery to soft beautiful greenery as you hike along the river. As you hike down, notice how the flora and fauna suddenly become more colorful, birdsong appears and see if you can spot a hummingbird hovering over a fuscia flower. The path eventually takes you to the village of **Huaran**, where the trekking portion of your journey ends.

Huaran is a local transportation hub from where you can get a *colectivo* to **Ollantaytambo** (S5 to S10; one hour; p53), where the archaeological site is well worth a visit. From Ollantaytambo, you can catch a train to **Machu Picchu Pueblo** (also known as Aguas Calientes; p180) and from there catch the bus or hike up to **Machu Picchu archaeological site** (p166). Make sure you book your accommodations in Machu Picchu Pueblo and your Machu Picchu citadel entry tickets well in advance.

Alternate Treks

Looking for even more great hikes in the Peruvian Andes? Visit obscure Inca ruins and take in vast peaks, glaciers, rainbow mountains and multicolored lakes with these five additional high-altitude hikes. You'll be heading firmly off the beaten track, so ensure you are properly equipped with your own camping and cooking gear.

Vesna Maric

Seven Lakes of Ausangate (p234)

ORORU/SHUTTERSTOCK

Hiker, Ausangate Mountain
JAN JERMAN/SHUTTERSTOCK

Ausangate

Solitude & Vast Expanses

ROUTE Pacchanta – Phinaya		**BEST FOR** Experienced hikers seeking solitude and vast expanses, who don't fear high altitudes
DISTANCE 79km	**TIME** 6 days	

AT 6372M, AUSANGATE is the highest peak in the Cusco region, and although this route doesn't reach the actual peak, this is a challenging high-mountain trek – the altitude is consistently over 4000m for the duration, and there are two passes over 5000m. You have to carry your own tent, cooking gear and food, and you must have good maps – physical as well as digital – and a compass. If you are an experienced hiker who likes a challenge, solitude, endless views and interacting with locals, this is the hike for you. You'll hike in the wild landscapes of the Andes, via some spectacular natural sights, passing puna meadows, alpaca-herding communities and glacier views along the way. You'll also see several 'rainbow mountains,' with those technicolor geological layers that are so incredible to witness, and may even spot condors and vicuña.

Starting from Cusco, get a local bus bound for Tinqui and then a taxi to Pacchanta, where you'll find the trailhead for the Ausangate Trek. Your first day consists of a gradual incline with amazing views of **Ausangate Mountain** and multicolored lagoons. The second day is hard work, crossing the **Jampa Pass** (5063m), with the **Palomani Pass** (5091m) following on day three. You will cross the **Condor Pass** (5400m) – a real challenge for your stamina and lungs – on day four. Many camp near the area's most famous and extensive lagoon, **Sibinacocha Lagoon**, a beautiful steely lake. Carry on up to the **Vicuña Mountain** (5350m) on day five, where the weather turns very harsh, and pitch your tent near the **Cascara Lagoon** (5000m). Day six is downhill toward the community of **Phinaya** (4000m), where you can pitch your tent and meet local people. From Phinaya, you can catch a *colectivo* (shared van) to Cusco.

Ancascocha

An Alternate Route to Machu Picchu

ROUTE Soqma Soqma – Ollantaytambo		BEST FOR
DISTANCE 61km	TIME 5 days	Those who want to see Inca ruins and spectacular nature on an alternative route to Machu Picchu

THIS FIVE-DAY TREK to Machu Picchu – via Inca archaeological sites, local agriculture and traditional villages – requires a high degree of self sufficiency. You must have your own camping and cooking gear, and carry your own food. While there are streams to refill water, there are zero services on the way. Good physical and digital maps are essential, and you can camp wherever you wish along the way.

There are several different Ancascocha routes, but most start in **Soqma Soqma** (3000m), a 1½-hour drive from Cusco – local buses will get you there. You will cross two high passes and see Salkantay and Veronica peaks in the distance.

Hiker, Ancascocha Trek
MARK GREEN/SHUTTERSTOCK

Day one passes by **Perolniyoc Waterfall**, crop-growing fields and the Inca archaeological site of **Racaypata**. Day two goes over **Kuychiccasa Pass** (4500m), with views of the Sacred Valley and descends to the community of **Ancascocha** (3900m), where you can camp. Day three includes the highest point of the hike – **Huayanay Pass** (4650m) – and the **Incaracay and Paucarcancha Inca sites**. You'll see the original Inca Trail in the distance, which you will be joining the following day. The archaeological sites of **Llactapata** (p186) and **Canabamba** (p62) are on the way. Most people finish this trek at **Ollantaytambo** (p53), from where you can get a train to Machu Picchu Pueblo (also known as Aguas Calientes; p180), and then continue on to Machu Picchu archaeological site (p166).

Seven Lakes of Ausangate

Stunning Scenery

ROUTE Pacchanta – Seven Lakes of Ausangate

DISTANCE 16km

TIME 5-6 hours

BEST FOR Those who want to see spectacular nature and multicolored lakes

DOABLE AS A day trip from Cusco, the Seven Lakes of Ausangate circuit is a beautiful hike to one of the most impressive sights you're likely to see anywhere – the different colored **Comercocha**, **Alqacocha**, **Patacocha**, **China Otorongo**, **Orco Otorongo** and **Azulcocha** glacial lakes, which owe their hues to the different sediment minerals they contain. The colors range from turquoise to lilac to pink and are quite otherworldly.

Start your trip from Cusco early in the morning and note that it is a three-hour drive to **Pacchanta village**, from where you begin the five-hour loop. This is a high-altitude walk that peaks at 4800m so make sure you're well acclimatized before you start. Bring your own water, food and snacks, and prepare for changing weather conditions. As always, make sure you have adequate maps if you're not going with a guide or someone who knows the area well.

On the way up, you will pass through valleys, streams and pastures, with impressive views of imposing Ausangate Mountain in the background.

There are **natural springs** *(S20)* in Pacchanta –bring swimming wear and towel – that are quite delightful for a soak at the end of the hike.

Seven Lakes of Ausangate
ORORU/SHUTTERSTOCK

Huchuy Qosqo ruins
ORORU/SHUTTERSTOCK

Huchuy Qosqo Ruins

Inca Ruins in a Day

ROUTE Camino Inca Huchuy Qosqo – Huchuy Qosqo ruins		**BEST FOR** Those who want to visit Inca ruins on a day hike
DISTANCE 18km	**TIME** 1 day	

THIS HIKE CAN be done as a day trip from Cusco. Start early, catching a taxi from central Cusco to Papitos Station, then get a *colectivo* to Laguna Piuray (S6, 45 minutes), from where you will get another taxi (S10 to S15, 20 minutes) to the Camino Inca Huchuy Qosqo, the trailhead for the walk.

The trail will take you past the **remains of Incan terraces and aqueducts**, and over a 4400m mountain pass with endless views of mountains and glaciers, after which you will approach the **Huchuy Qosqo ruins** *(per person S22)*. Known as Kakya Qawani by the Incas, Huchuy Qosqo means 'Little Cusco' in Quechua. Modeled on the Inca capital, it was established as a royal estate by Sapa Inca Viracocha – the somewhat mythical eighth Inca ruler – in around 1420 CE. You can easily spend an hour exploring these fascinating ruins before descending a serpentine path along a steep cliff face (allow two hours). When you reach the bottom of the steep path, take a right to cross the bridge, where there is a stop for *colectivos* back to Cusco.

The Huchuy Qosqo ruins can also be incorporated into a three-day, 24km hike from Lamay to Machu Picchu, via Ollantaytambo. You will need your own camping and cooking gear, and you can camp inside the Huchuy Qosqo ruins for no extra cost.

JULIA MOUNTAIN PHOTO/SHUTTERSTOCK

Rainbow Mountain

Iconic Photo Op

ROUTE Llactoc – Rainbow Mountain – Red Valley		**BEST FOR** Those who want to see fascinating geology
DISTANCE 7km	**TIME** 5 hours	

THIS IS A very popular route that most people complete with a guided tour because it involves long drives to and from the trailhead. Ensure you're well acclimatized before you embark on this relatively short trek, as you will reach over 5000m in altitude. Take plenty of water and snacks, and bring your own lunch unless it is provided by an organized tour.

It's a three-hour drive to **Llactoc** (4630m), the starting point for this hike. It's a 1½-hour hike uphill to reach **Vinicunca** (Rainbow Mountain, 5100m). Vinicunca's seven stunning colors were formed 24 million years ago. The photogenic multicolor effect is caused by the mineral composition of soil and rocks: the pinks are due to red clay; the whites, quartz sandstone; the greens, phyllites; the yellows, sulphurous minerals; and the lavender and purples, marl and silicates. Previously concealed beneath a glacier, the ice melted over two years from 2013 to 2015, and this popular tourist attraction was born. The colors are at their most vibrant during the early-morning hours on sunny days. The huge daily influx of tourists means that protective measures were introduced, so respecting designated trails is essential.

On your way up, you will see Ausangate Mountain (6372m). From Rainbow Mountain, most people then trek another 30 minutes to the **Red Valley** (5050m), followed by a two-hour descent back to Llactoc. From Llactoc, it's a three-hour drive back to Cusco.

Above: Red Valley mountains; Right: Rainbow Mountain

RIGHT: VICTOR DING/SHUTTERSTOCK

Toolkit

Hiker, Inca Trail
SHARPTOYOU/SHUTTERSTOCK

First Time

For more information on starting the journey, see Cusco City Guide (p34)

EXPLORING BY PRIVATE CAR

With public transportation so accessible and convenient, visitors all too often overlook the fact that a private car and an experienced driver can save a lot of time while also allowing you to tap into some locations that are removed from the tourist trail. Juan Javier Quispe Villalba *(WhatsApp: +51 902 888 881)* is a recommended English-speaking, Cusco-based driver.

Arrival

While Cusco's Aeropuerto Internacional Alejandro Velasco Astete sees arrivals from some South American destinations, most visitors arrive and depart through Lima. The 1½-hour Lima–Cusco flight is affordable and convenient so only the tirelessly intrepid are tempted by the 22-hour road trip over the high ridges of the Andes.

Visas

Citizens of the US, UK, South Africa, Japan, Australia, New Zealand and EU are automatically granted entry into Peru without a visa for tourism purposes. It seems to be luck of the draw whether officials stamp you with 30, 60 or 90 days. If you're planning a long stay remember to request this at the point of entry.

Customs

You can enter the country with one laptop and two mobile phones without paying tax. It is illegal to leave the country with any archaeological artifacts and, in some cases, items containing coca leaves. Even the smallest 'antique' souvenir can sometimes seem suspiciously valuable to a customs official.

Navigation

While you won't need to navigate yourself on the actual Inca Trail, it's reassuring to know where you are in the world. You can download a free South Peru map (147mb) through Maps.Me app. It will work offline and is handy when the signal drops, which can happen frequently, even in Cusco.

TRAVEL INSURANCE

Health insurance is vital. Even more so on a serious trek where there is very real potential for illness or injury. The bill for hospitalization in Peru (or repatriation from Peru) could be hefty.

ELECTRICITY 220V/60HZ

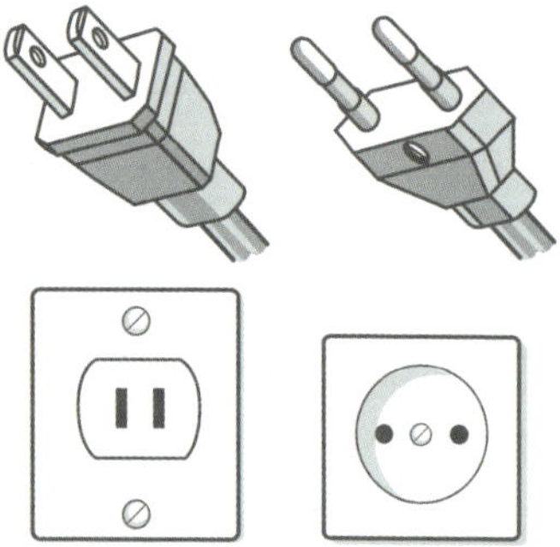

Type A　　Type C

AFRICA STUDIO/SHUTTERSTOCK

Money

Cash is King

While it's possible to pay with cards in tourist centers – ie at restaurants, hotels, travel agencies and large stores – cash is still king in Peru. Try to break large S200 (roughly US$60) and S100 (US$30) notes into smaller denominations since they'll frequently not be accepted for small purchases. In remote areas these big notes can sometimes be effectively worthless. Keep coins for snacks, bus tickets and buskers.

HOW MUCH IS a day on the Inca Trail?

All-inclusive costs per person on the four-day Inca Trail average around S600 per day.

Elsewhere

Museum entry	S10-20
Basic meal with drink	S30
Pisco sour	S25
Double room	S90-120
Large pizza	S50
Cappuccino	S20
Bus (Machu Picchu Pueblo–Machu Picchu archaeological site)	S82
Total (per day for two adults)	**S550**

'FREE' WALKING TOURS

You might find free walking tours in major tourist hubs throughout the region – most notably each afternoon from Cusco's Plaza de Armas. Often led by enthusiastic and very knowledgeable guides, they can provide unexpectedly colorful ways to get a local insight. Be aware though that these guides often survive from tips alone, so do plan on tipping them.

Currency Exchange & ATMs

Peru's official currency is the Sol (S). While you can change major international currencies at *casas de cambio* (currency exchanges) in international airports and tourist hubs, it is more practical, cheaper and safer to withdraw cash from ATMs. Many ATMs have a limit of S400 (necessitating multiple charges if you want to withdraw larger amounts) but Alfin Bank ATMs allow withdrawals of up to S2000.

Tipping Etiquette

Tipping is expected on the Inca Trail. Suggested amounts per guest for the four-day trail would be S150 for the team of porters and cooks, and S30 to S40 for each guide. Outside the Inca Trail, only high-end restaurants include a service charge on the bill. Tipping is not compulsory but in tourist-level restaurants it is gratefully received as a sign of your gratitude for good service.

Haggling

While the vast majority of Peruvians are fair-minded and hospitable, it should come as no surprise to learn that tourists regularly get overcharged. A smattering of Spanish can go a long way to limiting this unnecessary strain on your budget. Be respectful without being naive and be vigilant without being paranoid. Don't be afraid to haggle, but remember, while an extra dollar on a souvenir might make little difference to you, it can be a big contribution to a struggling family.

SHANA ESPINOZA/SHUTTERSTOCK

Packing

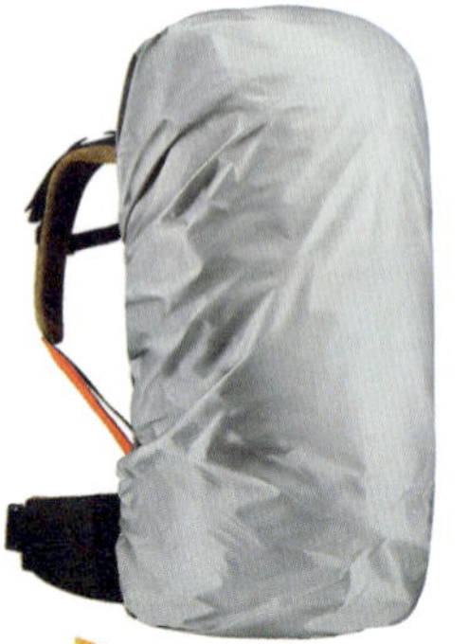

Picking the Pack

On the Inca Trail porters normally carry your extra clothes so a 20L to 25L day pack is optimal. Some hikers get by with smaller ones but since dry weather is never guaranteed in the Andes, a little extra space allows you to take a warm layer and wet-weather gear. Large packs must be left at the **luggage kiosk** *(S5)* before entering Machu Picchu.

Clothing

For a four-day Inca Trail hike:

- 1 pair of trusted **hiking boots/shoes**
- 2 pairs **hiking trousers**
- 1 pair **shorts**
- 4 quick-drying **T-shirts**
- 4 pairs **hiking socks**: merino wool is blister-friendly and quick-drying
- 4 sets of **underwear**
- Warm **jacket**
- Waterproof **poncho or raincoat**: consider oversize so you can wear it over your pack
- **Sunhat or cap**
- 1 pair **sport-sandals or flip-flops**
- **Buffs** (hiking neck gaiters) to stop your neck from burning on a sunny day, keep your cap on your head on a windy one and keep the dust out of your nose and mouth – they can even double as a facecloth

FIRST-AID KIT

SPF 50+ **sunblock** and **lip balm**
Vaseline and **sporting tape** to avoid blisters • **Compeed** blister plasters • Elasticated **knee/ankle support** wrap around your water-bottle to save space and keep water cool • De-activated **charcoal** for stomach problems • **Insect repellent** • **Antihistamine cream** for mosquito bites • **Electrolyte sachets** to add to your drinking water • **Coca leaves** or coca sweets to combat altitude sickness

TOILETRIES

You won't need much since very few hikers brave the icy water in Inca Trail showers.
Toothbrush and **toothpaste** • **Biodegradable soap** for the bowl of warm water that's delivered to your tent each morning • **Deodorant** • **Dental floss** – slip a **needle** into the plastic case and you have an instant and almost unbreakable sewing kit • **Ear-plugs** in case your tent-buddy snores! • Antiseptic **hand gel** • **Toilet paper**

Other Gear

Sunglasses are crucial to combat the glaring high-altitude sunlight

Binoculars might add a little weight, but they're worth it if only for the humming-birds!

Plastic bags, zip-locks and/or **roll-top waterproof bags** for keeping gear dry

Passport – crucial for passing various Inca Trail checkpoints

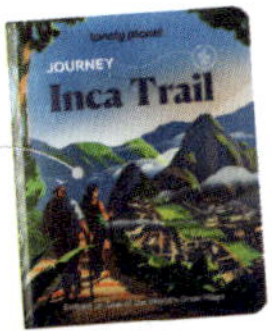

This guide-book – don't leave home without it!

Headtorch – especially useful for the 4am start on the last morning of hiking

Duct tape – the best way to transport this super-useful item is wrapped around your (always accessible) water bottle

Unlocked cellphone – purchase a local sim card in Cusco (Movistar, Claro or Entel are the most reliable)

Hiking poles with rubber tips (optional); be aware they must be left at the luggage kiosk before entering Machu Picchu

Thermal underwear and a **beanie** offer much-appreciated warmth at night

Water bottles – In addition to your main water bottle, carry a second bottle fitted with a water-filter (Lifestraw or similar), so that you can refuel from streams

Travel pillow although a fleece jacket, stuffed with your spare clothes is a convenient substitute

Sleeping bag can usually be rented from Inca Trail operators but some people prefer their own

Power bank for charging gadgets; a solar version can work well when strapped onto your pack

Trail mix – dried fruit, nuts, cookies, jelly sweets, chocolate raisins...

Access, Attitudes & Safety

ACCESSIBLE MACHU PICCHU

With more than 3000 precipitous steps and rugged paving, Machu Picchu is a challenge for travelers with restricted mobility. Fortunately, **Apumayo Expediciones** *(apumayo.com)* specializes in making Sacred Valley's archaeological sites accessible to everyone.

Crime

Street crime is rare in the Sacred Valley, but it is wise in urban centers (Cusco, for example) to avoid overt displays of wealth. It's safest to withdraw from ATMs in banks, commercial centers or stores during daylight hours rather than on the street. Don't carry more cash than is necessary and distribute it in different pockets. Invest in a smart tag so that you can keep a tab on bags left at hotels etc.

Avoid Drugs

You'll see ads for *ayahuasca* and San Pedro 'ceremonies' throughout the Sacred Valley, and coca leaves (a traditional remedy, see p112) are an accepted part of daily life in the Peruvian Andes. However, don't make the mistake of thinking drugs are tolerated in Peru: the country has draconian penalties for possession of even small quantities with prison sentences starting at a minimum of seven years. It is illegal to import coca leaves or coca tea into the UK or USA.

Wheelchair accessible sign, Machu Picchu (p166)

ABOVE: NEW AFRICA/SHUTTERSTOCK; LEFT: BETO SANTILLAN/SHUTTERSTOCK

LGBTIQ+

Same-sex activity has been legal between consenting adults over the age of 18 in Peru since 1924. However, while the country does not legally recognize same-sex marriages or partnerships among its own citizens, it does recognize them between foreigners. In tourist areas attitudes are more progressive but in rural communities, it can be unwise to flaunt sexuality of any kind.

HOW TO

ACCLIMATIZE

The Andes bisect Peru north to south reaching heights of over 6700m and forming a giant natural barrier between the coast and jungle. Many of the region's popular tourist sites are located above 3000m, making acclimatization an important consideration.

MARCELA RAMOS/SHUTTERSTOCK

Hiker gazes at Machu Picchu (p166)

Altitude Sickness Symptoms & Effects

Altitude sickness can occur anywhere above 2500m, but symptoms become more marked once you hit 3400m, roughly the height of Cuzco. The higher you go, the thinner the air gets – there is literally less oxygen in the atmosphere to breathe. The effects of this deprivation vary from person to person and are not necessarily related to your fitness.

Common symptoms include shortness of breath (even climbing the stairs can leave you gasping) and a headache, which can be intense and linger for hours or days. Other symptoms can include nausea, vomiting, dizziness and problems sleeping.

Severe altitude sickness can be dangerous and even deadly. Manifestations can include faintness, confusion, and lips and fingernails turning blue or grey. Cases may be complicated by fluid in the lungs (high-altitude pulmonary edema) or swelling of the brain (high-altitude cerebral edema). People experiencing such symptoms should descend to lower climes immediately and seek medical attention.

WHERE TO GET HIGH

Many of Peru's top tourist sights are located at altitude. Thin-air cities include Huaraz at 3052m, and Cuzco at 3399m, while Puno and Juliaca, close to Lake Titicaca, are both sited above 3800m. Spend at least three days in and around these places acclimatizing before you head higher into the mountains.

Adapting to Altitude

The good news is that the human body can readily adjust to higher altitudes over a period of a few days. The trick is not to gain height too quickly, increasing your elevation in increments. On day one, hike to 3500m; on day two, hit 4000m; on day three, break 4500m. At the end of each day, descend from your high point and sleep at a lower level.

To blunt the detrimental effects of altitude, drink plenty of water, eat sufficient quantities of carbohydrates and skip the alcohol. Ibuprofen and paracetamol can offer some relief. Acetazolamide, while effective, requires a doctor's prescription.

Health & Fitness

DOS & DONTS AT ALTITUDE

Do avoid strenuous activity for the first two to three days

Don't drink alcohol

Do eat light meals for the first few days

Do drink coca tea but avoid in evenings as it inhibits sleep

Fit for the Trail

With a little preparation – specifically acclimatization (p245) – most people of average fitness can manage the 43km four-day Inca Trail with a little determination. If you're in any way doubtful about your physical fitness, it may be wise to increase cardio workouts in the weeks prior to departure. A regimen of brisk 10km to 15km walks will improve stamina, while practicing lunges, squats and step-ups can help strengthen leg muscles and improve endurance.

Dealing with Altitude

The Inca Trail's greatest test derives from its altitude. It's fair to say that, at 4215m above sea level, Abra Warmiwañusqa (Dead Woman's Pass) is the major 'hurdle'. Much of the trail involves strenuous walking at altitudes over 3000m and *soroche* (altitude sickness) can affect people of all ages equally. It's a little-known fact that you may be more susceptible if you've suffered from it before.

BITING INSECTS

There is a risk of malaria in Peru, although it's extremely rare in the Andes. Dengue, yellow fever and zika virus are also widespread. Near Machu Picchu you might well encounter the voracious sand-flies known as *puma wakachi* – the fly that makes the puma cry.

Clinica Gold Medical *(goldmedical.com)* has highly recommended English-speaking clinicians in Cusco.

SATTA EKTRAKUL/SHUTTERSTOCK

Hikers, Inca Trail

AVIM WU/SHUTTERSTOCK

Hikers, Inca Trail

TOILETS

Most tour operators on the Inca Trail supply toilet tents ('porta-potties') and there are public toilets – usually squat toilets – at campsites and some rest areas. Toilet paper is binned and disposed of out of the sanctuary. Carry toilet paper in your day pack just in case you need to use a 'bush toilet' and take a ziplock bag so that you can dispose of the paper later. In general, public toilets (such as those in bus stations and markets) are often poorly maintained and infrequently cleaned. Keep a stash of toilet paper and hand-sanitizer handy.

STAYING HYDRATED

Dehydration is exacerbated at altitude and you're likely to find that flavored rehydration salts (with or without the addition of coca leaves) put a spring your step. Some experienced hikers set an alarm each hour to remind them to drink water. For others the frustrating weight of that 1L water bottle is reminder enough.

Preparation & Training

No matter how hard you train and prepare, the Inca Trail is likely to be something of a challenge for most people. Even if you are physically fit, few of us are in the habit of exercising at over 4000m above sea level. A series of 20km training walks – testing your footwear and pack for comfort – is advisable pre-trip training. If you have ongoing health issues, it's wise to seek advice from a doctor before departing.

Caring for Your Feet

The daily toll in kilometers is not so challenging that you're likely to suffer heavily from blisters, but a foot-preparation regimen during the weeks leading up to the hike can keep discomfort to a minimum. Softening the feet with nightly applications of petroleum jelly (such as Vaseline) for several weeks is the best guarantee against blisters. Keep dry socks with you on rainy days and carry antiseptic talc to dust your feet after drying them.

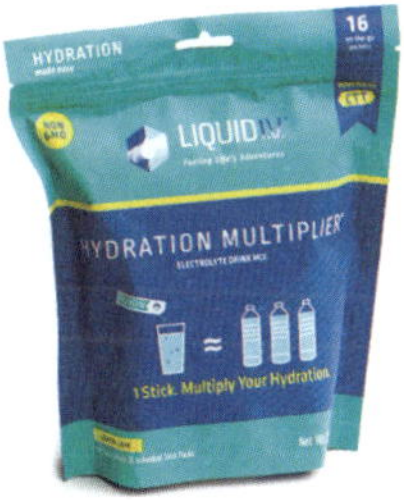

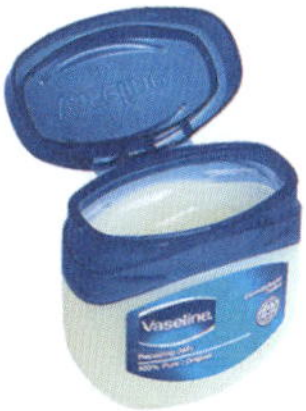

ARIF BUDI C/SHUTTERSTOCK, TADA IMAGES/SHUTTERSTOCK

Responsible Travel

GOOD TO KNOW

Sol y Luna Foundation – Cusco foundation making a real difference through education

Responsible-travel.com – travel while giving back to local communities

Worldpackers – help with agriculture across Peru.

Porters: Heroes of the Inca Trail

Porters have always been the 'backbone of the Inca Trail' – both figuratively and literally. Unlike alternative trails where pack animals such as mules and llamas are frequently used, the Inca Trail would cease to function were it not for the teams of porters who make it possible. While working conditions have improved massively since the days when they were expected to carry 30kg and even 40kg of equipment, their job remains a tough one with long days working at high altitude.

Has the Exploitation Ended?

It's natural when booking a holiday to try to limit damage to the budget but bear in mind that the easiest way for an Inca Trail operator to cut costs is to limit the number of porters or load them with heavier packs. While there are official checkpoints where these loads are weighed, experienced porters will tell you that the system is far from water-tight and that there are loopholes.

Environmental Awareness

Most tour operators these days are very careful about minimizing single-use plastics and about carrying all waste out of the area. Unfortunately - given Peru's often rainy highland climate - a vast number of disposable plastic ponchos make it onto the Inca Trail (to be ditched in bins at Machu Picchu citadel) each week. The most responsible companies are combatting this trend by issuing heavier-duty ponchos to hikers.

HOW TO

PICK A RESPONSIBLE OPERATOR

Servicio Nacional de Áreas Naturales Protegidas (SERNANP) has a list of accredited operators at visitaareasnaturales.sernanp.gob.pe. **Intrepid** *(intrepidtravel.com)*, **ExplorAndes** *(explorandes.com)*, **Llama Path** *(llamapath.com)*, **Inca Trail Reservations** *(incatrailreservations.com)* and **Salkantay Trekking** *(salkantaytrekking.com)* all have good reputations among porters.

MARK EVELEIGH

MARK EVELEIGH

Climate Change & Travel

It's impossible to ignore the impact we have when traveling; Lonely Planet urges all travellers to engage with their travel carbon footprint, which will mainly come from air travel. While there often isn't an alternative, travelers can look to minimize the number of flights they take, opt for newer aircrafts and use cleaner ground transportation, such as trains. One proposed solution – purchasing carbon offsets – unfortunately does not cancel out the impact of individual flights. While most destinations will depend on air travel for the foreseeable future, for now, pursuing ground-based travel where possible is the best course of action.

The **UN Carbon Offset Calculator** shows how flying impacts a household's emissions:

The **ICAO's carbon emissions calculator** allows visitors to analyse the CO2 generated by point-to-point journeys:

Community Projects in the Sacred Valley

Andean Colors *(andeancolors.com; p134)* was started by a small group of Quechua traditional weavers. They now lead hikes with llamas and empower their community by teaching textile classes. **AMA** *(amasacredvalley.com)* and **Awamaki** *(awamaki.org)* also work closely with highland communities and offer a chance to experience the unique Quechua lifestyle firsthand.

Llama

HOW TO

HAVE A POSITIVE IMPACT ON YOUR MACHU PICCHU VISIT

Machu Picchu continues to be a sacred place for the Quechua community and should be treated with respect.

Do not walk off the marked trail, stick to your circuit and don't sit or stand on the walls. While you are allowed to take water and small snacks, picnicking is not allowed, nor are single-use plastic bottles.

Hiking poles with metal tips should not be used anywhere on the Inca Trail. Rubber tips can be purchased in Cusco and Machu Picchu Pueblo. Neither hiking poles nor large bags (over about 30L) are allowed inside the Machu Picchu site. There's a **luggage kiosk** *(S5)* at the entrance. Take your sunblock with you as Inti beams powerfully on the stone plazas.

Drones, tripods and selfie sticks are not allowed into the site. You'll sometimes see large groups of hikers posing for photos but officially groups should number less than eight people.

While on the trail, take time to get to know your porters. Each has a specific duty from carrying the toilets and toilet tents to cooking and preparing food. It is often the older members of the team – veterans who might have been running across these hills for decades – who have the privilege of carrying the 20L water bags or the grocery supplies as these are loads that will lighten as the trail progresses.

A Day on the Trail

FOOD MATTERS

Hikers are invariably pleasantly surprised by both variety and quantity of meals on the Inca Trail.

Vegetarians, vegans and diabetics can be catered for with advance notice.

If morning coffee is important take supplies since sometimes only coca tea is available.

Morning

Rise early (around 5:30am) to enjoy the highland dawn. You'll normally get a bowl of hot water and a cup of coca tea delivered to your tent before a hearty breakfast – perhaps an omelet or porridge with coffee or more tea – is served at 6am. You'll be walking by 7am and will take it slow and steady throughout the morning. On the final morning, you'll vacate your tent by about 3:30am.

Midday

Having broken camp with fine-tuned efficiency, the porters and chefs will overtake you on the trail and will have prepared lunch – complete, as always, with dining tent, table and chairs – by the time you arrive. If there are some slower walkers among the guests, there might be some waiting time for front-runners so there's little point in racing ahead. Besides, you'll usually have 40 minutes or so to rest after lunch.

Evening

The day's walk usually comes to an end at around 5pm. You'll be greeted by the porters, who have already pitched your tent so, after a quick change of clothes, afternoon tea and snacks will be served. Then there's time either to rest in camp or to explore the surroundings. Dinner tends to be served at 7:30pm and you'll chat around the table by lamplight until tired hikers drift to bed, typically by 9pm.

ALONG THE WAY WE MET

ISAAC USCA MACHACCA

One of the most experienced and respected chefs on the Inca Trail

It's a real challenge being a chef on the Inca Trail but I love it. No two days are ever the same. We usually wake around 4am for breakfast, often catering for more than 30 people, including the staff. Afterwards we have to pack up quickly enough so that we can overtake the guests and have time to prepare lunch. Sometimes we're actually running – although chefs normally carry 2kg less weight than the porters since we have to be fast. In the afternoon, we're faced with the same challenge and it's often 10pm by the time we've tidied the kitchen tent and prepared for the next day.

ABOVE LEFT: KAYLAZARDI/SHUTTERSTOCK, MARK EVELEIGH

INCA TRAIL PROBLEM-BUSTER

How much luggage can I take? A 20L to 25L backpack should be sufficient for all your daytime needs. You're usually allocated an extra 5kg (including sleeping bag) to be transported by a porter, but which you can only access overnight. You can carry as much as you want in your day pack but try to keep it to a minimum: maximum 4kg is ideal.

What happens if the Inca Trail closes? The Inca Trail is closed each February for maintenance but it's not unheard of for heavy rain (even landslides) to temporarily close the trail at other times. Political unrest or demonstrations can also result in disruptions. Most operators can make alternative arrangements but additional costs often fall on the traveler. Consult the booking small print and check your insurance policy.

What happens if I fall ill and cannot go on? All reputable Inca Trail operators have a contingency plan in place for guests who – whether through sickness or injury – are unable to complete the trail. Extra expenses are invariably involved and these are usually covered by the guest.

What if I'm unable to book the dates I want? To avoid disappointment, book your place around four to six months in advance for high-season departures. If it's impossible to get dates that suit, there are alternative routes (p28) including the two-day Inca Trail (p148), which has its own advantages.

Hiker stretchered from trail due to altitude sickness

SL-PHOTOGRAPHY/SHUTTERSTOCK

Language

Spanish is Peru's official language. It's spoken almost ubiquitously and used in government, education and business. However, the country also has a significant number of Indigenous languages, including Quechua. Sometimes called Runa Simi (the Peoples' Language), Quechua is spoken by over five million Peruvians.

HANDY WORDS TO KNOW

Hello. Hola. o·la

Goodbye. Adiós. a·dyos

Yes/No. Sí. see/ No. no

Please. Por favor. por fa·vor

Thank you. Gracias. gra·cyas

5 Phrases to Know Before You Go

What time does it open/close?
¿A qué hora abre/cierra?

When is admission free?
¿Cuándo es la entrada gratuita?

Where can we go (salsa) dancing?
¿Dónde podemos ir a bailar (salsa)?

How do you say this in Quechua?
¿Cómo se dice ésto en quechua?

What are your happy hour specials?
¿Cuáles son las ofertas de 'la hora feliz'?

Greetings in Quechua

Hello **Imaynallan**

How are you? **Imaynallan kashanki?**

I'm fine **Allillanmi**

Until next time **Tupananchiskama**

What's your name? **Iman Sutiyki?**

My name is... **Sutiymi...**

Let's go! **Haku!**

Getting to Know People

What's your name? **¿Cómo te llamas?**

My name is... **Me llamo...**

Do you speak English? **¿Hablas inglés?**

I don't understand. **No entiendo.**

Directions & Navigation

Where is (the shop)? **¿Dónde está (la tienda)?**

What's the address? **¿Cuál es la dirección?**

Could you please write it down? **¿Puede escribirlo, por favor?**

Is this the path to ...? **¿Se va a ... por esta camino?**

Please tell me when we get to ... **¿Puede avisarme cuando lleguemos a ...?**

Signs

Open **Abierto**

Closed **Cerrado**

Entrance **Entrada**

Exit **Salida**

Women **Mujeres**

Men **Hombres**

Prohibited **Prohibido**

Toilets **Servicios** (sometimes just written as SSHH, ie Servicios Higiénicos)

Time

What time is it? **¿Qué hora es?**

It's (8) o'clock **Son las (ocho)**

in the morning. **de la mañana.**

in the afternoon. **de la tarde.**

in the evening. **de la noche.**

yesterday **ayer**

today **hoy**

tomorrow **mañana**

BETO SANTILLAN/SHUTTERSTOCK

Head Start

Just as a head start, a few words that will already be familiar to non-Spanish English speakers: armada, aficionado, conquistador, fiesta, guerrilla, macho, patio, plaza, salsa, sierra, siesta and vigilante.

Sound Familiar?

If you think Quechua sounds completely indecipherable and unlike anything you've heard before, you're not the only one. When the makers of Star Wars were searching for an 'alien' language for one of their characters (Greedo), it was Quechua that they finally settled upon.

Traveler converses with Quechua women

Emergencies

Help! **¡Socorro!**

Go away! **¡Váyase!**

I'm ill. **Estoy enfermo/a.** [m/f]

Call the police! **¡Llame a la policía!**

Call a doctor! **¡Llame a un médico!**

Numbers

1 **uno**

2 **dos**

3 **tres**

4 **cuatro**

5 **cinco**

6 **seis**

7 **siete**

8 **ocho**

9 **nueve**

10 **diez**

HOW TO ADDRESS PEOPLE

Señor (Mr), *Señora* (Ms/Mrs) and *Señorita* (Miss) tend to be used in everyday speech.

Doña, although rare, is used as a mark of respect toward older women.

Don is sometimes used as a respectful way to address men.

You may hear close friends calling each other *tío* (m) or *tía* (f), literally 'uncle' and 'aunt', but it's a slang habit and best avoided unless you are with a very familiar friend.

South Americans often use affectionate terms even with relative strangers, referring to each other as *papito* (literally 'little father') or *mamita* ('little mother').

Amigo/a (friend; m/f) is common too and is a safer bet for foreigners to use.

Index

Journey legs 000
Map pages **000**

Journey legs 000
Map pages **000**

THIS BOOK

Destination Editor
Alicia Johnson

Production Editor
Lauren O'Connell

Assisting Editor
Fionnuala Twomey, Clifton Wilkinson

Image Researcher
Catalina Aragón

Cartographer
Vojtech Bartos

Cover Illustration
Charlie Davis

Product Development
Anne Mason, James Smart,
Marc Backwell, Katerina Pavkova

Series Development Leadership
Darren O'Connell, Piers Pickard, Chris Zeiher

Thanks
Fergal Condon, Katie Connolly, Gwen Cotter, Melanie Dankel, Kellie Langdon, Saralinda Turner

Mapping data sources:
©Lonely Planet, ©OpenStreetMap, ©Natural Earth, ©GEBCO, ©Esri, ©NASA Earth Observatory, ©USGS-ASTER and the GIS User Community